# A Branch of the Sky

Fifty Years of Adventure, Tragedy, and
Restoration

in the

Sierra Nevada

by

Steve Sorensen

Mount Whitney, 14,505 feet

*A Branch of the Sky: Fifty Years of Adventure, Tragedy, and Restoration in the Sierra Nevada*

Copyright © 2018 Steven R. Sorensen
All rights reserved
Except for brief quotes used for reviews, no part of this work may be used or reproduced in any form.

Published by Picacho

5578 Coyote Ct.
Carlsbad, CA 92010

Email correspondence may be addressed to:
picacho67@gmail.com

Print Edition   ISBN 978-0-9629418-4-9

Ebook Edition   ISBN 978-0-9629418-8-7

Edited by Dinah McNichols

Cover illustration and design by Jessica Millis

For locating places mentioned in this book, interactive topographic maps are available at:
http://www.mytopo.com/maps/index.cfm
To center the map on the southern Sierra, enter Triple Divide Peak, California, USA, then zoom in or out, or search for more place names.

A PDF map of Sequoia and Kings Canyon National Park is available at:
https://www.nps.gov/seki/planyourvisit/upload/SEKImap1_2015.pdf

*It is believed that if a person thinks of a dead relative or friend, the ghost will come after him and he will become sick. A person must forget the dead, particularly those who have been dear to him, if he wishes to remain among the living.*

— Beatrice Blyth Whiting
"Paiute Sorcery: Sickness and Social Control"

# Table of Contents

Chapter One: A Fool's Education    7
Chapter Two: Going Up the Country    25
Chapter Three: Triple Divide    95
Chapter Four: Chubasco a Cappella    133
Chapter Five: God's Gardener    181
Chapter Six: Ghost Sickness    227
Photos    283
Author Profile    307

# A Branch of the Sky

# Chapter One: A Fool's Education

Fifty years ago I didn't believe in ghosts for the simple reason that I scarcely believed in death. Nobody close to me, other than elderly grandparents, had died, and the prospect that such a thing might happen to me or those I loved seemed so remote, I dismissed it as preposterous. But now that so many of my old friends have disappeared, I've been forced to reconsider. Their ghosts are real enough that I lie awake every night carrying on conversations with them in the dark. They come through the curtains of my room on a warm breeze, slipping into my dreams until they force me awake, and then we spend the remaining hours before daylight reliving things we did together long ago. In spite of their mischief, the ghosts mean no harm. It's just that their memories have grown weak, even weaker than mine, and they're starting to forget what it felt like to inhabit a body of flesh. I know I shouldn't indulge them, but I can't help myself. I want to relive those old memories as much as they do. So I begin telling them how we drank cold water straight from the creek in our cupped hands, crouched under foxtail pines to escape lightning, passed a bottle of whiskey over a dying fire, scraped our knuckles raw on tree bark and licked the blood, or lay in a hot spring on Kern River with beautiful women on a starry night.

In June of 1967, the day after I finished high school, I didn't bother to wait around for graduation ceremonies. Instead, I drove ninety-one miles from Fresno to Yosemite Valley, where I took a job as a busboy at the Yosemite Lodge cafeteria. My plan, if it's possible to say I planned anything at that age, was to become a rock climber on those magnificent walls of white granite. I had read about the exploits of Yosemite's big wall climbers like Warren Harding, Jim Bridwell, and Royal Robbins. Sometimes I'd even see them sitting around the courtyard at the lodge—catlike characters with scabbed elbows, torn clothing, and uncouth laughs—and somehow I had the notion that I could become like them. The only problem with my plan was that I knew almost nothing about rock climbing, and even though I lived and worked within sight of those granite walls, I had almost no time to learn. Yosemite Park and Curry Company, the notoriously cheap park concessioner at that time, worked all the restaurant and cafeteria employees in three shifts—breakfast, lunch, and dinner—with two-hour breaks between each shift, making the effective workday a miserable twelve-hour grind, six days a week.

Every day after the lunch shift, the cafeteria drudges like me would gather at a sandy beach along the Merced River, just below the lodge. In late June, the afternoon temperatures in Yosemite often reached the mid-nineties, and our hope was to take a refreshing splash in the river, followed by a nap in the warm sand, before dragging ourselves back to that food factory where hundreds of tourists waited in line to select their trays of tuna casserole, greasy meatloaf, and lime Jell-O. What they didn't eat would be served to us the following day as an unrecognizable, glutinous slop. None of us had actually dared to swim in the Merced River yet because the winter had left a heavy snowpack in the Sierra Nevada backcountry and the runoff hadn't even come close to reaching its peak. The Merced River was still an icy torrent at least two hundred feet wide.

One exceptionally hot afternoon, I was standing there beside the river, watching that hypnotic flow of whitecaps with a black guy about my age named Henderson. He was from Compton, built like a gladiator, and worked in the warehouse, where I'd seen him toss around boxes of canned goods like loaves of bread.

"I don't suppose anybody could swim across that river and live," Henderson said.

"I can swim across that river," I replied—I have no idea why, except that I was young and stupid and felt the need to show Henderson, and anybody else listening, including the attractive young women in bikinis nearby, that I was prepared for a life of risk.

"You a fool," Henderson replied, giving me a sly grin.

I had grown up in the San Joaquin Valley, had been camping and hiking in the southern Sierra Nevada all my life, and I knew that people drowned in rivers along the western slope of the Sierra every year. The Merced, San Joaquin, Kings, Kaweah, and Kern—they all claimed lives almost every spring and summer. The worst month for drownings was in fact June because that was usually when the runoff was at its peak. I hadn't really weighed the risk of swimming across the Merced on that afternoon, but it didn't really matter. I'd been challenged, and now I had to respond.

"I'll bet you five dollars I can swim across that river," I said.

"You even got five dollars?" Henderson asked.

Curry Company only paid us $1.10 per hour, and they deducted 35 cents per hour for room and board, so what I was wagering amounted to almost a day's pay. I pulled four ones and some change from my cutoff jeans and placed the money on a rock. "How about you?" I asked.

Henderson put a ten-dollar bill on the rock and took my four and change. "I'll be spending that ten dollars on beer in about fifteen minutes," he said.

I dropped my cutoffs—I was wearing boxer shorts underneath—and tossed them aside. Then I waded knee-deep into the river. When the current started gently pulling me in, I dove headfirst into the froth.

My plan was to sprint head down the entire way across. I knew what cold water could do to your muscles, cramping them up until they refused to work at all. But I was a surfer and a strong swimmer, and I figured I could easily get to the other side before the cramping started.

I stroked as hard and fast as I could for what felt like thirty seconds. I thought that should just about put me on the opposite shore. But when I looked up, gasping for breath, I saw that I wasn't even halfway across. And I had already been swept two hundred feet downstream! My only choice now was to try to power on to the other side before my muscles completely cramped up.

I did do one thing that helped—though surely by instinct, not reason. Rather than try to swim ninety degrees to the current, I turned downstream at a forty-five-degree angle so I was going partly with the current. I would bounce through the roughest parts with my head up, then swim hard through the flats.

When my hands finally scraped rock bottom, and I dragged myself to shore, I was at least six hundred feet downstream from where I'd started. After I'd caught my breath and was able to stand, I saw that my boxer shorts had come off and I was completely naked.

I used a fir branch to cover myself and began walking back upstream, tiptoeing painfully along the rocky riverbank. Henderson followed me on the opposite shore. Nobody else, not even the girls in bikinis, had waited around to see if I lived or died; like obedient drudges, they had all headed back to the lodge so they wouldn't be late for the evening shift.

To get back to the other side of the river again meant walking half a mile or so upstream, naked and barefoot, through tourist families picnicking along the river, crossing the arched rock bridge near the village, then walking back along

Northside Road to the lodge. I knew that if I didn't get back to the cafeteria in time for the dinner shift I might be fired and my dreams of becoming a rock climber would be shattered. But I also knew that Henderson had a car. So I pointed frantically toward the rock bridge and yelled above the roar of the rapids, "Drive around and pick me up!"

Henderson glanced up canyon, stared at the ground, looked across at me, put his hands on hips, then hollered above the roar of the river, "Okay! For ten bucks!"

~~~

All that summer I lived in one of Curry Company's moldy tent cabins with a dozen squeaky metal cots and a bare light bulb hanging from the ceiling. Rats and squirrels built their nests under the wooden floor. These were the same tent cabins where an outbreak of the deadly hantavirus occurred a few years later (humans acquire the hantavirus through contact with rodent feces, saliva, blood, or urine). All the male employees shared a dark, moldy, concrete shower room, where old pervert cooks and dishwashers propositioned the young busboys. One morning one of them tried to grab my ass in the shower, and I flung him against the block wall, fracturing his elbow. He never told anybody how his accident occurred, which probably saved my job.

As I said, this was 1967, the almost mythical summer of love. Strange things were happening all over the country, but especially in California, and Yosemite Valley had become the freak capital of the state. Hippies from San Francisco, just three hours away, would stream into Stoneman Meadow to camp illegally, drink wine, drop LSD, smoke pot, and sometimes run around naked all night long. (A few years later, on the Fourth of July, thirty park rangers rode into Stoneman Meadow on horseback, wearing knee-high leather boots, wielding billy clubs, and swinging ropes like whips, trying to break up one of those pagan celebrations. The hippies, who otherwise favored peace and love, pulled the rangers off their horses and beat the hell out them. That went down in park service lore as the Stoneman Meadow massacre.) Almost every night in Yosemite there were impromptu parties around a bonfire at Foresta, or else several of us would pile into a car and drive to Tuolumne Meadows just to sit along the creek and watch the reflection of moonlight in the rippling water. Sometimes on a Saturday night, we'd leave Yosemite after the dinner shift, drive to San Francisco to attend a concert of Jefferson Airplane or Country Joe and the Fish, and be back in Yosemite Valley in time to work the Sunday breakfast shift. There was always so much going on that summer, I was afraid to go to sleep for fear I'd miss what was going to happen next.

One of my tent mates that summer was a young Mennonite from Kansas named Doug Wiens. He was shorter than average, wiry, kept his blond hair clipped in a buzz cut, and wore blue work shirts buttoned up to the collar. He was so painfully shy, he could barely look people in the eye. Wiens had been born in the San Joaquin Valley, where his father had been a Mennonite pastor, and like me, he'd grown up exploring the Sierra Nevada. Later his family moved to Hillsboro, Kansas. But he longed to return to the Sierra Nevada, and as soon as he finished high school, he made his way west. That summer was Doug's first time away from home, and he was having an awkward time adjusting. He seemed so lonely and out of place, I couldn't help thinking he might have been happier if he'd stayed in Kansas.

My approach to being free for the first time in my life was completely different from the approach Wiens took. Yosemite Valley was full of enticing young women from all over the country eager to exercise their first taste of freedom, and I was just as eager to see that they exercised it with me. Many nights in a row, I'd drag myself back to our tent cabin just an hour before dawn, hoping to get a little rest before I had to go to work. Wiens would be awake by then, having slept the entire night, and sometimes we would talk. I could see that he found my behavior appalling, but he wasn't judgmental about it—more curious than anything.

"What made you want to come to Yosemite, anyway?" I asked him.

"I wanted to learn how to rock climb," he answered, in his soft, modest voice.

"Yeah, me too," I said wistfully. The summer was slipping away much too quickly and I hadn't so much as touched a climbing rope or hiked further than the few hundred yards to the base of Yosemite Falls.

"We should do some climbs together," he suggested. "Maybe we could help each other learn."

I didn't tell Wiens that I couldn't imagine him rock climbing, which, of course, required bristly facial hair, foul language, lots of body odor, and great daring with women. But, in fact, Wiens was a natural thrill seeker who as young as two years old had terrified his parents by doing front flips off the bed and trying to scale the side of the family piano. His return to California and Yosemite was the act of a determined young man pursuing what he knew to be his destiny. While I had spent the summer partying, squandering what little money I made on gasoline and girls, Wiens had used his earnings to buy himself a nylon rope, a swami belt, pitons, and a few carabiners. And he'd actually started teaching himself how to climb. By August he'd made friends with more experienced climbers, and on his days off he was starting to do short climbs on El Capitan. I was impressed by his quiet determination, and as the summer came to a close, I began to see that I had misjudged Doug Wiens. (At that age, I misjudged just about everything.) In less than ten years, he would become one of the most daring and tenacious American adventurers of his generation.

As it turned out, I didn't last too long as a Curry Company employee. I'd been promoted from busboy at the lodge to busboy at the restaurant next door, which was considered a giant leap in the career of a Curry Company employee, promising a bright future. But I hated the work and felt frustrated because I had learned nothing at all about rock climbing. By mid-September, I'd fallen in with two fellows my age who shared my craving for adventure. We spent fifty dollars on a 1952 Chevy station wagon, another ten dollars on a used differential that we installed ourselves, loaded the wagon with surfboards, quit our jobs, and drove 1500 miles to Mazatlán, Mexico. Curry Company was disappointed with my irresponsible behavior and banned me from future servitude. My career in the hospitality industry never recovered.

By late August of 1968, I was back in Yosemite Valley again, determined this time to make up for my slothful behavior of the previous year. I had already spent most of that summer at another miserable job in the San Joaquin Valley, saved almost all my earnings, and then quit. It didn't matter to me that I'd disappointed another employer, angered my parents, and abandoned my girlfriend of that time. I simply had to get back to Yosemite. It wasn't just the pleasure of Yosemite's intoxicating beauty, either. I knew my fate would be found somewhere in those mountains, and I had to be there, whatever the cost. But this time I was going to focus hard on the thing that mattered most to me: learning to climb rock. I took up residency at Camp 4, the renowned Yosemite Valley hangout for some of the greatest climbers in the world, but I was hopelessly intimidated and out of place among those grizzled veterans of the North America Wall, Half Dome, Lost Arrow, and many other awe-inspiring climbs. I was such a novice, I didn't know how to tie a bowline, properly coil a rope, or put

## A Fool's Education

on a swami belt. Not only was I completely inept as a climber, I couldn't even figure out how to get a foothold in that vertical world.

And then I ran into a friend from the previous summer, Dennis Miller, who was now running the bicycle shop at the lodge. He too wanted to learn how to rock climb, and he told me, "I know just the guy who can help us get started. He's the manager of the hot-dog stand at Camp Curry. He gets off at six, same as me." That didn't sound too promising to me, learning how to rock climb from the manager of the hot-dog stand, but I waited around until Dennis got off work, and together we drove over to Camp Curry in my VW bus.

This manager of the hot-dog stand was named Doug Tompkins. When Dennis introduced us, Tompkins was wearing a white apron with mustard stains all down the front. He was about six years older than I, handsome, dark-haired, and overflowing with energy and self-confidence. Originally from New York, Tompkins had been a high school dropout, competitive skier, and rock climber before moving to San Francisco. A few years before, while in his early twenties, he'd started the outdoor equipment company The North Face, which at that time was the most innovative maker of outdoor equipment in the world. He disliked the cheap gimmickry and shoddy design of outdoor products being sold at that time—folding cots, heavy canvas tents, metal canteens, clumsy packs. Most outdoor equipment was still based on military designs that hadn't changed much in years, and Tompkins saw that as an opportunity to make a living by designing better stuff.

Shortly before I met him, though, Tompkins had sold his share of The North Face to his business partner. I don't think it was an amicable split. The way he described it to me was, "I lost The North Face." But he didn't seem bitter about it. His plan was to use the money ($50,000, a lot in those days for a man still in his mid-twenties) to start another company, though

I don't think he'd decided yet what kind of company it would be. "All I want right now is a summer climbing in Yosemite," he said. To cover his living expenses, he took a job working for Curry Company, and the job they'd given him was manager of the hot-dog stand.

We swung by the little apartment Curry Company had given Tompkins for the summer, where he quickly changed clothes and gathered up some of the climbing gear he had lying all over the floor. He introduced us to a beautiful young woman with long blond hair, wearing a colorful summer dress. I assumed she was his wife, but I never saw her again.

Tompkins took Dennis and me to a place on the west end of the valley where there was a jumble of granite boulders. We were the only ones there, which allowed us to learn without being self-conscious about our complete ignorance of climbing. Tompkins spent a few minutes showing us some basic knots, slings, and rope management—but he didn't make a tedious lecture out of it. We were actually climbing rock within an hour, and we climbed until it was too dark to see. Driving back to his apartment, Tompkins said to Dennis and me, "You're both a couple of naturals. Come and pick me up tomorrow at the same time, and we'll do it again."

I don't know why Tompkins took Dennis and me under his wing that summer. He could have spent his free time with some of the best rock climbers in the world. So many accomplished climbers have big egos, and I suppose that's what drives them to the top. But Tompkins wasn't like that, at least not with Dennis and me. I think he had as much fun helping a couple of younger guys get started as he might have had with his more accomplished buddies. Also, I think just being in a natural environment like Yosemite was what was most important to him. More than anybody I'd ever met, Doug Tompkins needed to be outdoors.

One evening Tompkins took Dennis and me to a place called Bookends, just off the highway, below the tunnels, and just above the Merced River. The climb consisted of two parallel slabs with just enough room between them to inch your way up, like climbing through a chimney. He took a moment to show us the proper technique, then belayed us from the top. That's how Tompkins demystified climbing for us, by showing how it was mostly just basic instinct. Dennis and I were like two kids playing on the monkey bars at recess.

Tompkins liked to climb in the late afternoon, after work, when the hot valley was beginning to cool down and the light of the setting sun was so beautiful. On another evening just before dark, after we'd completed a climb on the Three Brothers, we sat on a ledge overlooking the Merced. Tompkins began talking about a project he'd been working on at The North Face, trying to develop domed tents using flexible Fiberglass wands. Domed tents, though rare, were around by then, but they still used aluminum poles that had poor flexion. Tompkins tried to describe how a dome tent using fiberglass poles could bend with snow loads and flex in the wind, making it much stronger than traditional tents using rigid center poles. He also talked about backpack frames of welded aluminum that were both lighter and stronger than traditional packs with wooden frames. He explained how the development of better steel pitons had made it possible for rock climbers to do things they'd never done before, like climbing El Capitan, but he warned us that the age of pitons in climbing was coming to an end.

"A few climbers are starting to say that pitons damage the rock and that we have no right to do that," he explained. "They believe the rock should always be left exactly the way we found it. There's a lot of thought right now going into pieces of removal hardware they call nuts or chocks."

I was impressed by his ability to think like a creative

engineer, his natural gift for business, plus his tremendous self-confidence. But it would be many years before I understood what a truly exceptional person Doug Tompkins was, and how lucky I had been to know him for those few short weeks.

Driving back to the village that evening, Tompkins told me something I wish I'd paid better attention to. "You're young enough and talented enough that you can do anything you want in rock climbing," he said. "The danger is that you don't understand yet how easy it is to get yourself killed in this sport. And that worries me. I've lost friends already, and I'll probably lose more. Just promise me you'll be as safe as possible."

A few days later, I met Tompkins at the hot-dog stand again, ready for another climb, but he told me with a pained look on his face, "I can't make it today, sorry. I'm supposed to meet with these executive types from Curry Company, and I can't figure out how to get out of it."

Tompkins knew about my low opinion of Curry Company and that I'd been banned from ever working there again. "What the hell do those knuckleheads want with you?" I asked.

"They want me to go to work for them," he replied.

"But you already work for them!" I pointed out. "You run their damn hot-dog stand."

"Yeah, but somebody told them I used to own The North Face, and now they figure I'm corporate material. They say they want to 'groom' me to be manager of the Ahwahnee."

The Ahwahnee Hotel is a majestic old structure of granite and pine logs, considered a rustic masterpiece and perhaps the most beautiful building in all the national parks. It was favored by rich tourists from all over the world, and its manager had to be a charming, sophisticated, and cultured individual, which Doug Tompkins certainly was.

"I suppose it's a step up from grilling hot dogs," I said. "But it's still working for Curry Company."

"I know," he said. "I've already done all that corporate bullshit. Maybe I'll start another company of my own someday, but the last thing I want right now is a permanent job working for these guys."

"Why don't you just tell them you're not interested?"

"Because," Tompkins said, "if I do that they'll probably fire me, and I'm not ready to leave Yosemite just yet."

As our climbing skills improved that summer, Dennis Miller and I tried more difficult climbs without Doug Tompkins's guidance. One day in early September, Dennis and I were on a climb at the base of El Capitan called Pine Tree. It started at the talus (loose rock) just above the valley floor and ended a few hundred feet higher at a ledge where a ponderosa pine grew from a crack in the rock. The climb was almost all vertical, but we completed it quickly and rappelled back to the base. When we tried to retrieve our rope, though, it wouldn't pull through—it was jammed in a crevice.

"No big deal," I told Dennis. "I'll just shimmy up the rope, clear it, then rappel back down."

"Use a prusik," Dennis said. "Do it right." (A prusik is a friction knot used to ascend or descend safely on fixed ropes.) And Dennis was correct—that's what I should have done.

"Naw, this will only take a couple minutes," I said. I was in excellent physical condition and so cocky that I didn't see the danger. Without another thought, I started up the rope.

I only got about halfway up when I couldn't go any farther. I'd failed to account for the fact that I was already tired from the earlier climb. I tried to rest my arms by letting my legs hold my weight on a nubbin (a small knob of rock), but that only saved me for a minute. My legs started wobbling—the dreaded effect climbers call sewing machine knee—and then I began sliding down the rope. At first my grip was still strong enough to slow my fall just a bit, but I gathered momentum quickly, and soon I was in a near free fall.

Luckily, my feet hit a rock ledge about twelve inches wide and I stuck there—otherwise I'd have fallen another fifty vertical feet, which almost certainly would have killed me. The skin on the palm of my hands was gone, yet, oddly, my hands didn't hurt at all. I ran the rope between my legs and over my shoulder, and I rappelled the rest of the way to the ground.

The next time I saw Doug Tompkins, a couple days later, I was embarrassed to show him my hands, which were now wrapped in bandages. He shook his head and laughed, "I already heard the whole story from Dennis. You're lucky, you know. Guys have gotten killed doing just what you did. Listen now—risk is part of climbing, but not foolish risk. If you expect to survive in a sport as dangerous as climbing, you have got to use better judgment than that!"

I told Tompkins I was headed for Utah, where I hoped to do some climbing in the Wasatch Range. Later, when we said goodbye, he gave me a big smile and a slap on the shoulder, and he gave me a hand-written copy of his climbing notes for Provo Canyon. Although I followed his amazing career over the next fifty years, I never saw Doug Tompkins again.

〰〰

By the spring of 1970, I was back in Fresno, more or less homeless, and usually hungry. I'd had a falling out with my parents over religion—they had it, I didn't—and I was less than welcome at their house now. There were places I could stay a night or two—a girlfriend's house when her parents were out of town, a friend's garage—but the only place I could count on

## A Fool's Education

was the back of my van. None of this worried me much, and I certainly didn't feel sorry for myself. The correlation between work and money, and money and food hadn't occurred to me yet, and I enjoyed flaunting my freedom in a stubborn way.

I was attending Fresno State, just a couple hours from three national parks: Yosemite, Sequoia and Kings Canyon. On a clear day, the snow-covered peaks of the southern Sierra looked close enough to hike to. On campus I felt at home in the company of climbers, skiers, and other outdoor junkies, clomping about in our ice-climbing boots and puffy down jackets. I was taking classes in math, physics, biology, botany, and geology—not working toward a degree in any of them, just studying whatever subject interested me in whatever order I was drawn to it. I also took plenty of courses in literature and creative writing. I'd been an avid and eclectic reader all my life, and I found that sitting in a classroom discussing the world's greatest literature was a pleasing and almost effortless way to pass the time.

For a university with a reputation as an agriculture school, Fresno State had a surprisingly good English department. Now and then William Saroyan, the great master of the short story who lived in Fresno, would stop by our writing classes and share his humor and insight. Beat poets from the Bay Area, like Gary Snyder, would come to speak on campus, and always there were young writers sitting around under the shade trees scribbling furiously in their notebooks. Fresno State had become a haven for people who valued the written word, and I was one of them.

I had no illusions about college professors teaching me much about writing, though. Most of them advised their students to choose a career other than writing, reflecting, I believe, their own bitter disappointments more than our future prospects. The only exception in my case was a journalism professor who praised everything I wrote for him and encouraged me to begin submitting feature stories for publication, which I did. Still, I didn't think of writing as a career choice, really. It was more like a compulsion. I needed to write, whether I got paid for it or not. So I just stumbled along, taking any course in any subject that interested me. It might not have made much sense to some people, but for a young journalist still learning to write, it was exactly the right thing to do.

In those days, like many people my age, I was out of sorts with the world. The United States was fighting an insane war in Vietnam that benefited nobody but the arms manufacturers and military officers eager for promotion. Kids my age were coming home from Asia dead, maimed, or suffering from emotional trauma that would end up troubling them all their lives. It was a different war than the one my parents' generation had experienced, but they didn't seem to understand that. I felt they'd consider it a noble thing if I died fighting for some miserable hill in Vietnam, just so the generals could abandon it that night and retake it the next day. In 1970, when my draft lottery number (fifty-three) came up low enough to guarantee I'd be drafted, I vowed I would go to Canada before I'd fight in that evil war. (I don't know why I didn't consider Mexico, which I knew had better surfing.) As it turned out, though, I failed the draft physical because I was deaf to high-frequency sound, something I'd always considered a great advantage but which apparently makes one unfit for shooting at people in a jungle in Vietnam. Still, I was angry with my country and pessimistic about the future. Other people my age were getting married and settling down in careers that looked like nothing but forty years of boredom to me. I wasn't buying into any of it, but I hadn't come up with a better plan yet, except to spend my time reading Shakespeare, Mark Twain, and the gonzo journalist Hunter S. Thompson.

Also around that time, I became aware that I had a powerful intolerance for being indoors. Even as a toddler growing up in

Fresno, I needed to break out. When my mother grew tired of trying to contain me indoors, she would pack me a hobo's bindle by placing a peanut butter sandwich in the center of a bandanna, tying the four corners together, and hanging it on the end of a stick. Then she'd turn me loose in the back yard, where I could see the snow-covered peaks of the Sierra Nevada, perhaps fifty miles away. So with my hobo's bindle on my shoulder, I'd tramp around the yard several times, creating the illusion of great distance, then retreat to the farthest corner, where I could eat my lunch while pondering those impossibly beautiful mountains.

As I grew older, my claustrophobia worsened. Schoolrooms without windows were mausoleums. Bedrooms with drawn curtains became tombs. Churches made me feel like I'd already been condemned to hell. Even outdoors, the foggy days, which are frequent during San Joaquin Valley winters, were like endless bad dreams. I needed to see blue sky at all times or I quickly became nervous and irritable. Yet I never thought my claustrophobia was abnormal. On the contrary, resisting confinement felt normal, even instinctual. Like most animals, people belong outdoors, where their chances of finding food, companionship, sex, and adventure are greatly improved. It seemed to me that the willingness of modern humans to shut themselves away in tiny cubicles for long hours at a time was the cause of so much neurotic behavior. Some people may be able to suppress the compulsion to break out of confinement for a while, but I never could.

In June of 1970, so broke I couldn't afford to put gas in my van, I accepted my brother's kind offer to work as an assistant in his dental office. It turned out to be one of at least a thousand jobs I'm not suited for. Though I learned a lot about dental work that month—even today I could pull a tooth if only I had a willing patient—I was desperate to find a way to get outdoors.

And then one day, there at the dental office, while I was extracting gold fillings from a box of teeth, I got a phone call from a young man named Don Stivers, who identified himself as a technician in the Resource Management Division at Sequoia and Kings Canyon National Parks. Don said, "We have an opening for a laborer on a backcountry crew. Your name came up on the hiring list. Would you be interested?"

"Hell, yes, I'd be interested!" I replied.

My brother, who'd been working on a patient in the next room, came running to see what I was hollering about. When I told him I was going to work for the park service, he was polite enough to pretend he was sorry to see me go.

Don Stivers grew up in the foothills town of Three Rivers, just outside Sequoia, where his family owned a motel on the Kaweah River. He went to Woodlake High, where he was a star on the track team. His senior year, Don could high jump six feet five, which won him a full scholarship to UCLA. He was a bright and hard-working young man, and when he was hired at Sequoia he quickly became the assistant to the chief of resource management. The morning he called me at the dentist office, he'd been given a stack of several dozen applications, which he winnowed down to ten. (My name was on the list because I'd scored high on the math portion of a civil service exam, making all those years of math classes for an English major miraculously worthwhile.) Don started calling the names on his stack of applications one by one, but was getting answers like "I'm not really interested." or "maybe." or "is there free housing?" My application was the last one, and when he heard my response, Don knew he'd found his man.

"Be at Ash Mountain headquarters Monday morning at eight o'clock," he said.

# Chapter Two: Going Up the Country

Just a few days later, I found myself at Charlotte Lake, deep in the backcountry of Kings Canyon National Park, where I'd been sent to help build a barbed-wire enclosure to protect the fragile meadow just below the lake. My crew of six and I drove by truck to the Onion Valley trailhead on the east side of the Sierra, a full day's drive, and the next morning we hiked over Kearsarge Pass, carrying our packs on our backs, while our tools and kitchen gear were packed in by mules. We camped at the lake, about 10,500 feet, among lodgepole and foxtail pines stunted by the extreme cold of winter. The intense sunlight, white granite, and occasional patches of snow, made it almost impossible to see without sunglasses. I felt like I'd spent most of my life as a blind salamander in a cave and only now was I seeing the Earth as it truly was.

The combined parks of Sequoia and Kings Canyon (which are managed as one) are roughly seventy miles long and thirty-five miles wide, and encompass more than 865,000 acres, beginning with the arid foothills on the west and ending with the snow-covered peaks along the Sierra Nevada crest. From cactus to ice, the parks span some of the most varied and rugged landscape in North America. About ninety-five percent of the land is designated wilderness, meaning there are no roads, permanent structures (except for a few backcountry ranger stations), or power lines, and the area is managed in such a way as to keep it as natural as possible. The parks are also surrounded by many smaller wilderness areas, making the southern Sierra Nevada one of the largest contiguous wilderness areas in the United States. Although the park visitation is high—in 1970, Kings Canyon alone received 1,019,000 visitors—only about five percent of park visitors ever venture into the backcountry.

My summer crew was called the Soil and Moisture Crew, and it varied in size from year to year, or even month to month, with as few as three workers or as many as twenty. The crew was an insignificant and often forgotten appendage of the Resource Management Division, which was also small in comparison to the much larger Ranger and Maintenance divisions. There was also an Interpretive Division to manage the park visitor centers, lead nature walks, and such. In those days, resource management crews fought wildfires, battled plant diseases (usually to no avail), cared for wildlife, removed hazardous trees, and conducted small scientific studies. The parks at that time had seven or eight trail crews working in the backcountry, and perhaps fifteen backcountry rangers. But there was only one Soil and Moisture Crew.

In some ways we were a vestige of the old Depression-era Civilian Conservation Corps, which had done a lot of good erosion-control work in parks and forests all across the West. The old CCC program ended in 1942, after the United States entered World War II. Once the war ended, the park service neither adequately funded erosion control work nor canceled it all together, as if our pitiful budget of less than $10,000 was so small, it wasn't worth the effort of some government accountant to "X" it out. So every summer our ragged band trudged into the backcountry in search of meadow protection projects, perfectly happy if the park service forgot about us altogether. The one great advantage our crew had over other park employees was that we were given the unusual privilege of working throughout the backcountry of both Sequoia and Kings Canyon, which meant that over time we saw more of the parks' wilderness areas than just about anybody.

The crew that first summer was an odd assortment that only

## Going Up the Country

the US government could throw together. For example, we had two guys named Art Norman. One was a fleshy, urbanized white kid who hated the outdoors; on Fridays after work, he'd go back to camp, zip himself up in his Korean War surplus sleeping bag, and come out only to eat or pee. The other Art Norman was a black six-foot-four retired Marine who weighed about 270 pounds; when we were splitting firewood with eight-pound sledges, throwing all our weight into each blow, Art would swing his sledge with one hand while telling jokes in his squeaky voice that sounded two octaves too high; he liked to say that the other Art Norman had been hired first, but the government always had to have a carbon copy of everything. Another employee was Mike Palmer, a photography student at Arizona State who wore about five pounds of turquoise jewelry around his neck and wrists; Mike was an ultra-marathon runner who liked to spend his time after work carving chunks of soapstone into marijuana pipes; later he became a master silversmith, as well. We had a primitive kitchen under a twenty-by-forty-foot rainfly, and some guys had their own tents. All I had was an old kapok sleeping bag, which I spread over a mattress of pine needles. A few guys hated living in the backcountry, and they either quit or were transferred. Those of us who survived, mostly younger guys like me, loved that life, and despite our differences we found a way to get along.

We worked forty hours a week, which left a lot of spare time in the evenings and on weekends. I spent my free time climbing everything in sight. Though most of the southern Sierra lacks the big vertical walls of Yosemite, there are many challenging peaks in the 13,000- to 14,000-foot range. I didn't have a climbing partner, but I found that with a light rope and a little hardware, I could climb just about anything by myself in the fast alpine style. One evening after work, starting from Vidette Meadow, I climbed 13,632-foot University Peak in fifty-five minutes. (I don't know why I was in such a hurry.) One

Saturday I made camp in Center Basin, then the next morning climbed 13,963-foot Mount Stanford, 13,855-foot Gregory's Monument, and 13,977-foot Mount Keith, all before lunch. The next weekend, after climbing 13,125-foot Mount Baxter, I got caught in a thunderstorm and spent the night in a talus cave without a sleeping bag. This was way more fun than wiping drool in a dentist office, and I couldn't get enough of it.

For several years I'd been thinking that the modern world of houses, apartments, shopping centers, roads, and parking lots was ugly and hellishly oppressive—a feeling I still have today. Looking back on my behavior at that time, I realize I was depressed by a world I considered intolerable. But after one summer living in the wilderness, I saw a future I wanted to be part of. I was astonished by the purity of that place. The air was so clear, the sky so blue, every crystal of rock so perfectly formed, every tree and lichen such a miracle of life. And it was almost completely devoid of man. Discovering the joy of pure nature became the greatest revelation of my life, and it's a joy that hasn't diminished one bit in fifty years.

That fall when I had to go back to Fresno State, I knew I would return to Sequoia and Kings Canyon the next summer if I could. There was no job security from one year to the next, but as long as you didn't smoke marijuana in the headquarters building or crash a park truck, you'd probably get hired back. The pay for a government laborer wasn't a lot, but it was double the minimum wage, and because I was living in the backcountry where I didn't have to pay rent and it was almost impossible to spend money, by the fall I'd saved enough money to live the remainder of the year. All in all, I felt pretty good about my new economic status.

I stumbled along in college, still taking an eclectic assortment of classes, and before I knew it, I'd acquired enough credits to graduate with a degree in English. I was almost an accidental graduate, not yet ready to leave the cozy cocoon of campus life. Gene Zumwalt, the much-beloved head of the English Department and an avid backpacker, advised me to pursue a graduate degree and apply for a teaching assistantship. I never did, but toying with the idea allowed me to hang around another year taking even more courses.

༄

In July of 1971, our four-man backcountry crew hiked into lower Rattlesnake Creek, about sixteen miles out of Mineral King Valley. In those days, that fantastically beautiful valley still belonged to the US Forest Service. The Disney Corporation had tried to turn it into a mega ski resort but lost a bitter legal battle to environmentalists, and a few years later Mineral King Valley became part of Sequoia National Park, where it always belonged. The valley is a major trailhead, with routes leading in all directions, and over the years I hiked out of there perhaps a hundred times.

Rattlesnake Canyon is a long, V-shaped canyon, and at 8,500 feet, where we were camped, it could be warm in the day but cold at night. We'd been building a series of drift fences through the canyon so stock parties would have a way to hold their horses and mules at night, keep them from "drifting," and so the grazing could be spread out to protect sensitive areas. We cut our posts of juniper or cedar, and stripped them of bark, dug post holes in the rocky ground, strung hundreds of yards of smooth wire, and fashioned our own swinging gates out of wood we cut on site. It was hard work, and at the end of the day, our half-naked bodies were smeared with sweat, sawdust, and grime. But to our minds, wilderness dirt wasn't dirty. We'd jump in the creek at the end of the day and come out smelling almost civilized. What little odor remained was masked by the campfire smoke that saturated our clothing. My crewmembers shared my horror of the urbanized world, and if only we'd had access to beer and women, we might never have stepped on a sidewalk again.

But we weren't quite savages yet. We ate what came out of a gunny sack or a can, drank coffee from Brazil, and ran our chainsaws on fuel that originated in the Middle East. We depended on a weekly resupply by mules from Ash Mountain headquarters, and that summer the park had a shortage of mule packers to make that two-day trip from the trailhead at Mineral King to where we were camped on Rattlesnake Creek. One Friday in July, our supervisor back at Ash Mountain called on the backcountry radio to tell us that our regular packer had quit; next week we'd be resupplied by a packer from Mineral King Pack Station, the private concessioner that catered mostly to rich dudes who wanted to experience wilderness with all the comforts of home.

Next Tuesday afternoon, the packer who rode into our camp leading a string of six mules was fifteen-year-old Craig Thorn, the son of a Three Rivers rancher. Even as a teenager, Craig was a skilled rock climber and talented backcountry skier. (In the late sixties, he was one of the skiers the Disney Corporation called upon to test the unpacked backcountry bowls above Mineral King Valley.) Craig handled his mules like an old hand, cussing and spitting Copenhagen, and ordering us greenhorns to stand back while he unpacked them himself, one by one. Then, after the mules had been unloaded, given a taste of oats, and turned loose, Craig offered each of us a Coors from the case he'd been working on for the past two days.

"Are any of those riding mules?" I asked.

Craig crushed his empty beer can in one hand, squinted at me like the Marlboro man, then said, "Well, sure. Irene there's a riding mule." He pointed Irene out to me, but when I approached her, she skittered away. Craig walked right up to her, snapped a lead rope to her leather halter, and brought her over to me.

"Go ahead," he said. "Jump right up on her back. She won't mind."

"What about a bridle?" I asked.

"You won't need it," he scoffed. "Just hold on to the halter real tight."

Craig bent over and locked his hands together for a stirrup, I placed one foot in there, and he launched me onto Irene's back.

Irene galloped about fifty yards up the trail, spun in a circle twice, then bucked me about eight feet into the air. Fortunately, I landed on a sand flat, mostly unhurt.

Craig laughed so hard, he had to sit down on the ground to keep from falling over. Then, to show there were no hard feelings, he brought Irene around again and jumped on her back himself. Craig lasted longer than the eight seconds needed to qualify as a bareback bronco ride, but when Irene finally threw him off, he landed in a pile of rocks with his legs bent under him in several ugly angles. We all ran to help him up, fearing he'd broken something, but Craig just hopped to his feet, dusted himself off, limped up the trail a ways, cussed a couple of times, and asked for another beer.

※

We completed our assignment there on Rattlesnake Creek in about four weeks and were ready to leave when headquarters notified us by radio that due to the shortage of packers, a pack train couldn't be sent in to pick us up for another week. When we asked what we should do in the meantime, we were told, "Make yourselves useful."

None of us minded staying another week. Rattlesnake Creek is lower in elevation than much of the backcountry, maybe a bit warm at times, but for us it was pure paradise. We were camped in lodgepole pines near the creek with dramatic views of the canyon walls above. We had a mountain of firewood, and we stayed up late every night playing poker on a table made from a tree round. The only problem was that we were running out of food. We still had some rice, potatoes, and a few canned goods, so we weren't going to starve, but we lacked meat or protein of any kind. Luckily, Rattlesnake Creek is full of trout—mostly goldens—though none of us had thought to bring any fishing gear. So we decided that the best way to make ourselves useful was to design our own fishing spears and see who could stick the most trout. Yes, we'd be fishing on government time, and getting paid for it, but the government had abandoned us to survive by our own wits. In our minds, finding a way to eat in the wilderness when nearly all our food had run out was making ourselves useful, and we didn't feel guilty about it.

Gary Hart, another Three Rivers boy, was the quickest to adapt to the situation. He put away his park service uniform and advised the rest of us to do the same. Perhaps anticipating just such an opportunity, he'd brought with him a piece of deerskin from which he'd fashioned a loincloth. Gary, who had been the center on Woodlake High School's valley championship football team, stood six foot one and weighed about 210 pounds. With a red bandana holding back his long hair, and a six-foot spear in his hand, he made a formidable savage. The rest of us tore up our T-shirts and reverted to wearing cloth loincloths, and because we were in the water most of the day, we cast our boots aside and went barefoot, too.

My own spear consisted of a straight cedar limb with a barbed piece of fence wire lashed to the tip. The others invented their own designs, and every morning we fanned out along the creek, studying the deeper pools where we figured we might have a chance to spear a big fish.

After a few days of this, we were all severely sunburned—sunscreen didn't exist yet, or at least we'd never heard of it—so we began smearing mud over our faces, shoulders, and chests. We soon learned about the problem of light refraction—that a fish in the water isn't really where it appears to be—and how to compensate by aiming slightly in front of the fish. Also, we discovered that to get close enough to a fish to spear it, you had to approach a pool with great stealth. One day I was so focused on sneaking up to an undisturbed pool that I stepped on a coiled rattlesnake. Even before I heard the rattle, I felt the slippery snake skin under my toes, and somehow I launched myself three feet into the air and landed five feet away. It was a survival mechanism I didn't even know I had.

One of the trout we speared came from a deep, clear pool on lower Rattlesnake Creek that could only be reached by climbing down a steep cliff. That poor fish had known only a worry-free life of many years until one day it was attacked by a clan of devolved primates with rock-climbing skills and crude fishing tools. I'd venture to guess that it weighed nearly five pounds, adjusting of course for normal exaggeration multiplied by the passing of time. We smoked our prize trout on an oak fire and ate it with blackened fingers, still wearing our loincloths, grunting our satisfaction but snarling at any member of the tribe who dared claim more than his share.

Soon we were spearing so many fish that we didn't need to work all day long anymore, so we devised another way to pass our afternoons. In the lower canyon we found a section of the creek where the water had carved a smooth but winding channel through solid granite. We could slide on our butts down the algae-slickened chute and land with a splash in the pool below—an exhilarating pastime that occupied our simplified minds for hours.

And then one carefree morning, as I was squatting on a granite boulder with my spear in my hand, staring intently into the creek, I heard a baritone voice shout, "What's the matter, you can't catch them on a hook?" Startled, I looked up and saw a cowboy on a horse leading a string of mules. Because of the roar of the rapids, I hadn't heard them approaching. The cowboy was wearing a park service uniform and a white straw cowboy hat. He was about fifty, skinny as a fence post, and looked as if he'd spent half his life on horseback riding into the wind. I was so startled and embarrassed, I chucked my spear into the bushes and hurried back to camp.

Slim Knutsen was born in Tulare County in 1919. He once told me that in his entire life he'd been to San Francisco once and Los Angeles twice, but no farther than that. He'd started packing mules at a young age, and by 1939 he was working at Cecil Pack Trains, out of Horse Corral Meadow, running supplies in to the federal Civilian Conservation Corps crews working in Kings Canyon. Over the years he worked at a number of jobs in farming and ranching, but his heart was always in the mountains, and when he finally got a chance to go to work full time as a mule packer for the park service, he took it.

Slim saw right away that our crew had degenerated into a band of mud-slathered savages, unshaven, half naked, living on fish and potatoes, and communicating mostly with hand signs. He had no authority over us, but he was thirty years wiser. That evening, after a supper of grilled steaks and fresh salad, he broke out a case of Budweiser and handed a can to each of us. He knew we'd been without beer for at least a week, and it was important to get us back on a proper diet as soon as possible. Then he said, "Tomorrow's a layover day for me and the stock. If you boys have finished your drift fences, I think it would be a good idea if we had us a little training session."

In the morning we all shaved and put on our park uniforms again, and after a breakfast of pancakes, bacon, and eggs, we lined up behind the tautline, where Slim had tied the six mules and his horse.

"Now, I saw by the way you fellows helped me unload the mules yesterday that you don't know squat about pack animals," he said. "We need to correct that situation before one of you damn fools gets yourself hurt or killed."

As Slim stepped toward the mules, they twitched their ears suspiciously and shifted their rumps to keep him in sight.

"Since you fellas are almost completely ignorant in these matters, I'll start right at the beginning—how to tell a mule's sex. Now, all the males here have been castrated, something I bet your mamas wished they'd had done to you. You'll notice by looking under their bellies, the males and females look pretty much the same most of the time. A male can alter his appearance when he's in the right mood, but we don't always have time to wait around for that to happen. The secret is to look not under their bellies, but under their tails."

Slim stepped toward a stout young mule with a crazy look in his eye and said, "Fortunately, it's easy for even morons like you to tell any mule's sex by thinking in terms of Morse code."

He lifted the mule's tail and continued. "Pot here is a male, and his mark is a dot." He pointed to the dot. Then Slim stepped toward the next mule and lifted its tail. "Mandy here is a female, and her mark is a dot-dash." Slim pointed to the dot-dash. Mandy added her own commentary by farting once, then issuing a mound of green, steaming turds.

By the end of the day, Slim had taught us the very basics of mule packing: brushing and currying, cleaning an animal's feet, touching their rump when you come up behind them so you won't get kicked, leading them with a hand under the chin and not from the end of a long rope, coiling a lash rope, folding a pack tarp, and more. We weren't packers—in my case, it would be a few more years before I dared call myself that—but at least we knew enough not to get hurt, and just maybe we'd be of some use helping a real packer.

That evening we were all sitting around the fire listening to FM radio. Reception in the mountains is always spotty, but we'd learned that it was better at night and that we could improve the reception by running a twenty-foot strand of fence wire up a lodgepole pine and clamping it to the tip of our radio's antennae. Because all of us except Slim were in our early twenties, we favored rock-and-roll stations, and 1971 was still in the golden age for our kind of music. One song I remember hearing a lot that summer was "Going Up the Country," a lively blues tune Canned

Heat had played at the Woodstock festival a couple years earlier. That song had become a kind of anthem for people of my generation who were disillusioned with the materialism of urban culture and felt a powerful need to get back to nature. In the high mountains, though, country-western radio stations usually have the best reception. Some of those country stations were only fifty miles away in the San Joaquin Valley, but others came from as far away as Arizona and Oklahoma. Most of the music we heard on those stations was pure hillbilly, but there was also a new country-rock fusion, with southern bands playing rock, and urban bands playing country, and some of that music almost spanned the gap between us and our packer, Slim Knutsen.

We were listening to a country-western station out of Bakersfield, when the disc jockey announced that he had a new song by Hank Williams Jr. called "Family Tradition." We appreciated Hank Jr. for his unrepentant rowdiness and his whiskey growl. We knew about his famous father, of course, but we hadn't really come to an understanding yet of what a giant Hank Williams Sr. had been in country music. When Slim heard the disc jockey say the name Hank Williams, though, he raised one hand, signaling for us to be quiet. But when he heard the opening of the song, he said, "That ain't Hank."

"No," I said, "it's his son, Hank Jr. Give him a chance. We think he's pretty good."

"Well, all right, if it's Hank's boy," he said. "Lemme listen and I'll decide for myself if he's any good or not."

I doubt that Hank Sr. ever had more fans anywhere in the world than in the San Joaquin Valley. During the Great Depression, the valley filled up with homeless farmworkers from Oklahoma, Texas, Arkansas, and all over the Midwest. They came fleeing the Dust Bowl, looking for work, and they brought their taste in music with them. Hank wrote about heartache and failure, drinking and love, loneliness, and sometimes religion, and he sang with a Southern twang that reminded the valley's Southern immigrants where they had come from.

The winter before I met Slim Knutsen, I'd been taking a

writing class from Pulitzer Prize-winning poet Phillip Levine. One evening the class was being held at the home of a talented young Fresno poet, Roberta Spear. As the students arrived, Roberta had a Hank Williams album playing quietly in the background. When Levine came through the front door, he stopped and asked, with a sour expression on his face, "What is that awful music?"

"That's Hank Williams," I said, not sure if he was joking. How could a poet of Levine's reputation not have heard of the most important person in American country music?

"Oh, I get it," Levine replied sarcastically. "He's some hillbilly star you kids think is cool this year."

Levine, who was originally from Detroit, had worked on an auto assembly line for a while and had somehow managed to parlay that into a reputation as a blue-collar poet. He even said once that there wasn't any blue-collar poetry until he started writing it. But the truth was, Phil Levine drove a BMW, lived on Van Ness Avenue (in Fresno's high-tone neighborhood in those days), played tennis in white shorts with a collegiate sweater tied around his neck, wore fine leather jackets that cost more than my annual tuition, and ridiculed hiking as something you were forced to do when the car breaks down. By watching Levine, I saw that a lot of American poetry had been commandeered by academics who isolated themselves from the language and culture around them. Their public images were as carefully cultivated as a politician's, and sometimes just as false.

Half the kids I went to school with in the San Joaquin Valley were Dust Bowl Okies, and another quarter were Mexican immigrants. The English we spoke was a mongrel language, but so was Shakespeare's, based mostly on German, but influenced also by the Celts, the Vikings, and the French. That's what makes English so wonderfully adaptable. It's a language almost without rules, which means there is no correct or incorrect way to use it. As Shakespeare demonstrated a thousand times, the more rules you break, the more useful English becomes. American folksingers like Bob Dylan, and beat poets like Gary Snyder all understood this, and I was beginning to understand it too. Living and working with cowboys, Mexicans, Native Americans, and Okies had become the best graduate course a student of English could possibly have. Today I can't remember a single line from any poem Phil Levine ever wrote, yet I can recite the lyrics to a dozen songs by Hank Williams—even more if I've had a beer or two.

That evening in our camp there on the Rattlesnake Creek, our packer Slim Knutsen listened patiently to Hank Jr.'s "Family Tradition":

> *I am very proud of my daddy's name*
>
> *Although his kind of music and mine ain't exactly the same.*
>
> *Stop and think it over, put yourself in my position,*
>
> *If I get stoned and sing all night long, it's a family tradition.*

When the song was over, we all looked toward Slim for his opinion. I don't think we needed his approval, exactly, but we were curious to know what he thought of a Hank who came from our generation. At first Slim was reluctant, or perhaps too polite, to tell us what he really thought. But we insisted. He finished his Budweiser, crushed the can, and tossed it into the fire. He rocked back on his stump, locked his fingers across one knee, spit sideways, and said, "Ah, hell, he can't hold a candle to his daddy."

On the western edge of Kings Canyon National Park, between the foothills and the high country, is a place called Redwood Mountain that contains the largest grove of giant sequoias in the world. (Sequoias of the Sierra Nevada are called giant sequoias, while the coastal sequoias are usually called redwoods.) Unlike other large groves of sequoias, such as the nearby Converse Grove that was almost entirely destroyed by loggers at the end of the nineteenth century, Redwood Mountain was miraculously preserved—not in perfectly pristine form, but pretty close to it.

Because giant sequoias have extremely shallow roots, and because some specimens are over three hundred feet tall, they can't grow in places where there are high winds—they would simply blow over. Also, the wood of giant sequoias is so brittle, the trees can't bend and sway in wind the way the coastal redwoods of northern California and Oregon are able to do. That brittle wood means giant sequoias aren't much good for most construction purposes. So in the nineteenth century, their wood was valued only for its exceptional resistance to rot. Some of the largest trees in the world were cut down, bucked into short lengths, and then split into fence posts, grape stakes, and shake shingles for the ranchers and farmers of the San Joaquin Valley. The awe-inspiring sequoias at Redwood Mountain had escaped that fate, but now they had other problems of their own.

In the 1960s, park service foresters began to see that the sequoias at Redwood Mountain weren't reproducing the way they should. You could hike the maze of trails around and across the mountain and see magnificent specimens that were 2,000 years old, 250 feet tall, and 30 feet in diameter, but there were few trees less than 100 years old, and almost no seedlings at all. The reason for that was fire suppression. Without fire, sequoia cones, which are about the size of a lemon, don't open to allow their seeds, which are no bigger than a baby's fingernail, to germinate. In order to correct that problem, fire had to be re-introduced to the sequoia groves, but it had to be done under carefully controlled conditions. A hundred years of dead wood had accumulated on the forest floor, and a wildfire would burn much hotter than it might have under natural conditions, causing damage or total destruction of the finest stand of sequoias in the world.

During the summer of 1972, park fire crews began cutting fire lines at Redwood Mountain in preparation for a big prescribed burn later that fall. In October my crew came out of the backcountry and joined in that work. We set up weather stations, and every morning and afternoon we monitored the temperature, humidity, and fuel moisture in anticipation of the time when conditions would be perfect to light our prescribed burn. But before that time came, there was one final task that had to be completed.

In the 1880s and 1890s, before there were large dams on the Kings, Kaweah, and Kern rivers, and a complex irrigation network in the San Joaquin Valley, many farmers had no choice but to bring their crops in as early as possible, before their ditches ran dry. Then, in late summer and early fall, with little else to do, they escaped with their families to the cool of the mountains. Some went to Mineral King, where they pretended to be mining for silver (no significant amount of silver was ever found there), some hunted, some loafed (which often amounts to the same thing), and some went to work making redwood roof shingles.

The first step in making roof shingles, or shakes as they were sometimes called, was to put one of those giant sequoias flat on the ground. Because the wood was so brittle, the tree might shatter when it hit the ground, rendering the wood useless, so the loggers would spend several days excavating a bed three feet deep and 200 feet long, where they expected the tree might fall. Then they lined the bed with hand-cut fir branches. Sequoias have very large butt swells (which add stability to their bases and make up a bit for their inadequate roots) so the loggers would have to build a crude scaffolding maybe ten feet high to get above the swell, where the smaller trees were only twelve feet in diameter. Using extra-long crosscut saws made by welding two standard saws together, a pair of loggers would make the undercut about a third of the way into the tree. Wielding double bit axes, they'd slice away a section as high as their heads; then from the other side, using their saw again, they'd make the backcut. If they had calculated the tree's lean correctly, it would fall on its own; if not, they'd have to drive steel wedges into the cut until they could pry it over. If the tree failed to land in the bed of firs the loggers had prepared, they would abandon the horrendous mess they'd made and move on to another tree. Judging by the number of shattered sequoias still lying beside hand-dug trenches, the loggers miscalculated the fall plenty of times.

Once the loggers had managed to fall a tree without shattering it to pieces, they began bucking the log into rounds. If their intention was to make shakes, their rounds would be only eighteen to twenty-four inches thick. They'd push the rounds over until they were flat on the ground, and with splitting wedges they'd break the rounds up into blocks. Then they'd sit down with a wooden mallet and a froe (a long-bladed knife with a vertical handle) and begin the long, tedious process of splitting the redwood into shakes. The advantage of the froe, by the way, is that it is struck by the mallet and not swung like an axe, and therefore it requires less energy to use, is more accurate, and much safer too.

(As a brief aside, the language of logging is different in the western United States than it is in the East. New York and Chicago might have most of the lexicographers, but west of the Rockies we have most of the loggers, and that allows us the right to describe our work however we wish. To the three-fingered sawyers who taught me how to use a chainsaw, you "fall a tree." In the past tense you "fell a tree." To loggers out West, there's no such word as "felled," and a "feller" is just a fellow hillbilly. A young writer working in the woods had to think about such things.)

Those San Joaquin Valley farmers on their shake-splitting holidays were hardheaded people, unreasonably diligent, with a tolerance for hard work we can scarcely imagine today. Over weeks and months, they amassed piles of shakes that were sometimes the size of a house. But apparently the market for shakes wasn't nearly as large as they'd anticipated because those mountains of redwood shakes were left there to gray in the sun for nearly a hundred years. When we came upon them in the 1970s, we could scrape the shakes with a fingernail, and just below the surface the redwood looked as fresh as the day it had been split. But the shakes were very dry, they posed a severe fire hazard to the sequoias surrounding them, and they had to be eliminated before we could safely light our prescribed burns.

I was assigned the task of burning those shingle piles with another park employee, Scott Erickson, who was about my age at that time, twenty-three. Scott was a so-called "hotshot" who'd been trained to parachute out of airplanes to fight fires in remote locations. He was very fit and self-assured, though not a chest pounder like some in that line of work. He was also an excellent rock climber who'd pioneered new routes on the granite walls of Tokopah Valley and other places in Sequoia. Those who'd climbed with him said he was daring but not reckless, and had great confidence in his own judgment. Scott was respected by everyone for his intelligence and even temperament.

One evening after supper, Scott and I hiked out to the shake piles at Redwood Mountain. We measured the fuel moisture and humidity, as we'd been taught; then, seeing conditions were just right, we set the largest shake pile on fire. It was a cool, clear evening, with a slight down-canyon breeze, so we lit the fire on the down canyon side of the pile. That way the fire would slowly back into the shakes rather than blow up in a wind-fed explosion of heat.

Our plan was working perfectly, but we soon saw that it might take all night for our blaze to consume the entire pile. So we settled down for an evening around the biggest campfire in Tulare County history. From our position, we could look west across the lower foothills to the San Joaquin Valley and, in the fading light, see the patchwork pattern of vineyards and orange groves that had become the most productive farmland in the world.

I must admit that in a way I felt like an arsonist, destroying with a single match the hard work of the men who had labored there so long ago. On the other hand, those people had no right to destroy trees that had been among the great natural wonders of the world and should have been preserved for future generations to enjoy. In a way, destroying their work was like destroying the ivory tusks taken from elephant poachers in Africa, and I didn't feel guilty about it.

To be fair, though, I don't believe it's right to judge people from a previous century by the standards we honor today. Those rugged woodcutters were still living under the illusion that our world contained endless resources. They had no idea how small this Earth would soon become. Even John Muir, perhaps the greatest preservationist of all time, made his living in the summer driving sheep into the Sierra Nevada high country, causing great harm to the fragile meadows there. People of that era just didn't understand how delicately balanced nature was, and how quickly it could be destroyed. While the shake makers may have put their own financial interests first, I prefer to think of them as good, hardworking people trying their best to get along in life.

As the twilight settled around us, Scott and I talked. I wanted to hear about his rock-climbing adventures and about parachuting out of planes. But Scott had other things on his mind. He was interested in computers, which scarcely existed at that time—personal computers didn't exist at all. Scott had somehow taught himself the basics of programming, and he was beginning to think that computers could be used to help organize wildland firefighting. Like other park employees, I'd been called on to help fight wildfires from time to time, and I knew what a logistical nightmare they could become. Often there were several agencies from all over the West responding to a large fire—the National Park Service, the California Division of Forestry, the Bureau of Land Management, the US Forest Service—and just communicating with one another was a big problem. When several fires were occurring at the same time, the agencies could scarcely keep track of where their equipment and personnel were at any given time. Often it seemed like the only way the agencies managed to control wildfires at all was by throwing huge amounts of manpower and equipment at them, like war, and the whole process was enormously chaotic, wasteful, and very expensive.

"By creating one database of all the equipment and personnel in the western United States," Scott said, "we could keep track of where every piece of equipment is at any time. We could manage the flow of personnel much more efficiently, too. I don't think it would be that hard. The agencies would be able to share resources, the cost savings would be huge, and the whole mess would just work so much more smoothly."

I really had no idea what he was talking about, and I wasn't even sure that putting order to chaos, as he wanted to do, was such a great idea. One thing I really liked about working for the park service was the endless bureaucratic confusion that put you in situations you could never have imagined. But I could see Scott's point of view, too, if I tried. He was just far more serious than most people I knew, more focused and determined, and he had such great vision at a young age.

As you might imagine, Scott Erickson quickly became a superstar in the National Park Service, leaping up a long and tedious ladder that took most employees decades to climb. In less than ten years, his dream of a computerized central firefighting system became a reality in the Boise Interagency Fire Center in Idaho, where he became the man who made it happen. The way government agencies attack large wildfires in the western United States today was created to a large extent by him.

Scott and I would run into each other again, many years later, under far different circumstances.

In the summer of 1973, my backcountry crew and I were working at another place named for the redwoods, Redwood Meadow, just a couple miles above the Middle Fork of the Kaweah, about twelve miles into the backcountry of Sequoia National Park. During the Great Depression, the Civilian Conservation Corps built a fine old cabin there, known as the Redwood Meadow cabin, which stands on a foundation of rough-hewn redwood slabs so large, they had to be dragged into place by teams of mules. It's a beautiful example of CCC craftsmanship. The crews often consisted of twenty or more young men, or boys, supervised by older men who were experts in their crafts, such as carpentry, masonry, and plumbing. The boys worked for thirty dollars a month plus meals, with the agreement that twenty-five dollars would be sent home to their families. During the Depression, that money kept many families from going hungry.

As much as I admired the Redwood cabin, though, I refused to sleep in it, and I even avoided going inside it if I could. Places become imbued with the spirit of the people who lived and worked there, and the more beautiful a place, the more likely it is to have spirits hanging around. It isn't something that can be measured in a scientific way, and religion can't explain it, either. It has to do with the way our imperfect minds try to make peace with death and the absence it leaves behind.

Because the cabin is built beneath a grove of firs, it receives little direct sunlight. The windows provide inadequate natural light, and there is no electricity for lighting. The place inflamed my claustrophobia so badly, I couldn't bear to be inside it for more than a minute or two. But the thing that makes the Redwood cabin truly uninhabitable, for me at least, is knowing that those young men in the CCC spent what might have been the happiest days of their lives working there. Then they went off to fight in World War II, and a lot of them never came back. Redwood cabin is infused with their memories. You can see the marks they made with their draw knives on the walls, see their fingerprints in the linseed oil coating the kitchen shelves. Even the dust in the corners is theirs. Now the cabin stands there unused and covered with snow for at least half the year. So it's only natural that ghosts would take it over, and as far as I'm concerned, they're welcome to it. It belongs to them.

Slim Knutsen had packed food and materials into the CCC crews at Redwood Meadow when he'd been not much more than a boy himself. Sometimes in the evening, standing around a campfire outside the cabin, Slim would tell us about those days, the men he'd known, and the work they'd done together some thirty-five years earlier. For us, thirty-five years seemed like a geological epoch, yet forty-five years have passed now since Slim first told me about those CCC boys, and my concept of time has changed considerably.

The reason we'd come to Redwood Meadow that summer was to improve the fence used to protect the most fragile portion of the meadow, which was sometimes grazed by pack stock. It was a flat meadow that tended to be boggy early in the summer; if stock were allowed to graze it too soon, a lot of damage could occur. In addition, a handsome grove of mature sequoias surrounded the meadow. Sequoias grow where there's ample ground moisture, which is why they're often found on the fringes of meadows. Our thinking was that if we lost Redwood Meadow to overgrazing, we might lose the grove of sequoias as well. An old fence, first built by the CCC to protect the meadow, had long ago fallen into disrepair, so we started rebuilding it, replacing the rotten posts and stringing new wire. Some of those old posts had been made from split redwood and were still perfectly usable; they just needed to be reset.

Using redwood for new posts, however, was no longer an option. It's a federal offense to use even dead and down sequoias for any purpose, and this law is taken very seriously by the park service. Even if a sequoia falls across the Generals Highway, the main thoroughfare through the parks, special permission from Washington must be granted before the tree can be cleared from the road. I think it's a wise law, though at times it seems wasteful. Cedars are almost as resistant to rot as sequoias, though, and fortunately there were plenty of cedars not far away. So we cut and limbed thirty cedar posts, and packed them by mule to the job site. When my four-man crew had completed the new fence, we still had a few workdays left at Redwood Meadow, and we began thinking about what else we might do that was more useful than spearing fish.

Some meadows are classified as stringer meadows, lying on a steep hillside, usually along a creek; they're wet in spring, firm by midsummer, and dry by fall. But Redwood Meadow is on a flat with poor drainage, and it often stays wet all summer. The creek leading into and out of the meadow is slow moving and tends to get boggy where the trail crosses it. In fact, the crossing below the meadow had been so badly trampled by hikers and stock that the fragile banks had become a muddy wallow. What the place needed, we decided, was a series of wooden footbridges—nothing elaborate, just practical. The problem was that none of us were very skilled carpenters, and except for our chainsaw, we had no woodworking tools of any kind.

One afternoon we were poking through the old tack shed at Redwood Meadow. It hadn't been used much since the CCC days, was being claimed by marmots and pack rats, and I'd been told by my supervisor back at Ash Mountain headquarters to clean it out. We found old gunny sacks of moldy oats used to feed pack animals, heaps of old baling wire (packers from Slim's era always saw some value in baling wire that my generation was blind to), ancient lanterns with busted globes, twisted horseshoes, cases of rusted nails, and rotted rope. And then in the very back of the tack shed, we uncovered an old metal bin. When we pried open its rusty hinges, we found the carpentry tools the CCC had used to build the cabin at Redwood Meadow: double-bit axes, log carriers, drawknives, and a brace and bits. Their wooden handles were still dark from the oil and sweat of men working there thirty-five years earlier.

The next day we began cutting cedar logs ten feet long and up to twenty-four inches in diameter. (The area where we cut the cedars was badly overgrown after a hundred years of fire suppression and needed to be thinned anyway.) We removed all the cedar bark using the drawknives, cut the log beams (called stringers) to length with our chainsaw, then dragged them to the boggy creek using two of the old CCC log carriers—like giant tongs with handles for a worker on each side. Next we cut stout cedar footings four feet long and two feet thick, smoothed their top surfaces, and placed them on opposite sides of the creek. We dragged the stringers into place by hand, then used the old CCC drawknives to smooth the upper edges. Using the CCC brace and bit, we bored holes through the stringers and into the footings, then fashioned pins of old rebar, which we drove through the stringers and footings to hold the bridges together.

This whole process of building four footbridges took four days. Because we were working in the water much of the time, often wearing only our underwear, at the end of each day we were covered from head to toe in mud. Before supper we'd hike down to Cliff Creek and jump off the granite ledges into a deep pool of clear water—the same place where the CCC boys had washed and played three decades earlier.

The most satisfying work I've ever done in my life was when I had a chance to use both my brain and my hands at the same time. And I've never known more satisfying work than building those simple cedar footbridges at Redwood Meadow. Some of the satisfaction came from knowing we were doing something to help the meadow, but I'm also certain that a lot of the satisfaction came from using those old tools, which might be considered obsolete today, in the same way the CCC workers had used them long ago.

Not all those CCC boys died in the war, of course. Some took permanent jobs with the park service and were finishing their careers just as I was beginning mine. I was lucky enough to know a few of them, and with time I gained a great appreciation for their plain habits and rustic humor, their indifference to hard work, and their simple decency. Most of all, I came to respect the way they had endured, at such a young age, a difficult time in American history. Through knowing and working with those fine men, I was able to partly overcome a distrust of my parents' generation.

♒

After working around giant sequoias for a few years, I came to believe that if humans have a soul, sequoias must have one, too. It used to be difficult for me to talk about such things for fear that park foresters, researchers, and the like would consider me unscientific, mystical, or perhaps just a fool. But I don't really care anymore. I met so many people who'd traveled thousands of miles just to see and touch a giant sequoia, and I saw the effect that experience had on them. Those old sequoias have character like no human I've ever known, and I don't think it's unreasonable to say they possess something like a soul, too. The problem for people like me, who believe in science but remain agnostic about the notion of ghosts, spirits, and souls, is that we're left with no words to describe things we see and feel in nature but can't explain. I work around the problem by assuming that spirit forces reside in our minds, not the external world, and I try to allow other people the freedom to believe whatever they want.

Whatever explanation we might prefer, there are powerful forces at work in those sequoia groves, and many people have something like a spiritual experience the first time they see them. The human desire to see and be near great trees is probably the biggest reason Sequoia National Park exists. But that desire has created a lot of problems, too. Forests aren't static. Trees grow, become old, and die, just like we do, and that means that living in and around great trees can be dangerous.

The second year I worked at Sequoia, before the snow on the

high passes had melted enough for my crew to head into the backcountry, we were staying at the Ash Mountain fire dorm (like a military barracks). We awoke early one morning in June to the sound of powerful winds howling down the Middle Fork of the Kaweah River. Although light down-canyon breezes at night are normal on the western slope of the Sierra, strong night winds are unusual. But there is a phenomenon on the western slope known as the Mono wind. It's a katabatic wind, similar to the notorious Santa Ana winds of southern California. Sometimes, rarely, high pressure over the Great Basin in Nevada and Utah forces air over the passes of the Sierra and down the canyons on the western slope. Mono winds are more common in Yosemite and the Sierra National Forest to the north, but they're almost unheard of farther south.

Of the sixty-seven sequoia groves in existence, fifty-nine are located south of the Kings River. Sequoias have shallow roots, often only about four feet deep, and their roots extend laterally only a short way beyond their trunks. It seems odd, but the largest trees in the world blow over rather easily. A short hike through almost any grove of giant sequoias will reveal magnificent specimens that stood for more than a thousand years and then, one day, simply fell over. How can that be? The answer, I believe, is that even though Mono winds are a rare event in the southern Sierra, they do occur.

But why are Mono winds less common in the south? The reason is partly that the Sierra Nevada is higher in the south—all the peaks over 14,000 feet are at the southern end—but also in the south there are actually two ranges, the Sierra Nevada and the Kaweah Range, separated by the deep Kern River Canyon. If you think of wind as high pressure flowing to low pressure, then in order for Mono winds to reach Giant Forest, high pressure air in the Owens Valley would have to spill over the highest passes of the southern Sierra, sweep across the upper Kern Canyon, rise over the passes in the Kaweah Range, and flow into the mid-elevation areas above the foothills. That is a very unlikely event. Nevertheless, Mono Winds found their way to Giant Forest that June day in 1971, and it was a disaster.

Giant Forest in those days was a classic example of poor park planning. For seventy years the park service had allowed the concessioner to build more than three hundred buildings under the largest trees in the world. The structures included a lodge, store, restaurant, warehouses, and dozens of cabins and tent cabins; there were also parking lots, a trash incinerator, a maze of service roads, and more. A lot of it was destroyed that day, not just by falling sequoias, but by falling white firs, red firs, and sugar pines. Almost the entire Giant Forest plateau was a tangle of jackstrawed trees, and the forestry crew I was working on spent several weeks trying to untangle it. We weren't allowed to touch the largest, or so-called monarch sequoias, not even those now lying on top of buildings or secondary roads; they were all preserved as part of the park heritage. But the rest of Giant Forest was changed forever, and for the better. In just a few years, almost all the buildings in Giant Forest had been removed, and the park concessioner had been relocated to the Clover Creek area, a few miles away, where sequoias don't grow.

Although there have been a few people killed by falling trees in Sequoia and Kings Canyon over the years, I've always considered it a miracle that far more people haven't been killed or injured. Every spring and fall, I worked on a hazardous tree crew that moved from one end of the parks to the other, cutting down some of the largest and most hazardous trees, including firs, pines, and cedars—but never sequoias. Most of us on that crew were in our early twenties and really too young and impulsive to be trusted with such dangerous work. Fortunately, we were trained and supervised by a very experienced tree worker named Charlie Castro, a Paiute who'd grown up in Yosemite Valley. We sometimes affectionately called him, "Chainsaw Charlie."

Learning how to fall big trees followed the old apprentice system. First you're a laborer, trusted to drag limbs and carry fuel and tools for the experienced workers. Then you become an axman, allowed to cut limbs from the fallen trees, first by ax, then by small chainsaw. Once you learn to handle and maintain a small chainsaw, you're promoted to sawyer, using a larger saw to buck up fallen trees. The final step is to become a faller, and only a few tree workers make it to that level.

Charlie selected the new fallers himself, though any sawyer

# Going Up the Country

was allowed to listen in on the training sessions and begin to learn the craft. Charlie showed us how to read a big tree's lean by walking around the base and gazing up the bole, or trunk. He showed us how to judge the quality of a tree's wood by thumping on it with an eight-pound sledge. He taught us to study the tree's tip and branches for "widowmakers"—dead or rotten parts that fall off when a falling tree begins to lean. Charlie taught us the three basic cuts: the undercut, which determines the direction a tree will fall; the topcut, which opens the bottom cut and allows the tree to fall the first forty-five degrees; and the backcut, which almost, but not quite, joins the other two cuts and allows the tree to begin falling. He explained the absolute necessity of leaving a strip of uncut wood, the hinge, to guide the tree in its fall. He explained how a tree with good wood at the base can be "pulled," using nothing but well-placed cuts to coax it to fall up to ninety degrees away from its lean. And he demonstrated, literally hundreds of times, how a tree can be felled 180 degrees from its lean by using steel wedges and, in some cases, ropes.

Like many of my fellow workers, I became fascinated with that work. I knew that if I wanted a career as a writer, it might take a few years before I'd be able to make my living that way, and until then I'd need a more practical way to support myself. Falling big trees was interesting and exciting and, most important, it could only be done outdoors.

In the 1970s the number of annual visitors to Sequoia and Kings Canyon was growing rapidly, just as the population of the country grew. The increased number of visitors meant a greater likelihood of accidents or fatalities caused by falling trees. And gradually the park service began to accept responsibility for doing more to ensure visitor safety. If a camper is killed in his tent by a tree blowing over in the night, is it an act of God? Or should the park service have done a better job of providing the camper with a safe place to pitch his tent? The answer might seem obvious now, but in the 1970s it was a hotly contested issue. I once had rabid environmentalists screaming at me that I was violating federal law, and God's will, by putting a chainsaw blade to any tree inside the boundaries of a national park. Other people thought campers should accept responsibility for their own safety, and that the government had no business spending taxpayer money pampering them. Still others felt there were too many people on the planet anyway, and natural disasters were just nature's way of culling the herd.

I'm certain that our hazardous tree crew saved dozens, if not hundreds, of lives in those years. We took our jobs very seriously, not just for our safety, but for the welfare of millions of visitors who didn't understand the dangers of the environment they were in. But we also had a helluva lot of fun doing it.

There were four or five of us at that time who'd been trained to fall trees by Charlie Castro. We were all at about the same level of proficiency in tree falling, and we were highly competitive with each other. Every day we were dropping some of the biggest trees left on the western slope of the Sierra, many of them fifty or sixty inches in diameter (some up to eighty inches in diameter) and as much as 250 feet tall. Most of the trees were either dead or dying, and almost all of them were rotten. Many of the large firs, either red or white, were practically hollow, with just a rim of fairly solid wood around the base. We were working in campgrounds, around buildings, power lines, water lines, and roads. In addition, our goal was to fall the hazardous trees without damaging the healthy trees around them, and sometimes those other trees were sequoias. If we so much as scuffed a sequoia, we could have been in big trouble. As a result, we became very proficient at dropping even the sloppiest trees in the narrowest of places.

We used to play a game called "hit the peg." When our turn to fall a tree came around, we'd drive a peg into the ground to mark the exact spot where we wanted the tree to go. At the end of the day, the faller who came closest to hitting his pegs enjoyed dinner at the others' expense, either at the restaurant at Stony Creek or at Grant Grove.

Red firs and white firs grow more rapidly than pines, and their wood is tough and fibrous, which makes it an ideal choice for construction purposes. Before World War II, many houses in California were framed with two-by-fours from one of the fir species, but today the wood from the Douglas fir (which is not a true fir) is more commonly used for construction. The firs grow readily in shade, which gives them an advantage over pines and cedars, and that's why the firs often crowd out the other conifers, creating bleak and unhealthy monocultures where practically nothing else grows. Man's suppression of fire over the past 150 years has made the problem worse by favoring trees that can grow in the shade of a dense canopy.

Our hazardous tree crew came to think of white firs and red firs as almost weeds. We called them "piss firs" because of the foul odor of their decaying wood. Inside some mature firs, there are large pockets where fetid water accumulates. Often when we were in the process of cutting down a sixty-inch white fir, our chainsaws would penetrate one of those pockets, and the foul water would be flung back on us by the teeth of the chain. We'd curse and moan, but there was nothing we could do about it—the smell was already splattered all over our clothes. When we returned to Ash Mountain headquarters at the end of the day, the office workers heading to their cars in the parking lot would take one sniff of us and make a wide detour.

Falling white firs and red firs can also be treacherous. A tree that appears to be solid at ground level could be badly rotten a hundred feet up. As soon as the backcut was completed and the tree began to lean toward its line of fall, the balance was upset and the entire middle section of the tree might collapse. I saw this happen many times. To minimize the risk, a faller always worked with a spotter who stood about fifty feet away. The spotter maintained eye contact with the faller while also trying to keep watch on the upper portion of the tree. If the tree suddenly began to collapse, the spotter made a hand sign by slicing his thumb across his own throat, which meant "Get the hell out of there right now!" The faller then left the saw in the cut and sprinted away from the tree as quickly as possible. We all had this happen to us, but because the collapse of the tree happens in relative slow motion, and because we were young and nimble of foot, nobody I knew ever got hurt that way. Once, though, I was spotting for my friend Mike Gililland, when a red fir collapsed so quickly, practically exploded, that he couldn't get completely out of the way in time. Mike was showered with a couple hundred pounds of rotten wood and foul-smelling water. Fortunately, none of the pieces were large enough to hurt him, though he was knocked to the ground and smelled like a sewer for the rest of the day.

Once, in Dorst campground, Bill Paleck, a University of Arizona graduate who later became superintendent of North Cascades National Park, was cutting into a red fir that had a large cat face (a rotted out hollow at ground level) when the chain of his saw suddenly turned blood red. He looked at me—I was his spotter—and I gave him the cut-throat sign.

"What in the hell is that!" Bill shouted.

"Looks like blood to me," I said.

"Trees don't bleed!"

We talked it over for a few minutes and decided that what certainly appeared to be blood had to be some form of putrid fir rot we 'd never seen before. Bill fired up his chainsaw again and finished falling the tree. After the tree hit the ground and we were able to examine the bole, we saw there was a large hollow section inside where a raccoon had taken refuge. Bill had severed the raccoon's tail. As soon as we backed off and left it alone, the terrified raccoon, which appeared to be otherwise unhurt, scampered off into the woods.

Sometimes we encountered hazardous trees next to buildings and power lines. The trees had to be removed, but we simply had no direction in which we could safely fall them. The solution was for a worker with spurs and a flipline to climb high in the tree, tie in with a safety line, and, using a small chainsaw, bring the tree down in sections.

Finding workers who had the physical agility, the courage, and the desire to be tree climbers wasn't easy. Jack Townley, one of the finest climbers I ever saw, told me how he got started: "When I got out of prison," he said, "I was laying in a cheap motel room down in Visalia, in the winter, with pneumonia, drinking cough syrup straight out of the bottle. I was hungry and broke but I didn't want to go back to prison, so I took a minimum-wage job picking peaches. That led to a job pruning peach trees, which led to climbing trees, and eventually I was hired by a tree-trimming service."

The best tree climbers I've known had very high strength-to-weight ratios, an exceptional sense of balance, and were quick. Often climbers are short. Jack Townley, though, was over six feet tall, but his legs were thin and he probably didn't weigh more than 150 pounds. I think he might have been the finest natural athlete I've ever seen. If it hadn't been for his troubled youth, he might have become a track athlete, boxer, or rodeo rider. Watching Jack swing from a tree 175 feet in the air while dangling a chainsaw in one hand was like watching a ballet dancer. He'd roll his head from side to side as he worked, like a praying mantis, as if that somehow helped him judge the task in a way others couldn't. Park visitors who happened to pass by a site where we were working would often stop, get out of their cars, and take pictures of Jack high in some lightning-scarred sugar pine, just a dark, graceful silhouette with the summer sun behind him.

～～
～～

The most experienced tree climber on that crew was our boss, Charlie Castro, who'd learned to climb trees as a boy growing up in Yosemite Valley. I asked him once if he'd done any rock climbing in Yosemite, and he said, "A good rock climber took me climbing with him once. But it didn't feel right to me. I wasn't comfortable. Later, I took that guy tree climbing with me, and he said that scared the hell out of *him*!"

Charlie excelled at everything he set his mind to. Besides being the sort of person who easily made new friends almost every day, he played drums in a popular Dixieland jazz band that toured the world, and he was a skilled fire boss who worked on wildfires all over the West. Charlie was also the only person I know with a sequoia tree named after him; he once rigged a 290-foot sequoia in the Redwood Mountain Grove with ropes and a crude elevator system so professional botanists could study the tree at their leisure, and that tree was later named the Castro Tree in his honor.

Charlie was asked once to appear in an episode of a silly TV series about Yosemite called *Sierra*. The way the plot had been written, Charlie was supposed to have been working high in a tree when he became injured and couldn't get down. The show's star, a Hollywood actor playing a park ranger, then had to rescue him. Charlie told the producers he'd be happy to appear in their drama, for a fee, but they'd have to rewrite the script so the ranger was trapped in the tree and Charlie was the one who did the rescuing. At that time, Charlie was one of the few people in the country who knew how to safely stage such a thing, so the producers had no choice but to go along with his demand. They rewrote the script and Charlie became the hero. Although I never saw the episode myself, I loved hearing Charlie tell about it.

What Charlie Castro was most known for, though, was extinguishing a fire in the California Tree. In 1967 the California Tree in Grant Grove was struck by lightning, and a fire began to smolder inside the trunk, which had been partially hollowed out by previous fires. While sequoias have very thick, fire-resistant bark, once a fire becomes established within the bole of the tree, that insulation works against the tree, allowing the fire to grow even hotter. Lightning-caused fires in sequoias within the park boundaries are normally allowed to burn, the reasons being that lightning is a natural element, sequoias have evolved in the presence of fire, and the process shouldn't be tampered with by man. But the California Tree is located on a popular hiking loop frequented by hundreds of visitors every day of the summer, the tree was dropping sparks and ash on the trail below, and there was a serious danger that part of the upper tree might collapse, showering down tons of burning wood on hikers below. So the decision was made to have Charlie climb the California Tree and extinguish the fire, if possible.

Charlie was thirty-one at the time and in his climbing prime. If anybody could do that job, he could. But the California Tree was so large, it couldn't be climbed by conventional means. Usually when there are no low-lying limbs, a tree climber ascends by use of steel climbing spurs and a flipline. The climber tosses one free end of the rope around the tree, catches it with his other hand, then ties it off on his belt. If the rope is properly adjusted, he can flip the rope a foot or two higher, climb up using his spurs, then complete the process over and over until he reaches a limb. A flipline for a tree four feet in diameter is about thirteen feet long. But the California Tree is twenty-two feet in diameter, and any flipline used to climb it would have to be seventy feet long—utterly impossible to manage. In addition, the lowest limb on the California Tree was about ninety feet from the ground.

What Charlie did was climb a fir next to the California Tree until he was as high as its lowest limb. He then threw a rope over to the limb, secured the rope, swung over to the California Tree, and ascended the rope using a prusik knot (which tree climbers call a monkey fist). From there he threw his rope up to the next limb and prusiked to it. As he climbed, he was being showered by hot cinders from above, and there was a danger that his rope might be burned. Eventually, he managed to reach a point higher than the fire. After tying in securely, he slung a work rope over a limb above him and lowered both ends to the ground, so his ground crew could attach a fire hose to one end. With the ground crew pulling on the other end of the rope, they raised the fire hose and nozzle to Charlie, over two hundred feet in the air. He tied off the hose on the limb above him (a hose that long, when filled with water, would weigh hundreds of pounds) and he began spraying a stream of water into the hollowed-out center of the California Tree. To his surprise, a thick column of steam and ash erupted from the tree and splattered him in the face. Eventually, though, he managed to fully extinguish the fire.

Back on the ground, after working twelve hours on the burning tree, Charlie was greeted by the park's chief ranger, who awarded him with a six pack of beer.

*※*

In the fall of 1973, I was working with the hazardous tree crew at Grant Grove when Charlie Castro announced that our crew needed more tree climbers. The three climbers the crew already had couldn't manage the workload any longer. "There aren't any tree climbers to be hired," he said. "At least not any crazy enough to climb these trees. So I'm gonna see if I can teach some of you myself."

There were about twelve guys on the tree crew at that time, and Charlie selected four of us: Frank Walter, a six-foot-one, three-hundred-pound farm boy from Woodville; Mike Gililland, an excellent tree faller from Springville; Tim Stubbs, a botany student and surfer from San Diego; and me. Our training session began with Charlie leaping up and grabbing the lowest branch of a sugar pine with one arm, doing five one-armed pull-ups, hanging there with his arm cocked at ninety degrees, slamming his biceps with his free hand, and growling, "There's something wrong with a man who can't do a one-armed pull-up!"

One by one we had to demonstrate our ability to do a one-armed pull-up, which immediately ended Frank's tree climbing career. Charlie showed us how to strap on climbing spurs and spike our way a few feet up a tree. Then he showed us how to buckle on a leather climbing belt. He separated the strands of a flipline to show us that the core was made of steel cable, and he explained that if one of us was clumsy enough to nick the flipline with our chainsaw, we had a decent chance of surviving. He showed us how to tie a monkey knot and use it for ascending or descending on a fixed line. And that was about it. We were already fallers, so he didn't need to teach us that. The only difference was that we'd be using a chainsaw so small it looked like a toy, and we'd be using it 150 feet in the air. We had a quick lunch, and then it was time for Charlie to see if we had learned anything.

My assignment was to climb a dead sugar pine more than 225 feet tall and sixty inches in diameter, and take out a fifty-foot section of the top. It was a beautiful tree—or at least had been. It still had most of its orange needles, though some of them were already beginning to fall to the ground. The bark was still thick and firmly attached to the tree, though I could see large pitch balls around the base, which meant the tree had been attacked by bark beetles. The only defense conifers have against invading beetles is to ooze out pitch through the bore holes. Sometimes a healthy tree can win that battle, but this time the beetles had won, and now the tree was rapidly dying.

As I began to climb the sugar pine, dragging my long rappel rope behind me, I noticed for the first time that sugar pines grow in spirals and that you can actually feel the ridges along each twist of the bole. I found the climbing to be easy, even enjoyable—perhaps because of some primitive tree-climbing instinct humans have. What young boy or girl doesn't enjoy climbing a tree? The limbs in this sugar pine were evenly spaced, so the climbing was hardly more difficult than climbing stairs. I really didn't need to use my climbing spurs at all.

I had only been climbing a few minutes when Charlie called up, "That's high enough! Tie in now and take her down!"

At that height, the sugar pine was only about twenty inches in diameter, so flipping my safety line around the bole with my right hand was easy. I caught the loose end with my left hand and fastened the line to my belt. At that point, even if I slipped, I'd only fall a couple feet before the rope caught on the tree's bark and the friction stopped me. I might have the skin removed from my face, and my shirt shredded, but I would otherwise be okay. I set my spurs deep into the bark, leaned back to catch my breath, and looked around.

I was surprised to see how high I was. Somehow I hadn't even noticed on the way up. But I'd been rock climbing much higher many times, with far more exposure, and I felt secure, almost cozy, in that tree. As I looked around me, though, I saw that what had started out as a beautiful day had now become cloudy, and a light breeze from the south had begun to sway the tree just slightly, back and forth.

The Sierra Nevada is renowned for its beautiful summer weather, which is unusual in most mountain regions around the world, where summer rain is more common. Almost all precipitation in the Sierra comes in the form of snow in the winter and spring, and for most of the summer the skies are a deep blue, almost cobalt. But every few years a different weather pattern develops when tropical moisture begins to move up through Mexico, Arizona, and the Owens Valley. As the warm clouds rise over the Sierra Nevada, they cool quickly and begin to dump their heavy loads in the high country. Those violent squalls are sometimes called *chubascos*, a Spanish word that sounds to me like an explosion of wind and rain, which is exactly what a *chubasco* is. The first time I ever heard that word used it was by an old cowboy who spoke some border Spanish and knew that almost everything about the cowboy tradition, from the chaps, lasso, hackamore, and even the word "cowboy," had come up from Mexico. In the Sierra Nevada, a *chubasco* morning often begins clear and dry. A wispy cloud appears in midmorning, by noon the sky is a turbulent gray, thunder and lightning soon follow, and before long violent thrashings of wind and rain are sweeping across the southeastern ridges. In some years, that daily *chubasco* pattern will continue all summer and into the fall.

I'd dragged up a small chainsaw on a short rope behind me. I pulled the saw up to me and quickly made my undercut and topcut in the tree. Then I swung around to the other side and began to make my backcut. As soon as I saw the cut beginning to open the slightest bit, I shut off the saw and quickly lowered it away from me. There are so many ways even a small saw can hurt you—the chain, the dog teeth, and the hot muffler—and I didn't want it anywhere near me if something went wrong.

So far everything had gone perfectly. I felt confident and at ease. Compared to the rock climbing I'd done, this was easy. But as the top of the tree leaned away, gravity and leverage pulled the remainder of the tree with it, perhaps ten feet, until the cut's hinge finally broke, and the top fell into space and began its long, slow-motion descent. Then the rest of the tree, with me attached, swung back in the other direction, a full eight feet, and it continued swinging back and forth, like a metronome, until the energy had been expended. This was something I hadn't expected, and I didn't like the feel of it one bit. The sensation left me feeling nauseated, and even worse, I now had the irrational fear that the sugar pine was no longer firmly attached to the ground—that it might fall over on its own at any moment. I also knew from my experience falling sugar pines that their wood is more brittle than that of other pines, and because this tree was half dead, its wood was more brittle than a healthy tree. It didn't help that the increasing wind was now catching the sugar pine's very long limbs below me and causing the trunk to sway even more.

I was ashamed to feel my legs beginning to tremble with sewing machine knee, just as they had on the side of El Capitan a few years earlier. After taking a couple deep breaths, though, I realized that I no longer had any reason to be in that tree. My task had been completed, and I was free to rappel down any time I wanted. But fear is irrational. When I tied the prusik knot from the pigtail of my safety belt to my climbing rope, I was unwilling to test my weight on it. The prusik is a friction knot—it's loose when tied but tightens when weight is applied. I'd used the knot with complete confidence hundreds of times while rock climbing, but in a tree I no longer trusted it.

Looking down, I could see Charlie with his hands on his hips, glaring up at me impatiently. To stall, I untied the prusik and retied it, as if I hadn't tied it correctly the first time, though I knew very well I had. And then I retied it again. By now the wind was swirling the treetops around me, and I had the sensation of being on a boat in a violent sea. Looking northeast toward the Kings Canyon gorge and the granite peaks beyond, I could see flashes of lightning, followed by the crack of thunder and long echoes rumbling across that enormous landscape.

I knew that tall trees are struck by lightning quite frequently. All old sequoias, for example, are covered with lightning scars. I'd worked on wildfires in the backcountry where the only thing burning was one tall snag that had been struck by lightning. The odds weren't great that the tree I happened to be in would be struck by lightning on this day, but they weren't impossible either, and they seemed to be increasing by the minute.

I found myself thinking about one beautiful sugar pine I'd seen once—it was about the same height and diameter as the one I was trapped in now. The tree had been struck by a bolt of lightning at the very tip, and the lighting had stripped off a long piece of wood about four inches wide and two inches thick that spiraled around the tree three or four times, all the way to the ground. What a frightening display of power that had been, I thought, and how horrible it would be to have the same thing happen to this tree. Still, I couldn't find the will to do what I knew had to be done.

Finally, a bolt of lightning struck a tree not four hundred yards away. Even worse, that tree was lower than I was. Charlie offered his encouragement by calling up to me, "Sorensen, you better get your sorry ass down out of that tree before the lightning knocks you down!"

Seeing that I really had little choice, that I could either die by lightning or die by hitting the ground, I took a deep breath, kicked my spurs loose from the bark, pushed myself away from the tree—and the prusik held. Ten seconds later my feet touched the ground, though my legs wouldn't hold me upright, and I collapsed to my knees.

※

Another tree climber on our hazardous tree crew in those days was Truman James. He came from the foothills below Yosemite, around Mariposa, and he was a Chukchansi, a branch of the Yokuts. Truman was thirty-five when I first met him in 1974. He was about five foot seven, wiry and strong, not as athletically gifted as some climbers, but he made up for that with great tenacity and hard work. For me, Truman was a working-class hero. He showed up on time every morning with a black metal lunch pail in one hand and a thermos of coffee in the other. When there was hard work to be done, nobody jumped in quicker than he did, and he always did his work with a smile. In the years I knew Truman, I never heard him complain about anything, and I never heard another worker say a bad word about him.

Whenever I remember Truman James, I think about a wonderful day we spent working together on the hazardous tree crew in October of 1975. There were a lot of dead trees at Cedar Grove that year. All four campgrounds had been closed, and the road into Cedar Grove had been closed as well, so we could work without having to worry about injuring park visitors. After work we had that beautiful valley all to ourselves.

Cedar Grove is a long, narrow, glacial valley, much like Yosemite, though drier, with fewer waterfalls, and without the huge visitor use. There are high granite walls rising almost vertically from the valley floor. The light in autumn is a warm golden color by day, and at dusk the canyon walls glow pink. The south fork of the Kings River meanders through the canyon, and sometimes after work we'd catch large brown trout in its deep pools. At the east end of the valley, at Copper Creek, lies the site of an ancient Native American village, where we'd find obsidian arrowheads and soapstone beads after the fall rains brought them to the surface. Just a few yards away, on the banks of the Kings, lies a large, flat-topped granite rock some people call Muir's Pulpit because it's said that John Muir himself delivered long-winded lectures there. I like to think of that rock as a place where children dove into the clear water of the Kings while their mothers, grinding acorns, watched from the nearby banks.

The days were still warm in Cedar Grove that October, but the nights were growing chilly, as the alpine air flowed down from the high peaks after the sun went down. We were living in the fire dorm, a typical park service warehouse for workers, with thin plywood walls, a leaky roof, one disgusting shower, and creaky metal cots. There were a lot of hazardous trees to be removed that year, and although our eight-man crew had been working at a furious pace, the night before we were supposed to leave we still hadn't completed the job. Charlie was there, Truman, Frank Walter, Mike Gililland, Don Stivers, and a few more. We were a compatible bunch, even though we came from wildly different backgrounds. We respected one another and enjoyed the time we spent together. We started drinking beer that night, then whiskey, playing poker at the long kitchen table on a red-checkered tablecloth. In a fit of macho drunkenness, we staged an arm-wrestling contest, then gorged ourselves on apple pies that our cook had baked for us. Knowing this would be our last night together that year, we stayed up late telling tree-falling stories and other lies.

The next morning we woke to the annoying crackle of Charlie's park radio. It was the dispatcher at Ash Mountain coming on at 7:45 a.m., which meant we'd all overslept. We jumped out of bed, yanked on our filthy work clothes stained with pine pitch and chainsaw oil, gulped down a quick cup of coffee, and hurried out the door without breakfast.

The only place where we hadn't finished our work yet was Sentinel Campground. There were about thirty trees there that needed to be removed, which was a lot for one day. The trees weren't so large—they averaged maybe twenty-four inches in diameter. But it was still an unreasonable amount of work for a small crew, and most of us really didn't see how it could be done.

Heavy clouds were hanging low over the valley, and a blustery wind was beginning to blow. High above the canyon walls, craggy spires disappeared in the clouds, then burst into view again, like watching an old black-and-white movie. We split up into crews of two, a faller and a spotter, and we began working our way through the campground, slamming down trees wherever we could find a hole in the forest to put them. After we fell a tree, we worked together to limb it, then bucked the trees into sixteen-foot lengths to be used as bumper logs along the park roads. Every stump had to be flushed at ground level in order to make the area appear as natural as possible, and that took time. We worked at a furious pace, but we were young, we'd been doing this kind of work for months, and somehow we enjoyed it.

As it turned out, some of the trees were so rotten, they were of no use as bumper logs, which meant we'd have to do the long, tedious work of bucking and splitting them so we could haul them away in a dump truck. But then Charlie Castro showed us a trick we'd never seen before. He told me to put on climbing spurs and scramble up one of the rotten trees, hauling a thick work rope, called a "bull rope," behind me. I tied the bull rope off with a bowline, then rappelled down. Charlie tied the other end of the bull rope to the hitch on our five-ton stakeside truck. When Charlie gave the order, the driver of the truck inched away until the rope became taut. Then, shifting into compound gear, the driver crawled the truck just a bit more until, eventually, the tree snapped. The advantages of that method were that the tree was no longer a hazard, it looked as if it had fallen naturally, and there was very little cleanup—the debris would be used as firewood by campers the following spring.

On the next tree there wasn't room to maneuver the stakeside truck, so Charlie showed us one more trick. He took a big steel snatch block (a heavy-duty pulley) from the bin of his pickup and showed us how to attach it by a steel cable to a nearby tree. Then he ran the bull rope through the snatch block so the truck could pull the tree from a ninety-degree angle. We thought that method was so clever, we laughed out loud, then began applying it as quickly as we could.

By then the wind was whipping the tips of the tallest pines back and forth and snapping off dead branches high in the cedars. We were pelted with hail, which soon turned into wet snow that melted as soon as it touched our clothes. Before long we were all soaking wet, but we didn't much care. We were so close to finishing the job, none of us even wanted to stop for lunch. So we kept working at that manic pace until, finally, we heard Charlie hollering at us to shut off our saws. Charlie studied his clipboard one more time, glanced up canyon, then down canyon, and said, "That's it, guys. Let's go back to the barn and get something to eat."

Back at the dorm, our cook had prepared platters of bacon, ham, pancakes, *huevos rancheros*, and a gallon of hot coffee. We stripped off our wet clothes and hung them by the gas stove so we'd have something dry to wear on the drive back to Ash Mountain. Then we sat around that long kitchen table in our underwear and socks and, at three in the afternoon, ate the biggest breakfast of our lives.

The chief of resource management in those days, my boss, was

George Briggs. He came from a wealthy East Coast family, was well educated, and had been an officer in the Marine Corps before joining the park service. George was an expert in wildland firefighting and spent much of each summer acting as fire boss on large fires all over the West. Later he used that expertise to begin implementing some of the first prescribed burns in Sequoia and Kings Canyon National Parks. Because of his Marine Corps background, he had an authoritative management style that sometimes was almost comical in its heavy-handedness: barking orders in a gruff voice, inflicting penalties for minor uniform infractions, and swaggering through our workshop on a Monday morning like General Patton inspecting his troops. All he lacked was a riding crop. Perhaps because George came from the East Coast, he felt he had to act tough to get the respect of cowboys and loggers out west. I even heard once that he'd knocked out a guy's teeth in a poker game in Yosemite, which is about as western as you can get. And because he was a bit shorter than average, he always wore Wight's firefighting boots, with two-and-a-half-inch heels, even in the office. But George had a soft side, too, especially for anybody he saw as an underdog, and we loved him for that. Unlike other supervisors in the park, George made it a practice to hire minorities or anybody else he figured could use a break. Our crew had the only black man working in the park in those days, as well as an ex-con on methadone, several Native Americans, a Mexican cook, and even a few dumb college kids who didn't know which end of a chainsaw to grab hold of.

If George could be a bit authoritative at times, *his* bosses, hard-assed officers from World War II, could be downright dictatorial, and it grated on George when they tried to tell *him* what to do. When he started hiring longhairs who wore turquoise jewelry with their park uniforms, and mule packers who smoked marijuana instead of Marlboros, George's bosses came down hard on him, and that fired up a spirit of rebellion in him. Or maybe he was just having a midlife crisis, I don't know. After divorcing his rather delicate wife, who never liked Three Rivers anyway, George started hanging out with a pretty cowgirl from town, and then everything started to change. The next time he came into the backcountry to inspect our work, rather than riding in on a horse like some British cavalry officer, he hiked in carrying a backpack, wearing a red bandanna around his hair, and somewhere along the trail he had even cut off the legs of his park service trousers above the knee. Not long after that, George quit the park service, bought a large plot of land in British Columbia (I heard 600 acres) and moved there with his new wife. Don Stivers, the technician who'd hired me, went up there to visit him once and came back saying our old chief of resource management was working part time on a brush-cutting crew for the Canadian government.

But before that, back in 1971, George Briggs took one of the boldest steps I ever saw any park service administrator take, something that will forever endear him to me. He started hiring young Navajos from Ramah, New Mexico, seven or eight of them in one summer. The Bureau of Indian Affairs is in the Department of the Interior, like the National Park Service, so the arrangement probably started back in Washington, D.C., with some jobs or acculturation program. But no other division chief in the park had the courage to hire them—just George.

That was my first year as foreman of the resources management backcountry crew, and in addition to four of my old crewmembers, all the Navajos were assigned to me: Curtis Cohoe, his brother Ernie, Amos Pino, Jerry Martine, David Beaver, Damon Charley, Roy Beaver, and more. Except for Ernie, none of them could speak much English. If you had four of them together, they might be able to make a complete English sentence. But they were bright and they learned English quickly, while I failed miserably at learning Navajo. Sometimes around the campfire at night, I'd try to imitate the Navajo I'd heard them speaking that day: "*Ish lan a he!*" I would say, and the Navajos would fall off their stools and roll in the dirt with laughter. Then one of them would tell me, "You didn't say even one word right."

The Navajos on our crew had grown up on a beautiful but remote part of the reservation, about forty miles southeast of Gallup, and this was the first time they'd ever been away from home. They were skinny and bowlegged, and most of them had scars on their young faces from knife wounds and automobile accidents. When we were working in the backcountry, they always hiked together in single file, and when they came to a creek or river, they trudged right on through with their boots on, almost as if it weren't even there. They told me Navajo tales of corpse powder and skinwalkers, and when they cut each other's hair around the campfire, every single hair went from the barber's hand, into the owner's hand, and then into the fire, so nobody could use the hair to witchcraft them later. Once, when they received news that a friend back home had been killed in a car accident, they stayed up all night long, singing and drumming on empty coffee cans to ease their lost friend into the next world.

Working in the backcountry was too much like the reservation to be of much interest to the Navajos, and not at all what they'd expected when they first heard they were going to California. But they enjoyed the Three Rivers honky-tonk life. They were too young to drink in the bars, but they were allowed in the beer taverns, and on Friday and Saturday night they'd hitchhike the five miles down from Ash Mountain. One of the taverns was managed by Tom Pappas, who'd worked in Hollywood before moving to Three Rivers. Tom had a caged black bear that he'd let out sometimes so he and the bear could put on a wrestling display. He and the Navajos became fast friends, even though Tom was at least forty years older, they could speak little English, and he could speak no Navajo. Sometimes on a Friday night, I'd stop in at Tom's place to check on them, but the Navajos seemed happy spending their free time there, so I didn't interfere. More than once on Monday morning, though, when they failed to show up for work at Ash Mountain, I found them sleeping in the grass alongside the highway between Three Rivers and the park. I scolded Curtis Cohoe about that once, and his reply was, "Bears sleep in the grass. Why not me?"

Once, in the backcountry at Woods Creek, when tensions had been high all week, Curtis took offense to something Mike Palmer had said at breakfast. Mike shrugged and started down the trail toward the job site, but Curtis picked up a double-bit ax and ran after him, swinging the ax like a tomahawk. I called to Mike in warning, but he just turned around and stood there, watching as

Curtis raised the ax with both hands over his head. Mike didn't show the slightest fear, and I think that might have saved his life. Curtis lowered the ax and continued walking on up the trail. As it turned out, the misunderstanding was due to the language difference, and later Mike and Curtis became good friends.

The Navajos could also be fearless to the point of being fatalistic. They simply weren't concerned with dying in the same way most of us were. One Sunday afternoon in the backcountry, while we were camped at East Lake, Mike Palmer, Curtis Cohoe, and I decided to hike up to Reflection Lake, just a mile or so away, to have a look around. We'd never been there before. After we'd strolled around Reflection Lake, we decided to climb up to Milly's Foot Pass to have a better view. From there it was only a jaunt to the top of Mount Genevra, at 13,055 feet, so on a lark, we climbed that too. Rather than return by the same route, we saw that we could descend to the basin on the other side, cross to Lucy's Foot Pass, and make a complete loop back to East Lake. The day was getting long, but we were enjoying ourselves and in no hurry.

After we'd crossed Lucy's Foot Pass, we came to a place where the route down had been completely eroded into a steep, gravelly chute. We couldn't see the bottom of the chute, and we had no rope, so it was simply a matter of committing blindly to the route or not. It would be foolish to do such a thing—just beyond our vision, the chute might drop a hundred vertical feet or more. The only sane alternative was to return the way we'd come, but it was starting to get dark. We had no flashlight, sleeping bags, matches, or even jackets. Turning back would mean a long cold night out. A gusty wind started blowing gravel and sand up the chute and into our faces. The three of us were hunched down there cursing our foolishness, when Curtis suddenly said, "I'll go." And before I could stop him, he slid down the chute on his skinny butt. Mike and I watched him disappear over the edge, but with the wind howling around us, we couldn't hear a thing. And then we heard Curtis call up to us, "It's okay! Come on!"

Well, it wasn't quite okay. Mike and I slid down the chute, went over the edge, skipped once or twice, then landed hard on the rock ledge, where Curtis stood laughing at us. But at least we made it back to camp.

Those young Navajos could be wild and unpredictable, and sometimes they got themselves, and me, into trouble. I was criticized by my supervisors for not taking a firmer hand in controlling them, but I'd seen how tough they were, how hard they worked, and I didn't feel it was my place to play disciplinarian with them.

One Saturday night back at the Ash Mountain fire dorm, the Navajos got into some serious mischief. They disliked Ash Mountain headquarters as much as we did and jokingly called it "Fort Defiance," the Arizona base Kit Carson used when he was trying to destroy the Navajo nation. I wasn't responsible for them on the weekend, and that particular weekend I wasn't even around. They got hold of a case of beer, and by the time they'd finished it, they were in full revolt. Around two in the morning, the area ranger was summoned to the dorm because three of the Navajos were hanging one of their buddies over the parapet of the two-story roof by his ankles. The way they explained it to me later, that young man happened to have been part Zuni, and according to the Navajos, Zunis eat dogs. The ranger investigated the incident, and it turned out that Mike Palmer had been the one who'd bought the Navajos the beer. His punishment was to be pulled off our backcountry crew, which he dearly loved, for the rest of the summer.

Some of the Navajos, like Curtis, came back to Sequoia to work with us every summer, and I learned to rely on their judgment when mine failed. Once we were in Sugarloaf Meadow building check dams—small log dams placed in creeks to stop erosion. The Sugarloaf area is part of Kings Canyon, which didn't become a national park until 1940; before that, Sugarloaf had been badly overgrazed by cattle, resulting in serious damage to the meadow. The creek banks had begun to slough off, the meandering pattern of the creek's course became a straight channel, and little by little, the surrounding vegetation began to die as the meadow's water table dropped. Without some intervention to correct the problem, the entire meadow could have been lost. Back in the 1930s and early 1940s, the CCC had built a series of check dams that had done an effective job of correcting the erosion in the lower portion of Sugarloaf Meadow, but they'd never finished the job, maybe because the start of war put an end to the CCC program. So in 1974, my crew was sent to Sugarloaf Meadow to complete the work the CCC had begun.

I'd had no training in erosion control and had never built a check dam. The CCC, under the guidance of skilled leaders, had built thousands of them all over the West, but those boys, and their expertise, were long gone. Furthermore, by the 1970s almost all erosion control work was done with the aid of machinery; one backhoe could easily do the work of a hundred men. But backhoes weren't permitted in the wilderness, and neither was any other sort of machinery except chainsaws. Why my supervisors figured that three white college kids and six Navajos were best suited for that job, I don't know.

Sugarloaf Creek was at its seasonal low when we arrived, not dry, but with maybe three inches of water flowing in the bottom. It was a pretty good time to build a dam, so with the help of an old forest service manual, we went to work. We started by choosing the location, which was the narrowest part of the gully below the erosion. The gully there was about twelve feet across and maybe ten feet deep. The next step was to cut notches into the banks, about four feet on each side, to receive the logs we intended to place there—otherwise, the water at high level would undermine the dam, rendering it useless. After we'd measured the distance from one side to the other, we saw that our logs would have to be twenty feet long, and maybe twenty inches in diameter, which meant (using log-scaling formulas) they'd weigh something like 2,000 pounds each!

I knew the old CCC boys had used mules to move logs that big, but that method was quickly becoming a lost art. Slim Knutsen, our packer, could have helped us, but he was busy keeping our crew, and others, supplied by making runs back and forth to the front country. Fortunately, acquiring the logs wasn't a problem. The receding water table caused by the erosion had already killed a strip of lodgepole pines just 200 feet away, and they were about the size we needed. We fell six of them, limbed them, removed the butt swell, then measured and cut them into lengths. Then I sat down in the shade and tried to figure out what to do next.

Nothing I'd learned in my nineteenth-century British poetry class had taught me how to levitate a ton of dead wood across a twelve-foot-wide gully, and French 101 hadn't taught me a single word of Navajo. Curtis Cohoe could see my dilemma—white guy doesn't have a clue—so he said, kindly but firmly, "Lemme do it." And from then on, speaking only Navajo, Curtis supervised that job.

Moving the cut logs to the gully wasn't all that complicated. We cut the unused tree tips into rollers, and with log carriers we placed the rollers under the logs and inched them along slowly, like Egyptian slaves moving stone blocks. But the rollers were useless once we reached the gully. How could we get the logs to leap over the creek and fall into our notches? Curtis's plan, which I just sat and watched unfold, was to build a tripod eight feet high on the opposite bank, using three tree tips and some manila rope for lashing. A work rope went from our log, across the gully, and over the top of the tripod. To ease the friction on the rope, Curtis lashed a broken but very smooth shovel handle across the top of the tripod. Then, fifteen feet beyond the tripod, he drove a stake deep into the ground at a forty-five-degree angle. I could see what his plan was now, but it seemed to me that without a pulley, his plan wouldn't work.

What Curtis did, while I watched with humble fascination, was make a long trucker's hitch, which is a primitive pulley using only rope. It took him all of a minute. We gathered on the far side of the creek, put on our work gloves, grabbed hold of the work rope, and pulled. With the first tug, the tip of that 2,000-pound log raised into the air and lurched two feet toward us. We pulled again, and then again. By now the log was halfway across, but Curtis needed to reset the trucker's hitch. One of the Navajos stood a stout pole under the log to hold it up while Curtis made his adjustment. And in ten more minutes, that log fell into our notches as if it were a child's tinker toy. It was the finest example of intuitive engineering I've ever seen.

Later that evening, back at camp, I asked Curtis, who at that time was no more than twenty years old, how he'd learned to do work like that. He just shrugged and said, "I never did that before."

※

Mike Palmer wasn't with us the remainder of that summer because he was being punished by the park service for buying the Navajos the beer that had fueled their late-night rampage at the Ash Mountain fire dorm. Palmer was assigned to a crew that hiked around the middle elevations of the park all summer in 100-degree heat looking for blister rust. That's such a peculiar job that it deserves an explanation of its own.

Blister rust is a fungal disease of white pines, which in the southern Sierra Nevada are the sugar pine and the western white pine. The disease was unknown in North America until the early twentieth century, when infected pine seedlings were unwittingly imported from Europe. In order for the disease to complete its life cycle, it requires a second host, which in the Sierra Nevada includes two species of *Ribes*: gooseberries and currants. During the Great Depression, large crews of young men were sent out to scour the mountains all over the West to root out every currant and gooseberry they could find. Why they didn't realize it was an impossible task, I don't know. I once asked a PhD forester who'd worked on those blister rust crews during the Depression that question, and his answer was, "Of course we knew it was impossible to eradicate every gooseberry and currant in the western United States. But look how much good came from it. Those blister rust crews put an entire generation of foresters through college!"

Today gooseberries and currants can be found throughout Sequoia and Kings Canyon in great abundance, and blister rust is still in the parks as well. For many years, the approach to controlling the disease was to send out crews to walk the park's entire middle elevation areas every year to identify infected white pines. When they found a tree with the telltale canker on its branches, the canker was removed by pruning, thereby preventing the disease from spreading. That approach wasn't effective either, due to the large number of acres that had to be walked each year, and the vast number of trees that had to be inspected. Today the US Forest Service has developed strains of white pines that are resistant to blister rust, and it's hoped that seedlings from those trees can be planted in sufficient numbers to replace the sugar pines and western white pines as they die.

Working on the blister rust crew was considered the worst assignment in the resource management division. The middle elevation areas in Sequoia and Kings Canyon are not only hot in the summer, but steep and rugged, with almost no trails. The wonderful thing about some of those remote places, though, is that they're almost completely undeveloped, making them perhaps the most undisturbed wilderness in the parks. Mike Palmer was an endurance trail runner who could finish fifty-mile jogs through the backcountry, and not even the blister rust crew could hinder his determination. He accepted his punishment with good cheer, and by the end of the summer his misdeed had been forgiven (or perhaps forgotten), and he was working with us in the backcountry again.

The cook for my backcountry crew in those days was Jimmy Castro. His mother was a bilingual Mexican American, but Jimmy's father was a Native American from the Tule Indian Reservation, in the foothills above Porterville. Most of the people living on the Tule Reservation were from one of the Yokuts tribes that populated the San Joaquin Valley and the Sierra Nevada foothills before the arrival of the Spanish and American settlers. So even though Jimmy grew up speaking Spanish and was treated as a Mexican immigrant by the predominantly white, middle-class culture of Tulare County, he could trace his heritage back to people who'd lived on that land for hundreds of years.

In 1959, when Jimmy was only ten, his father left his mother and their eight children, and Jimmy scarcely saw him again for several years. His mother worked as a teacher's aide, but she struggled to raise the family on her own, and sometimes on weekends the whole family had to work in the orchards and vineyards of Tulare County to supplement their income. They lived in the poorest part of Visalia, just a block from Oval Park, known in those days as Spike Park, where junkies could be seen shooting up heroin at all times of the day or night. It was one of the most violent, drug-infested neighborhoods in the San Joaquin Valley. Jimmy was so angry and ashamed of his family's poverty that when the school nutritionist would come to his classroom and ask each of the kids what they were eating at home, Jimmy would lie and say he was eating chicken, milk, and cottage cheese like the other kids, rather than the beans and tortillas he had for every meal. His father, whom Jimmy still dearly loved, would show up at their house now and then, usually on a Saturday afternoon, dressed in new cowboy garb, with a pint bottle in his back pocket.

Every age group in Jimmy's neighborhood had its own gang—the Lonelies, the Dixie Cup Gang, the Night Walkers—but Jimmy's was called the Syndicate. If you weren't a member of a gang, you were at the mercy of those who were. During a BB gun fight, Jimmy was shot in the eye, and though he didn't lose the eye, he started gradually losing his sight in it. He stopped going to school and got into fights with other gangs and even with the police. Eventually he got arrested and was sent to the county youth detention center, called Boys Camp in those days. And, in an odd way, that turned out to be one of the luckiest things that ever happened to him. Not only did he receive some wise counseling from teachers who understood what he was going through, but after six months in the detention center, Jimmy qualified for a work release program and was sent to Sequoia National Park to cut fire lines at Ash Mountain. It was the first time he'd worked in the mountains, and he loved it.

Jimmy's long-range goal was to get a full-time job with the California Division of Forestry, but because of his bad eye, he couldn't pass the vision test. He had surgery on the eye to relieve the pressure, but his vision kept getting worse. He continued to work seasonally for the park service, though.

"One day in the summer of 1969, they told me I was going to go work on a bridge," Jimmy told me. "There had been really heavy rains that winter, and I knew bridges were out all over, but what I imagined was a big concrete bridge on the highway somewhere. The next thing I knew, I was in a helicopter flying to Kern River, twenty-five miles in the backcountry. Until then I'd never been camping in my life, and I didn't even know there *was* a backcountry."

In those days Sequoia only had one trail crew foreman, and he was a sixty-five-year-old legend, Emery "Mac" McCool. When Jimmy stepped out of the helicopter, McCool was standing there wearing his old yellow hardhat, pitted with dents signifying how many times that hat had saved his life. During World War II, McCool had worked at the naval shipyard at Vallejo, where a cable had snapped one day and robbed him of half his nose. He had been a minor league baseball player, a catcher, and after having suffered several fractures of his left hand, he had an indentation the shape of a baseball in his palm. He put out his huge right hand to shake Jimmy's, and asked, "What's your name, Bubb?"

"Jimmy Castro."

"Do you know Salvador Castro?" McCool asked, still grasping Jimmy's hand.

"Salvador is my uncle," Jimmy replied.

"Well, I played a lotta baseball with your uncle down in Visalia."

McCool, and his counterpart in Kings Canyon, Thad Moorehead, were immortalized in Gary Snyder's poem "Bubbs Creek Haircut," about backpacking in the fifties:

> *hiking up Bubbs creek saw the trail crew tent*
> *in a scraggly grove of creekside lodgepole pine*

> talked to the guy, he says
> "If you see McCool on the other trail crew over there
> tell him Moorehead says to go to hell."

And then later:

> we ran on that other trail crew
> setting up new camp in the drizzly pine
> cussing and slapping bugs, 4 days from road,
> we saw McCool, & he said tell that Moorehead
> KISS MY ASS

In later years, Sequoia and Kings Canyon produced many other colorful trail crew foremen: Rocky Camine, a wiry knot of muscle who liked to be called "the riprap king"; Jack Oliphant, who wore starched khakis and a powder-blue ascot to work every day and, even in the backcountry, kept his flowing mane of silvery hair properly tinted and coiffed; and Duck Brooks, said to have gone gambling in Nevada while the park service thought he was in the backcountry working on trails. But McCool had all of Sequoia to himself in those days. One of McCool's duties was to periodically ride a horse (later the park helicopter) to the top of Mount Whitney and dump the contents of the outhouse over the steep eastern escarpment. Accepting that disgusting job with good humor, he had the words "Sanitation Engineer" stenciled onto his hardhat.

McCool always took an empty coffee can to bed with him every night so he wouldn't have to get out of the tent to urinate. In the morning, coming out to light the fire, he would fling the contents of the coffee can into the brush and announce to his still-sleeping workers, "Damn near pissed a quart last night!" Then he would order them out of their bags by bellowing a string of obscenities. But in spite of his gruff behavior, McCool was dearly loved by those lucky enough to have worked for him.

McCool's crew was rebuilding the washed-out bridge across Kern River that summer, a labor-intensive task for only the most experienced trail crew foremen. Without the help of machinery, he had to temporarily divert the river, build new abutments of rock and cement, then drag huge log stringers into place using only a tripod, pulleys, and winch. Jimmy Castro started as just another laborer, but one morning before work McCool watched Jimmy cook himself an elaborate breakfast of bacon, fried potatoes, and *huevos rancheros*, while the other four workers gagged down their bowls of cold cereal. "Hey, Bubb," McCool said. "You think you could cook that same breakfast for everybody?"

"Sure, I could," Jimmy said. "As long as somebody else washes the dishes."

From then on, around three o'clock every afternoon, McCool would say to Jimmy, "Why don't you head on back to camp now and get dinner started. We'll be in around five."

Jimmy would ask, "What should I cook?"

"Cook anything you want, Bubb" McCool replied. "We'll eat it."

By the time the crew got back to camp, Jimmy would have a platter full of chicken enchiladas, a bowl of Spanish rice, a pot of beans, a fresh salad, and a hot peach cobbler. The next day he might make a pot of *sopa de albóndigas* with fresh flour tortillas. The day after that, he'd make beef tacos with corn tortilla chips and hot salsa. Food like that, for men working hard at high elevation, meant an awful lot, and it meant even more to McCool, whose job it was to keep his crew happy while they were living under primitive conditions, without the comfort of wives, mothers, or girlfriends to coddle them.

McCool did another clever thing that helped make working in the backcountry a bit more comfortable. Just up the trail from the bridge site was Kern Hot Springs, where scalding hot water oozed from the hillside just fifteen feet above the ice-cold river. After the spring floods, the site had become just a muddy wallow where hikers scooped out a pit to collect the hot water, but McCool had a better plan. He excavated a proper hole the size of a bathtub, partly filled it with wet cement, then used a fifty-gallon drum to mold a depression in the cement. After the cement had dried, he removed the drum and had a nicely shaped bathtub, just the right size for one person, or maybe two if they were both willing. He built a smaller cement box above the tub to collect the hot water, and ran a steel pipe from the box to the tub. Over the years, countless hikers have soaked their weary bones in that bathtub while staring at Chagoopa Falls on the craggy cliffs to the west, or gazing up at a dark sky full of stars on a cold night.

Jimmy Castro and Mac McCool became friends, and what an improbable pair they were—the gnarled old trail crew foreman and the Mexican gang member. Just a few years later, when McCool was lying in a hospital bed dying of cancer, Jimmy went to visit him. "Mac was in pretty bad shape," Jimmy said. "He had a tube in his throat and he couldn't speak at all. But when he looked up and saw me standing there by his bed, he reached out with that big old hand and squeezed my hand, and I could see by his eyes that he was happy to see me."

The first day I'd met Jimmy, in the Ash Mountain parking lot, it was because he'd been assigned to our hazardous tree crew. He was about thirty pounds overweight then, and some of his friends called him Gordo—"fatty" in Spanish. He wore his short hair straight back, tied with a red bandanna, like a San Joaquin Valley *cholo*. He had a loud, irreverent laugh, like a mule's bray, that was his way of telling us, and the park service, that he didn't take us too seriously.

The whole crew piled into our Dodge Power Wagon and headed up the hill to work at Giant Forest that day. Most of us were young bachelors without the sense to make ourselves a decent breakfast, but Jimmy was already married by then, and he came to work with two big, hot burritos made of fresh flour tortillas, scrambled eggs, and bacon, wrapped in aluminum foil. As soon as he opened the foil, that wonderful aroma filled the cab, and we all started begging him for just one bite. Jimmy said something like,

"I don't understand why you guys aren't married. Are you all gay, or what?" But then he generously handed us one of the burritos to pass around. The next day Jimmy came to work with four burritos, and the day after that he had two burritos for every guy in the truck.

"Tell your wife we'll pay her to make us burritos every day!" somebody said.

Jimmy threw back his head and laughed, then gave us a stare that wasn't at all funny. His bad eye was slowly turning white, but with his other eye, Jimmy could look right through you. "She doesn't want your money," he said. "She just feels sorry for you—a bunch of white guys too scared to get married and too lazy to cook for yourself."

Frank Walter, the 300-pound worker who'd failed Charlie Castro's one-arm pull-up test, was another member of the hazardous tree crew we all came to love. Frank was nineteen when he first came to work with us. Woodville, where he'd grown up, was a tiny farm town in Tulare County where the men met every afternoon at the only gas station to drink, gamble, and watch sports on TV. Frank slicked his reddish-brown hair back like Elvis, drove an orange Dodge Charger, drank beer like it was water and whiskey like it was beer, and chain-smoked Camels. He looked about ten years older than he was, and even at nineteen he was already working as a bartender on the weekends. Frank usually wore blue work shirts with the sleeves cut off, maybe to show off his arms, which were bigger than my thighs. The first time we saw Frank in his new park service uniform, we teased him by saying it didn't look quite right on him. "What you should do, Frank," I said, "is cut those sleeves off like all your other shirts and just tattoo the park emblem right on your arm."

Having grown up on a farm, Frank wasn't afraid of hard work but was experienced enough to avoid it if he could. He was good with machinery, could fix anything broken, and became an expert tree faller in a short time. He might have made a better backcountry foreman than I, except that he hated hiking, didn't care for the backcountry at all, and loathed having to write daily work reports, something I could do in either nonfiction or fiction form, as necessary.

In early July of 1973, our crew was headed to Evolution Valley, one of the most beautiful and remote sections of Kings Canyon. On Monday morning, we loaded ourselves and our backpacks into a six-passenger truck and drove to Florence Lake, about 150 miles north, where we'd begin hiking the 18 miles or so into Evolution Valley. All our camp gear and tools would be flown in by helicopter from Ash Mountain. We spent that first night at a forest service campground called Jackass Flat, had an early supper of canned stew, sat around a picnic table playing a few hands of poker by Coleman lantern, then retired early in anticipation of the long hike we'd have the next day. Frank, who'd cracked the seal on a new quart of Jim Beam, stayed up late drinking alone by lantern light.

While most of us looked forward to backpacking into a part of the wilderness we'd never seen before, Frank despised the thought. Worse, he feared it. Frank was as strong as a bear, but dragging that three-hundred-pound body, plus a sixty-pound pack, uphill for eight hours was painful for him. He'd actually lost a few pounds in the preceding days, trying to get in shape, but he knew in his heart he wasn't ready.

Frank might have had a hard time understanding why the rest of us enjoyed the backcountry so much, but he'd listened to our stories and knew we always had great fun there and he didn't want to miss out on it. He could be highly emotional, displaying enormous love and affection sometimes, and heartbreaking despondency at others. More than once I'd seen him break down in tears trying to express himself. Frank's younger days, which he'd never talk about much, must not have been pleasant ones, and that, I think, made the promise of our crew's camaraderie a special attraction for him. More than anybody I've ever known, Frank needed friendship and acceptance.

The next morning I was up at first light, anxious to get moving. It had been an unusually cold night for that elevation. I'd slept warmly enough in my down bag, under the boughs of a lodgepole pine, but I saw that frost had settled on the meadow. After I got dressed, I went to the picnic table to get a fire started, and I saw that the lantern we'd used the night before was still burning. I went around to wake the others one by one, but when I went to Frank's sleeping bag, it was empty. In fact, the bag looked as if it hadn't been slept in at all.

We fanned out in all directions, and in just a few minutes one of the Navajos found him. Frank was halfway across Jackass Meadow, lying face down, passed out drunk, in his cutoff shirt sleeves, with a layer of frost on his back. Thank god he was alive.

We got Frank to his feet and helped him back to camp. We put him in his sleeping bag beside the fire and gave him hot coffee. He was okay, but in no condition to go on an eighteen-mile hike, so he sadly returned to Ash Mountain with our truck. In the following days, he came down with pneumonia and missed several days of work. But he was young, still very strong, and he recovered. I don't believe Frank ever made another attempt at backpacking. From then on he worked only in the front country with Charlie Castro and the hazardous tree crew.

♒

That summer working in Evolution Valley turned out to be one of the finest summers I ever spent in the mountains. The valley is located at the northernmost tip of Kings Canyon, at an elevation of 9,500 feet. Because of its orientation, which is generally east to west, it receives sun fairly early in the morning and loses it late in the day. The valley has long meadows of brilliant green, cold meandering streams, and snow-capped peaks with bold faces of glistening granite. There's a quality about that place that is so seductive, it's a wonder that anybody who has spent much time there ever returns to the commonplace world. Just knowing that such a place exists has helped me endure difficult times in my life.

Because the John Muir Trail passes through Evolution Valley, there was usually a lot of traffic, though most of the hikers were on strict schedules and didn't stay long. We didn't object to watching them pass through; on the contrary, they made our days more interesting. I recall meeting a serious-minded film student from UCLA who was making a movie of the John Muir Trail by exposing one frame every few yards. We met a young hippie couple from the Owens Valley who had a baby with them; they'd brought along a goat to carry most of their belongings, with the added benefit of having fresh goat's milk every day for their child. (Goats are banned in the backcountry today because of the risk of introducing diseases to the endangered bighorn sheep.) And we took in a bewildered young man from LA who'd just gone through a shattering divorce; he'd never been backpacking before and scarcely knew the basics of building a fire or cooking a meal on a gas stove. After seeing the fragile state of his mental health, we invited him to stay at our camp for a few days until he was in better control of his emotions; he was a considerate guest and could be very funny at times, and we enjoyed having him around.

Because of Evolution Valley's exceptional beauty, it was also popular with stock parties—mostly paying customers escorted by the private pack stations. The packers had their own semi-secret camps tucked away in places most people would never see, and except for when we passed them on the trail, we hardly knew they were there. Anybody looking for peace and quiet could walk a mile up any side canyon, or climb any bench (a fairly flat section in otherwise sloped terrain), and find perfect solitude.

We set up camp at McClure Meadow, not far from the ranger station, which was really just a tent cabin on a wooden frame, and we walked to the job sites every day. We'd come to Evolution Valley to rebuild the series of drift fences that separated the meadows in the canyon so they wouldn't be overgrazed. We were fortunate to have plenty of junipers the right size for fence posts; after the bark is stripped off, juniper posts can last many years in that dry, granite soil. The crew was mostly Navajos that summer, and those young men had been building wire fences all their lives. They required little supervision and no instruction at all. My job was to make sure the work was done with as little impact as possible so that when we were finished, the fences looked as if they had always been a part of the landscape. Often the hardest part of a backcountry foreman's job is to keep his workers happy, but that wasn't a problem that summer. We all knew we were living in a very special place and that we were lucky to be there.

Jimmy Castro was on the crew, and we worked out an agreement whereby he spent half day on the job and the other half cooking dinner for the rest of us. When we came back to camp in the late afternoon, Jimmy was there in his white apron with a big smile on his face, singing, "That's the sound of the men working on the chain gang," from the Sam Cooke song. He was always telling us jokes, some of which he had to translate from Spanish: "You know what it sounds like when a Mexican starts his motorcycle? *Cabrón! Puta, puta, puta, puta, puta. . . .*" And at night around the campfire, he'd entertain us with tales of survival back in the barrio, where everybody had a nickname, like Ratón, or Pinky, and he and his friends were always trying to outwit the police.

Jimmy liked to act as if nothing mattered all that much, like nothing anybody said or did could ever get to him. It was just prison survival strategy, crude and sometimes insensitive. But he went out of his way to look after the Navajos, who were young and vulnerable, and he wasn't afraid to correct anybody on the crew if he thought their behavior was selfish or inconsiderate. Jimmy's advice sometimes had a biting edge, with a touch of sarcasm and mocking humor, but he was never cruel. And he was right about so many things, we learned to trust him and value his advice. Jimmy also knew I'd traveled around Mexico some and was trying to learn Spanish, so he would help me with my pronunciation or recite to me Mexican folktales his mother had told him, like *La Llorona*. But then he'd warn me, "Just remember, Sorensen, you can learn to speak Spanish and how to cook *enchiladas de pollo*, and all that. But only God can make you a Mexican!"

We had a female visitor stay with us that summer, a young woman by the name of Phoebe, if I recall. She was a strong lusty blonde who loved backpacking, loved the Sierra Nevada, and loved park employees. Perhaps the best way to describe Phoebe is to say she was a sort of groupie. Phoebe spent her first night there at the ranger station, but when we came in from work the following afternoon, we found Phoebe sunning herself, fully naked, by the creek in front of our camp. Her freshly washed underwear, which came in a delightful variety of colors, was drying atop the willows.

The ranger at McClure Meadow that summer was Randy Morgenson, and our relations with him had been strained. We usually got along okay with backcountry rangers wherever we went, but Morgenson seemed to resent our presence in his valley, camped so close to his ranger station, with our horses and mules desecrating his meadow with their manure (which after all was just fertilizer). I didn't want to do anything that would make our relationship with Morgenson worse, so I said to Phoebe, "I thought you were staying over at the ranger's place?"

"Ah, he's no fun," she replied. "Can I hang out with you guys for a few days?"

Other trail crew foremen had told me about Phoebe and the arrangements they'd worked out with her in the past. I was in a serious relationship at the time, and after seeing the sad condition of our divorced visitor, I wasn't willing to jeopardize it. But I figured my crew members worked for the government eight hours a day and what they did the rest of the time was their business. "As long as you help out with the camp and kitchen chores, I don't mind," I told her.

Phoebe would spend her mornings hiking and exploring by herself, then help Jimmy in the kitchen in the afternoon. When the crew came home after work, she'd invite one of them to hop on her back, give him a piggyback ride down to our swimming hole at the creek, and then frolic with them, all naked in the water, until they were clean enough for supper. Phoebe was a funny and lively guest, we all enjoyed having her around, and she certainly made my job that summer easier. But after she took up with us, our relationship with Ranger Morgenson turned ice cold.

One evening a couple of middle-aged men from the Bay Area who were hiking part of the John Muir Trail set up their pole tent just a few yards from our camp—normally a violation of backcountry etiquette, but they seemed unsure of themselves, so we didn't say anything about it. They retired soon after dark, but later that evening we heard them shouting angrily at each other. We saw their little tent shaking violently, we heard them throwing blows at each other, and we heard their cries of pain. And then suddenly it stopped. A moment later, one of the men emerged from the tent, shyly approached our campfire, where we were sitting on tree rounds playing poker, and said in the oddest, Tiny Tim-like voice, "I'm afraid I've had an accident bumping into the pole of the tent, and now I've dislocated my shoulder."

I'd never seen a dislocated shoulder before and didn't have the slightest idea how to treat it. But the man was wearing a thin T-shirt, I could clearly see the head of the humerus bulging out in an unnatural and frightening way, and I knew something had to be done.

Jimmy Castro, who knew a lot of Mexican home remedies, said, "I saw that happen once to a guy in a street fight, and I know exactly what to do." Jimmy had the man lie face up on the ground, then placed his boot on the man's chest and began tugging on his wrist. The poor man howled in pain.

"Wait a second, Jimmy," I said. "Lemme call the park dispatcher. Maybe she hasn't gone home for the night."

Fortunately, the park dispatcher was still at her desk. She called a Three Rivers doctor at his home and patched our calls so we could hear his advice over the radio. The first thing the doctor said was, "Under no circumstances should you try to pull on the arm. That could result in serious injury to the nerves. Your patient will probably have to be flown out by helicopter in the morning, but there is one thing you might try."

The doctor instructed us to have the man lie face down on a table with his arm dangling over the side, attach a five-pound weight to his wrist, then have him rest in that position for twenty minutes. If the shoulder muscles relaxed on their own, the weight might gently pull the humerus back into its socket. We had two roll-up tables for our kitchen, so we cleared them of dishes and utensils, pushed them together, and helped the man lie down on them. We decided that our cast-iron Dutch oven lid weighed about five pounds, so I pulled off my leather belt and used it to strap the lid to the man's wrist. Then we went back to our card game and forgot all about him.

I'm not sure how much time passed, but it was more than twenty minutes—perhaps twice that long. Finally the man, not wanting to trouble us, tried to squirm off the tables by himself, but the flimsy table legs buckled, and he slid into the dirt. We ran over to help him up, but I had to unstrap the Dutch oven lid from his wrist before he could stand. When he did, he raised his injured arm over his head, rotated the arm 360 degrees, and announced himself healed. We offered him a shot of whiskey, but he declined, and after thanking us profusely, he went back to his tent. The next morning he and his companion were gone before daylight.

☙

One Sunday morning that August, I set off by myself to explore the spectacular country around us. I'd heard about an unnamed lake not too far away from our camp that was said to have exceptionally good fishing. Many of the lakes in the backcountry had been stocked with trout more than a hundred years ago by mule packers hauling five-gallon cans of fingerlings. The fish were mostly golden trout and rainbows, though there were some brookies and brown trout as well. Later, the California Department of Fish and Game stocked more backcountry lakes by releasing fingerlings from airplanes. But the success of both those operations was spotty. Some backcountry lakes are entirely without fish, some produce an abundance of average-sized fish, but every now and then the most intrepid fishermen discover a lake that produces fish of exceptional size. And then they do their best to keep that lake a secret.

The lake I was looking for was on a bench high above Evolution Valley. There was no trail there, and the most logical route was straight up the canyon side. So I started climbing through large, gnarled junipers that filled the warm morning air with their spicy aroma. By the time I reached the bench around noon, there were a few wispy clouds forming to the south, tumbling and rolling, disappearing and then quickly reforming. It was that *chubasco* pattern I'd seen before, carrying tropical moisture up from Mexico. The sky still looked calm enough, but I knew that could change quickly.

I was disappointed when I first saw the lake. It looked shallow, without much vegetation surrounding it. The inlet, where the best fishing is usually found, was scarcely a trickle, and I didn't see any water at all flowing from the outlet. One thing fishermen like to see in a backcountry lake is a cliff, or at least a steep incline, that continues into the lake. Those deep, cobalt waters are often where big fish hang out when they aren't actively feeding. But I saw nothing like that there. The lake seemed drab, lifeless, even a bit ugly.

I started by casting flies at the inlet, but except for a little interest from some small fish, I wasn't having any luck. Before I could try the outlet, the sky had turned dark gray, and I could hear the sound of thunder not so far away. Powerful blasts of wind raked across the basin, stirring up flurries of foxtail pine needles that stung me in the face. Soon I saw lightning striking on the ridges above the lake.

The odds of being struck by lightning, for most people, are slim. But for people who spend their whole lives outdoors, especially in the mountains, the odds fatten quickly. My friend and neighbor in Three Rivers, Gary Kenwood, was hit by lightning once, and every time he told me that story, my scalp prickled and itched. In the early seventies, Gary was leading a string of mules across Milestone Basin, high in the Kaweahs. "I could see it was clouding up and would probably rain," he told me, "but I still had a long way to go that day and didn't want to stop. After a while, lightning started striking not far away, and I was thinking I might *have* to stop. I started leading the mules across Milestone Creek,

## Going Up the Country

and then the next thing I knew, I was lying on my back in the creek, staring up at the sky. It took me awhile to even remember where I was. I sat up and saw that my horse and mules had continued on across the creek and were grazing on the other side. Eventually, I was able to drag myself out of the water and get moving again."

So, thinking about Gary's story, I took shelter under a big foxtail pine, which didn't give me much comfort either. Practically every foxtail pine above 10,000 feet has a lightning scar. Some have several. Still, I hunkered down under its broad limbs but away from the fat base, which I figured, if struck by lightning, would carry the charge to ground.

The wind blew, and the rain fell hard for about an hour, until muddy rivulets were flowing into the lake. And then suddenly it stopped. The clouds broke up, and soon I was seeing patches of blue sky.

I had a hunch that if there were any fish in this lake they would begin to feed more actively when they saw the rivulets flowing, bringing dead insects and anything else edible from the slopes above. I gave up on fly fishing, switched to a spinning reel, and tied on a white rooster tail, a feathered lure with a light weight and a whirling strip of shiny aluminum. I cast it as far as I could into the lake, counted to five while the lure sank, then jerked the tip and began reeling the line in as quickly as I could. Within five minutes I'd caught three golden trout/rainbow hybrids. The smallest was nineteen inches, the next was twenty-one, and the largest was twenty-three.

Later that evening, back at camp, those three fish, with their heads and tails removed, filled an eighteen-inch skillet.

〰️〰️

By late August we'd completed our work on the drift fences in Evolution Valley and had begun repairing a network of check dams built by the CCC back in the 1940s. Most of the meadows in the canyon had been overgrazed by cattle long before Kings Canyon had become a park, but the log dams had successfully restored the meadows to good condition. At that high elevation and in such cold water, there wasn't much rot in the log dams, but some of them had been undermined or washed out in floods, and they needed work. We even added a few dams where we thought more were needed.

Before Labor Day, we had an early snowstorm that caught a lot of backpackers by surprise. It wasn't weather from the north; rather it was another big tropical storm coming up from the south. Tropical storms usually bring a lot of rain, but at that elevation and that late in the season, the rain quickly became snow. We were comfortable enough in our camp, but a lot of the backpackers passing through Evolution Valley on the John Muir Trail weren't prepared for weather that foul. Summer in the Sierra can be so seductive, with day after day of crystal blue skies, warm days, and only mildly cold nights, and it's easy to fall into the trap of thinking it will always be like that. The trend of speed hiking the John Muir Trail was beginning to catch on, and many of the hikers were traveling without tents, and wearing just light summer clothing and running shoes. Also, many of them had caches waiting along the route ahead, but the weather had slowed their progress, and now they were running out of food.

By the second day of the storm, weary backpackers were stopping by our camp to ask if they could rest awhile, dry their feet, and warm themselves by our fire. We took in everybody who asked, and soon we were sheltering ten people, fifteen people, then twenty or more. I pulled the crew off our job site and put them to work cutting and splitting firewood. We built two large fires, then three, and still backpackers kept coming. We had one large rainfly that was twenty by forty feet, but because of the heavy snow, we had to pitch it at steep angles so the snow would slough off, and this reduced the space for shelter. Some of the backpackers were clearly exhausted, some showed early signs of hypothermia, and some were scared.

Mike Palmer made a cardboard sign that read, "Hungry Chuck's Trail Kitchen—Come on in!" He propped the sign up on the trail so hesitant backpackers would know they were welcome. Jimmy Castro made a gallon pot of strong, black, cowboy coffee, then started a big batch of beans with bacon in our Dutch oven. The Navajos went to work making fry bread, a staple back on the reservation in Ramah. It consists of just flour, shortening, salt, and baking powder. They mixed and kneaded the bread by hand, then used a ketchup bottle to roll it out. Jimmy scooped out big spoonfuls of lard into our cast-iron skillet, and the Navajos began turning out stacks of hot, greasy fry bread. We had a gallon can of government surplus strawberry jam, and we set that out where everybody could reach it. The shivering backpackers stumbled into our kitchen, holding out their pitiful little plastic cups like homeless beggars. We gave them each a ladle of hot beans and a slab of fry bread the size of a dinner plate, then pointed them to the strawberry jam.

An hour before dark, our guests began thinking about where they would spend the night. The most exhausted crawled into their damp sleeping bags, under the rainfly, close to the fire, and refused to move. But we managed to coax some of them under the shelter of foxtail pines nearby. Eventually, one of the hikers called out to me, "I thought there was a ranger station here at McClure Meadow!"

"Well, there is," I said. "But unfortunately it has a ranger in it."

"That's government property," he said. "Why can't we spend the night there?"

"It's not up to me," I shrugged. "You'd have to talk to him."

All that summer, Randy Morgenson had behaved as if we were a threat to his privacy. We'd invited him to dinner several times—trail crews, which are resupplied by stock every week, always eat far better than backcountry rangers—but he refused. I didn't take it as a personal affront because I'd seen him treat other people with the same aloofness. When he went on patrols, he often made a practice of going to the most remote locations, where he was unlikely to see park visitors. That gave him great knowledge of the backcountry, but I don't think it helped the visitors very much. One day I happened to come up behind him on the trail as a party of backpackers approached from the other direction. Morgenson, whose job it was to make contact with park visitors, slipped into the trees and hid so he wouldn't have to speak with them.

Morgenson wasn't the only disgruntled backcountry ranger I knew. Backcountry rangers are paid poorly—about half what an experienced trail crew foreman is paid. They're expected to collect a seasonal quota of trash in their area and to break up illegal fire rings, which makes them more like maintenance workers than law enforcement officers. In Morgenson's era, many backcountry rangers weren't even trained in law enforcement or emergency medicine. They couldn't sharpen a chainsaw, saddle a horse, pack a mule, build a log bridge, or fashion a riprap wall. Many of them resented pack stock, ignoring the fact that neither their cozy ranger station nor the trail leading to it would exist without those animals. Park visitors were sometimes awed by backcountry rangers, with their clean uniforms and gold badges, but other backcountry workers weren't, and that rankled them.

Some of the backpackers at our camp began insisting that I lead them to the McClure Meadow ranger station, which I eventually did. Then I slid into the shadows, curious to see what would happen next. The bedraggled backpackers huddled outside Morgenson's tent cabin like pitchfork peasants storming the lord's castle. They could see a golden candle glowing inside, so they knew he was there, and they began shouting for him to come out. When Morgenson finally threw open the door, he was dressed in full uniform, with an amused look on his face.

"We're cold and wet!" one of the backpackers shouted. "We want to spend the night in the ranger station!"

Morgenson, a short thin man with a full beard, was holding a steaming cup of tea in one hand. "I'm sorry, but you can't do that," he said. "I pay rent here. This is my personal residence."

"Taxpayers paid for it!" they hollered back. "It belongs to us as much as it belongs to you!"

Morgenson looked beyond the rabble-rousers and found me lurking in the dark shadows. He knew now who to blame for his predicament.

"You are responsible for your own safety in the backcountry," he announced to the crowd. "Anybody who travels in the wilderness without an adequate tent, sleeping bag, and warm clothing is risking his life. If you don't know that, you shouldn't be here."

"But we are here," someone shouted back. "And we're cold!"

I didn't need to hear any more. I slipped farther into the darkness, then turned back to camp. Half an hour later, most of the angry backpackers came back, too. I don't know what happened to the rest of them, though I believe a few backpackers did succeed in gaining entry to the ranger station that night.

Randy Morgenson did his best to avoid me and my crew for the rest of that summer. Over the years, I worked many places where he was the area ranger, but he never forgave me for the role I'd played in the riot at McClure Meadow. Perhaps I'd offended him in other ways, too. I don't really know.

A few years later, I saw Randy Morgenson again at the Cort Gallery in Three Rivers. He had a show there of photographs he'd taken in the backcountry. I happened to be in town during the opening and decided to stop by. We had many good friends in common, and I wanted to reach out, to let him know I held no bad feelings for him. I'd seen a cartoon in the *New Yorker* that I thought was something a backcountry ranger might appreciate, so I cut it out and took it with me to the gallery that night.

The cartoon showed two bighorn sheep at a cocktail party, standing upright, wearing turtleneck sweaters, and holding martinis. One sheep was saying something like this to the other: "So I found myself becoming more and more isolated, and I decided if I was going to survive, I had better try to change."

When I handed the cartoon to Morgenson, he read it quickly, then handed it back.

"I don't get it," he said.

Evolution Valley

# Chapter Three: Triple Divide

A year after that wonderful summer in Evolution Valley, a bunch of us were celebrating the Fourth of July at a barbecue at Mike Gililland's house in Springville, a foothills town much like Three Rivers, but on the Tule River just to the south. Frank Walter, who had left the park service to try his hand at cotton farming, was there too with his beautiful bride, Karen. Mike Gililland had just bought a new Suzuki 500, a powerful street bike, and we were taking turns trying it out. We'd all been drinking beer, but it was early, and I, at least, was far from drunk. When my turn on the motorcycle came around, I put on Mike's helmet but was wearing nothing else except a pair of cutoff jeans. I roared off up Highway 190, going faster than I should have, when I came to a bridge over the Tule River. There was a sweeping turn before the bridge, and a gravel side road entered the highway at the same place. I leaned hard into that turn, and as soon as my tires hit the gravel, the bike slid out from under me. The bike hit the bridge railing and shattered into pieces, while I continued straight ahead, tumbling and sliding down the asphalt road. By the time I got to my feet, I looked like a raw steak ready for the barbecue grill.

A car coming the other way stopped immediately and offered help. I left the bike where it was, hopped in the car, and pointed down the road. In just a couple minutes, I was back at Mike's house.

I hadn't broken any bones, but I'd lost a lot of skin, as well as a few chunks of flesh, and I knew I needed to go to the hospital. First, though, I wanted to clean my wounds before the blood began to dry. Dirt and pieces of asphalt had been ground into the flesh, and they would be much more difficult, and painful, to remove if I waited. I removed my cutoff jeans, hopped into Gililland's shower, and with soap and a brush began scrubbing my entire body. But there were large portions I couldn't reach. Mike Palmer, at my insistence, stepped into the shower and scrubbed the places I couldn't reach, like my butt and lower back.

"Just promise me you won't ever tell anybody I did this," he said.

After being released from the hospital that afternoon, I had to figure out what to do next. My crew was scheduled to go into the backcountry on Monday, but there was no way I could go with them. I'd been staying at the fire dorm at Ash Mountain, but I couldn't go back there in my condition. Who would take care of me? Who would feed me, give me my pain medication, and change my dressings? As it turned out, Frank Walter and Karen insisted that I go home with them.

Like so many seasonal park employees, Frank had decided he couldn't make it as a married man working just six months out of the year. He'd signed a lease on a large piece of farmland in Tulare County that came with a small house. Frank knew how to farm, he'd been doing it all his life, and he figured if anybody could make a go of it, he could. Karen, whom I hadn't met until that day, was a tall, dark-haired, curvaceous woman with alabaster skin and a Tulare County accent as thick as Frank's. She had an office job in Visalia, though I can't recall now what it was. I was impressed by her, and I figured she was exactly the motivation Frank needed to give up his bad habits, his drinking and carousing, and start a better life.

It was just before dusk when we arrived at their house. I was on codeine, barely awake, and I can't say now with any certainty exactly where it was. But theirs was the only house in sight, with nothing but endless rows of cotton in every direction. Frank helped me to the bed in their spare room, and

I fell asleep almost instantly. I didn't wake until noon the next day, when he came in from the fields to make us lunch.

Frank brought me a cup of noodle soup and sat down in the chair next to the bed. His blue work shirt not only had both its sleeves, but it was starched and pressed. Even his blue jeans had creases in them, and his hair was trimmed and slicked back neatly. But he wasn't smiling.

"Tell me the truth, Frank," I teased. "How did you ever get a woman like that to marry you?"

"I still can't figure it out," he muttered. "But to be honest about it, Sorensen, I'm a bit scared."

"Scared of what? You've got everything here. Your own house, a new job working for yourself, and a gorgeous wife."

"I never been this lucky in my life," Frank admitted. "Maybe I don't think I deserve none of it. Maybe I'm just afraid I'll screw it up."

"You deserve it, Frank," I said. "Karen obviously loves you. And you've been farming your whole life. There's no reason why you can't make this work."

When Karen came home from work that evening, she and Frank helped me out of bed so she could change my bloody sheets. Then they both sat and talked with me until I fell asleep.

Later that night, when I woke to take my pain medication, it was so quiet in the house, I could hear Frank and Karen making love in the next room. A cool breeze flowing down from the Sierra Nevada fluttered the lace curtains next to my bed and reminded me that I needed to get back to the mountains.

Every day for the next five days, Frank came home and had lunch with me, and every evening Karen came home from work and washed my bloody sheets. I'll never forget the kindness they showed me.

After a few more days, I returned to Ash Mountain and limped upstairs to my tiny room, a grim and depressing place, like having your own drawer at the morgue. Perhaps a quarter of my body was caked with thick scabs, and though I was no longer in pain, I couldn't move without lurching from side to side like a mummy. I figured I needed at least another week of healing before I could go back to work, so I had no choice but to lie there naked in my tiny cinder-block room, on a bare mattress, staring up at the acoustic ceiling stained brown by cigarette smoke. Once again, though, I was saved by the kindness and compassion of a friend and fellow worker. This time it was Tighe Geoghegan, our short, bossy fire dispatcher.

Tighe came from Connecticut and had graduated from Smith College, where she'd majored in classical studies. Her science education had ended with Aristotle, something I liked to tease her about, but her mind worked so quickly, and her ability to absorb and process information was so great, I thought she was easily the most competent person working in the park. She'd spent one season at the Ash Mountain entrance station, a tedious job, and had gotten herself into trouble with the chief ranger by carrying on a scandalous relationship with a married ranger. But in the end, it didn't matter because her talent made her too valuable to dismiss. In her second year, she was promoted to dispatcher, a GS-5 position that barely paid minimum wage.

Tighe lived in Three Rivers, way out on North Fork Drive, in a tin-roofed hippy shack on Mankins Creek, with squirrels living in the walls and most of the siding pecked through by woodpeckers. It was a charming, soulful place, and Tighe held parties there almost every weekend for an eclectic mix of park service refugees, Three Rivers artists and craftsmen, and East Coast intellectuals who'd come out west to slum with her awhile. If you had no place to go and nothing to do on a Saturday night in that lonely little redneck town, you were at least welcome at Tighe's place, as long as you showed up with a bottle of wine or a six-pack of beer.

After I'd spent just one dreary night in the fire dorm, Tighe came bursting into my room, shouting, "Goddamnit, Sorensen! I can't get any work done knowing you're up here bleeding all over the place! Get off that bed right now, you sonofabitch, and quit feeling sorry for yourself, because I'm taking you home!"

With the help of two fire guards, I limped downstairs and carefully folded myself into Tighe's Opel Kadett, which ran on only three cylinders, but which she refused to fix because she believed that machines eventually heal themselves. It was her lunchtime, but she used those thirty minutes to set me up on the sofa in her living room, where I could play Bob Dylan records on her phonograph, watch squirrels frolic in the black oak outside the window, and fall asleep listening to the soothing sound of Mankins Creek.

Mike Gililland's insurance covered the totaled Suzuki 500, by the way, but I was responsible for the $1,000 deductible, which amounted to about a month's pay.

※
※

Later that summer, after I was back on the job again, one of the Navajos on my crew, Jerry Martine, came to me and said he was worried about me. He said I was having too many accidents, too many cuts, sprains, and then the foolish disaster on the motorcycle.

"I've been accident-prone all my life," I told Jerry. "Maybe I just need to slow down and try to be more careful."

Jerry shook his head. "Every Monday morning we have

safety talks. Safety talks, safety talks. Talk about it all you want, but it never does any good. You still have accidents."

"Yeah, maybe that's true. What do you think I should do?"

"I don't think it's you causing the accidents," Jerry said. "Sometimes bad people can make bad things happen to you just for the fun of it. Ghosts can do that, too. I think maybe somebody's trying to witchcraft you."

"I can't think of anybody who would do that," I said. "But even if they were, what could I do to stop it?"

"You're a white-eye. Maybe it won't work for you," Jerry said. "But back in Ramah, when somebody tries to witchcraft us, we wear a little bag of corn pollen around our neck for protection. I'd try that if I was you."

I didn't know much about Navajo religion, but I was impressed by the trust and belief Jerry and the other Navajos had for their traditions. While I, and just about everybody I knew, had lost faith and interest in our religions, my Navajo friends still believed in theirs. That weekend I drove out in the valley by Hanford and found a mature stand of corn with long, golden tassels. The only problem was that it wasn't corn grown for human consumption, but silage, meant to be fed as fodder for pigs and dairy cows. I wasn't sure if that mattered or not. By placing a paper sack over the tassels and shaking the stalks, I soon gathered what I figured to be enough pollen to do the job. Then I asked an ex-girlfriend if she'd sew me a small pouch out of an old scrap of denim. I explained to her about the witchcrafting, but she said I deserved whatever curse had been placed on me, and more. With one last favor, she could be free of me forever, so she sewed me the pouch and I wore it on a leather thong around my neck for the rest of that year.

That winter, after I was laid off by the park service, I moved to the little beach town of Encinitas, in north San Diego County, and started working as a writer for the *San Diego Reader*, a scrappy, irreverent, and rapidly growing weekly that was having trouble finding writers. That job not only provided a pathway to a career as a journalist, it gave me a chance to see how other writers went about their business, and it provided the guidance and discipline of professional editors, which I'd never had before. The editors at the *Reader* gave me the freedom to write about anything within the geographical boundaries of San Diego and Imperial counties, and northern Baja—a big territory that included the Anza Borrego desert, Camp Pendleton Marine Corps Base, and the Pacific coastline. To satisfy my need to be outdoors, I started surfing every morning before I had to sit down at my writing desk, and to soothe my claustrophobia, I made sure my desk had a view of the ocean. But as fortunate as I was to have a writing job like that, I knew I couldn't bear a summer away from the backcountry of the Sierra Nevada. Wilderness couldn't be just a two-week summer escapade. I needed that freedom, that space, and those beautiful blue skies. So I worked out a deal with the *Reader*'s publisher, Jim Holman, who understood that like a lot of young writers, I was too undisciplined to accept orders. The deal was, I could work at the paper for six months in the winter and spring, then return to my park service job at Sequoia and Kings Canyon for the summer and fall. And for a few years, I had the best of both worlds.

Beginning in the summer of 1975, my backcountry crew began working on a shift of ten days on, four days off. That allowed us plenty of free time in the backcountry for climbing, fishing, or exploring obscure corners of the park where people rarely went. But Sequoia and Kings Canyon is a big place. If our next assignment was in a distant area of the park, it would usually be necessary for us to return to Ash Mountain headquarters to retool and resupply, and that meant four boring days in a place we loathed.

Part of the problem was that Ash Mountain was located in a narrow part of the V-shaped Middle Fork Canyon, surrounded by high ridges that aggravated my claustrophobia. The headquarters compound itself looked as if the government had tried to save a little money by reusing the plans for military barracks. The rectangular buildings, of ugly brown brick, were surrounded by a cyclone fence. On a hot day, which was just about every day there in the summer, the asphalt parking lots raised the air temperature to well over a hundred degrees. Ash Mountain had a military oppressiveness to it, and the fact that I'd never been in the military made me feel like an infiltrator. Clean-shaven, zombie functionaries in nylon uniforms marched through the halls with bundles of memorandums tucked under their arms, trying to remember what park they'd worked at before their last transfer. And the GS-12s, in their air-conditioned offices, eyed me suspiciously through their mirrored windows.

Just about the only thing that made Ash Mountain tolerable was a wonderful swimming hole on the Kaweah River, just below the maintenance shop, with cold, clear pools among huge granite boulders. Backcountry refugees like me could hide out there all day, swimming in the grottoes or sunning on the smooth rocks. At night we'd sneak our girlfriends (if we were lucky enough to have one) down the trail to frolic naked in the moonlit pools or sleep on the warm sand.

The only other thing that made Ash Mountain tolerable for me in those days was to go sit in the air-conditioned fire dispatch office and watch Tighe Geoghegan work. She always knew everything going in every corner of the park, including a lot of things some people wished she didn't know, and it was always delightful to sit and watch her in action. She'd be following the progress of firefighters working on a lightning strike in Roaring River, applying red toenail polish to one bare foot perched on the desk, while confessing to me her infatuation with the Oakland A's star pitcher Catfish Hunter. One day while I was sitting there, she had to arrange a delivery of porta potties to a fire in Kings Canyon. She called the fire boss on one of the open radio channels and said in her cheeriest voice, "Peter Potter from Porterville is here with a load of porta potties and wants to know where to put them." I could hear office workers all over Ash Mountain laughing out loud.

Sometimes I thought Tighe was the only truly competent person working at that place. You could have eliminated the top five positions in the park, all held by men with military backgrounds, saved a few hundred thousand dollars, and the park would probably have run more efficiently. But if you lost a GS-5 dispatcher like Tighe, the park's day-to-day operations would have spiraled into chaos.

Once I was working as falling boss on a very nasty fire in Cedar Grove that had become a huge, interagency fiasco with hundreds of firefighters from all over the West. After several days, the fire was still blazing wildly out of control, and we were all hot, tired, and frustrated. The fire boss was clearly in over his head, and Tighe was working twelve-hour shifts back at Ash Mountain trying to help him put some order to the madness. One afternoon, over the radio, Tighe berated one of the line bosses for leaving his post before a replacement arrived, and a forest service firefighter working next to me said, "That's about the mouthiest dispatcher I ever heard. You guys always let her talk to you like that?"

"Tighe's the only person in this whole mess with the least bit of sense," I replied. "She can say or do whatever she wants."

Still, even with Tighe for entertainment, four days off at Ash Mountain could be a dull and demoralizing experience, and I knew I had to come up with something to keep me busy.

The fire cache at Ash Mountain always had a room full of busted, broke-down chainsaws that nobody ever got around to fixing. The fire crews consisted mostly of college guys who were competent sawyers but not very good at chainsaw repairs, and they were usually out fighting fires most of the summer, anyway. To send the saws to a repair shop outside the park would have cost more than most of those old saws were worth. So they just lay there until one day I proposed a solution to Ray Warren, the assistant fire management officer: If he'd hire me on my days off under the emergency firefighter fund, I'd work in the fire cache repairing the heap of broken chainsaws. It was a good deal for me because I could keep busy while earning extra money on my days off, and it was a good deal for Ray because he was getting his chainsaws fixed at a bargain price. Ray thought it over for a moment, then said, "All right, let's give it a try."

I'd never had any formal training in chainsaw repair. I learned it on my own the way most backcountry workers do. When a saw breaks down, and you need that saw to complete a job, you figure out a way to get it running again. We always carried a few basic spare parts in the backcountry, like a spark plug, carburetor rebuild kit, and a spare magneto, but our tools were rarely more than just an open-end wrench and a universal chainsaw tool. So I became a chainsaw mechanic out of necessity.

Ray Warren and I knew that a lot of those old saws were never going to run again. They had fatal internal damages, like a cracked head or badly scored cylinder, but they still had a lot of parts that could be salvaged. Because the park often bought several models of the same saw, many of the parts were interchangeable. So I'd spend all day tinkering with heaps of blackened machinery, and by the end of the day, the fire cache would have three or four chainsaws running almost like new again.

One Saturday morning, I was working in the fire cache when Ray came in and said, "Stop whatever you're doing. We need you at the Woodlake airport in thirty minutes. Here, you can take my truck." And he tossed me his keys.

During fire season, the park kept a twin-engine airplane, on contract with a private company, to make two reconnaissance flights over Sequoia and Kings Canyon every day. The purpose was to quickly locate lightning strikes or man-caused fires so they could be extinguished before they got out of control. Putting out a one-acre fire might cost only a few hundred dollars, while putting out a fire that had grown to several hundred acres might end up costing more than a hundred thousand dollars. So it made sense to watch vigilantly for fires and respond quickly. In the old days, that kind of monitoring had been done from fire lookout towers, but Sequoia and Kings Canyon had grown, and there were vast sections of the backcountry that couldn't be seen from the towers. After adding up the cost of maintaining the towers and paying the salaries of the lookouts, it was not only more effective to do the reconnaissance by plane, it was cheaper, too.

The problem was that the young pilots flying those planes often knew little or nothing about the backcountry. They didn't know the boundaries, the prominent peaks, the major passes, or the canyons and rivers. They might be able to read a map, but trying to read a map while flying a plane in the mountains isn't a good idea. The solution was to send along a spotter who knew the backcountry firsthand. Most employees who knew the backcountry were *in* the backcountry, so on that day I happened to be just the guy the park service needed.

The route from Ash Mountain to the Woodlake airport passed through Three Rivers and around Lake Kaweah before descending to the flat San Joaquin Valley. That area below Terminus Dam, where the Kaweah River meets the valley floor, is mostly orange orchards now, but just 150 years ago it was a paradise on earth, with gigantic black oaks and an abundance of deer and other wildlife that supported the densest population of Native Americans in California. When Lake Kaweah was filled in 1962, five separate pictograph sites behind the dam were flooded. Most of the Yokuts who had lived there died of smallpox and measles in the 1800s, or were later relocated to reservations, but I couldn't drive through that place without thinking about the people who once lived there.

Because I'd been working with a lot of Native Americans, I often found myself considering the differences between their way of life and mine. Even though they came from cultures as far apart as Navajo, Paiute, and Yokuts, I saw that they had some things in common: a modest sense of their own importance, an earthy sense of humor, and a fearlessness than bordered on fatalism. I didn't want to adopt their ways, but I welcomed the chance to learn about their cultures. The park had a small library at Ash Mountain, including a good collection of academic books and pamphlets on Native Americans, so whenever I came out of the backcountry, I'd borrow as many as the librarian would let me have, plus a few more when she wasn't looking. That summer I'd been reading *Myths of the Owens Valley Paiute* by Julian H. Steward. The stories were oral folktales recorded but unedited by an anthropologist, which gave them an odd, sometimes awkward tone. But if you could imagine how they would sound being told by a talented storyteller around a campfire on a cold winter night, they were funny, informative, and delightful. Here's an excerpt from one of my favorites, called "Origin of Fire":

> *Long ago the people had no fire. The only way they could cook meat was to get black rocks which were hot from the sun and use them for cooking.*
>
> *One day a piece of ash came floating through the air and dropped near Coyote. Coyote went over and looked at it. He walked all around and looked at it, wondering what it was. Then he picked it up. "I wonder what this can be and where it came from?" He went everywhere asking the people about it. They could not understand what it was. Then Wolf said, "This must be the ash of some fire. This must be tule ash from way back over the mountains (to the west)." Wolf thought that some tules had burned and somehow had been carried across the mountains, probably by a whirlwind. The people all wondered where the ash came from.*
>
> *Coyote said, "Somebody will have to go way up in the sky and look for the fire. He will have to go up on a branch of the sky and see where this ash came from. Let us see; who can do that? What man can we get to fly way up in the sky?" They looked around for someone.*
>
> *Then Coyote said, "I can go up there. Just wait." Coyote began to run around, hallooing; then he gave a big yelp and jumped straight up. He fell back on the ground. "I am going to do it this time." He ran around again, made a big noise, and jumped up with all his might. He went up only a little way and fell back on the ground.*

Later in the story, after Eagle and Hawk also failed to get a glimpse of the fire, Crow was able to soar high enough to see over the Sierra Nevada and find the source of the burning ash. The people, under Coyote's blundering leadership, were eventually able to cross over and acquire their own fire.

Coyote is a common figure in Native American literature all across the West. He's a trickster, and sometimes a lecherous fool, who has great ambition but often fails. His misadventures are meant to be instructive to a young audience as lessons in how not to behave. But I suspect a lot of his appeal was pure comedy, too, like our modern Coyote and Roadrunner cartoons. After reading a lot of Coyote tales, I started to think of Coyote as something like the antihero in American novels and films. He's Jack Nicholson in *One Flew Over the Cuckoo's Nest*, a flawed character with great appeal who fails tragically, but in a way that makes us admire him. It's hard not to like a character who's on the path to destruction but having a wonderful time along the way.

In those days I came to admire Coyote more than I probably should have. I was never able to buy into the stifling bureaucratic structure of the park service. I liked the work and appreciated the paycheck, but I knew I had no future in such a rigid and militaristic culture. I thought playing the fool like coyote whenever I thought I could get away with it, taking advantage of the chaos inherent in government work, might buy me enough time to find another way to make a living. Eventually I had some T-shirts printed with a big coyote paw print on the back, and I was wearing one that day as I drove to the Woodlake airport.

The pilot I met at the airport (I can't recall his name.) was a clean-cut young man, just a few years older than I. He was enthusiastic about flying but had no real interest in Sequoia or the mountains in general. To him it was all just terrain to be maneuvered like some video game. We took off from the airport and headed east, crossing Redwood Mountain, Big Meadow, and Horse Corral. At Williams Meadow, an exceptionally long meadow where I'd spent a lot of time building check dams, the pilot circled around a couple of times before saying over the headset, "I always figured that would be a good place to land if I ever had to."

From the air, Williams Meadow looked like a groomed golf course, but on the ground, it was something else. "It's all hummocks," I said, "Some of them three or four feet high. Please don't try to land there while I'm your passenger."

The pilot blanched. "Well, where *could* I land if I had to?"

"Woodlake airport," I replied, pointing back the way we'd come. "There's nothing even close to flat in these mountains."

We cruised over Roaring River, often a hot spot for lightning strikes, but didn't see any smoke. We circled over Deadman and Cloud canyons, where I'd also spent a lot of time. It felt wonderful to glide so effortlessly over the Whale's Back, which would require most of a hard day to cross on foot. The speed and freedom of flying low over the mountains made me feel almost giddy, but I also felt oddly disoriented. All the landmarks I knew so well were more or less where they were supposed to be, but the distances between them didn't match the model in my head. Everything looked either elongated or compressed, and I realized my sense of distance on the ground had been distorted by the effort it took to travel by foot over the rugged terrain.

As we passed directly over Triple Divide Peak, I asked the pilot if we could circle around it.

"Do you see a fire?" he asked.

"No," I replied. "Let's do it just for fun."

Triple Divide had a special interest for me because it stood at the center of that entire wilderness kingdom. A raindrop falling on the very top of Triple Divide might flow north into the Kings River, southeast into the Kern, or southwest into the Kaweah. That otherwise unimpressive peak, of only 12,640 feet, fed water to three distinct watersheds that together drained more than a million acres of the highest and most rugged landscape on the Pacific slope. As we circled the rocky summit once, then twice, I tried to memorize an image of that entire landscape by folding it like origami and cramming it into an empty place in my brain where I'd never forget it. This wasn't a map I was looking at, a scale model, or a written description. This was the real deal, seen with a vividness and clarity that was shocking. I said nothing to the pilot, but it was an important moment for me, even an emotional one.

We continued flying north toward Kings Canyon, with the intention of heading up Bubbs Creek toward the crest of the Sierra, when the pilot yawned and said, "I hate to say this, but I got to bed late last night, and now I'm feeling drowsy. If I can just close my eyes for a few minutes, I know I'll be okay."

"Not while I'm your passenger!" I said.

"Why don't you take over for a few minutes?" he suggested.

I looked down at the duplicate set of controls in front of me. "I don't know how to fly an airplane!"

"Flying's easy," he scoffed. "Landing's the tricky part. Look." And he showed me how you pushed in on the steering wheel to lose altitude, pulled back to gain altitude, then steered left or right, just like a car. "Nothing to it." He slouched down in his seat and pulled his baseball cap over his eyes. "Wake me up if anything goes wrong. And no matter what happens, don't try to land without me."

I immediately thought of Coyote trying and failing to jump high enough to grab hold of a branch of the sky. Now, for at least a few minutes, I had hold of that branch, and I intended to see as much as I possibly could.

The first thing I did after the pilot went to sleep was change course. I'd hiked up Bubbs Creek many times, and it lacked appeal. What I really wanted to see was the lower Middle Fork of the Kings River, which has no trail and is nearly inaccessible. I knew that only a handful of people had ever seen it, and now I could be one of them. In just a couple minutes, I was flying over the junction of the South Fork and Middle Fork of the

Kings River. I turned northeast into the rugged canyon itself, and from the air it looked enticing, with steep canyon walls and shimmering pools of water over white granite. But in just a couple of minutes, that forbidden journey was over. From Tehipite Valley I continued on to Evolution Valley, circled it once out of pure nostalgia, got a good look at snow-covered Mount Darwin, then flew north toward LeConte Canyon. I was having fun now and would have liked to keep flying all day.

When the pilot finally woke, he looked around and said, "Whoa! This doesn't look familiar! Where are we?"

"We just crossed the Oregon border," I said. "I've always wanted to see Crater Lake from the air."

The pilot sat up straight. "You're kidding, right?"

"This is LeConte Canyon."

As the pilot turned the plane around, he muttered, "My instructions were to stay south of Bubbs Creek."

"That makes sense," I nodded. "Not much to burn, really, up here in the rocks."

We crossed over the Kings-Kern Divide and entered a land I knew almost by heart. As we glided over Lake South America, I could see the breezes rippling across the surface of the water. The twisted foxtail pines, a brilliant amber against the white granite, looked as if they'd augured their way up out of the ground. At the Tyndall Creek snow survey cabin, I could see the summer ranger lazily chopping firewood in the front yard. Over the Bighorn Plateau, I spotted a herd of bighorn sheep moving along the side of Tawny Point. The air at that elevation was perfectly clear, and the detail available to the eye was astonishing. The sky overhead was an impossible shade of blue that seemed to go on for eternity. The intricate complexity of the landscape, with layers upon layers of beauty, baffled me and made me wonder what it could mean. I didn't like thinking about nature, or wilderness, in religious terms, but it was hard to explain all this without some kind of grand miracle. And rather than seeing that hidden paradise as a collection of place names and topographic lines, as you would on a map, I saw it as one organic body, an entire wilderness. More importantly, I saw it as a sacred place, a temple, with white spires glistening in the sunlight.

As we continued flying low over the Kern plateau, it occurred to me that wilderness doesn't have to be in remote places like the Brooks Range of Alaska or the southern Andes. Two hundred years ago, it was the rugged inaccessibility that protected wilderness. But no place is truly inaccessible anymore. If it weren't for laws put in place by people with heart and vision, this would all be ski resorts, gambling casinos, shabby amusement parks, and the faces of politicians carved into rock. What I was seeing in front of me was one of the largest wilderness areas in North America, including not only Sequoia and Kings Canyon, but Golden Trout to the south, and Ansel Adams, John Muir, and Yosemite to the north. And it made perfect sense that it was right in the middle of the most populated state in the country, where people driven half mad by civilization could find solace.

I suppose you could say I had an epiphany that day, that the veil was pulled back and I saw Earth with truer eyes. It didn't matter that I had reached that height in a manmade contraption rather than by my own legs. I saw what I saw. The vision wasn't a false one. I've never forgotten it, and I've never been the same again because of it. What had started out as a dull day repairing chainsaws had suddenly become the closest thing to a spiritual experience I would ever have.

We continued flying along the western flank of the 14,000-footers: Russell, Whitney, Muir, and finally, Langley. We were getting low on fuel, and I knew it was about time for us to head back to Woodlake. The pilot circled around a couple times to gain enough altitude to cross back over the Kaweahs, when suddenly one of the engines quit. It didn't cough and sputter—it just stopped. The pilot tried several times to get it started again, but the engine refused. If it had been a chainsaw, I might have checked a fuel line, dried the spark plug, maybe taken a coffee break to think about it. But of course it wasn't, and there wasn't a thing I could do to help.

"Well, that's why we have two engines, right?" I asked. "One quits, you still have another?"

"Not exactly," the pilot said. "With one engine we can descend gradually, but we can't ascend. Do you know the elevation at Kaweah Gap?"

"It's about ten thousand six hundred feet," I said.

"And it's all downhill from there, right?"

I had once jogged from Big Arroyo, over Kaweah Gap, to Giant Forest, a distance of about twenty miles, and as I closed my eyes I could visualize the route clearly in my mind. "Yeah, straight down the Middle Fork to Three Rivers."

"What's the deal with that abandoned airport in Three Rivers? Could we land there if we had to?"

"Maybe," I said, not really sure. "But the reason they closed it was because there'd been so many fatalities there. Woodlake is the nearest real airport."

There was a bit of turbulence as we crossed over Kaweah Gap—just the normal up-canyon winds at midday—but I could see the pilot struggling to control the plane. I could see, too, by the instrument panel in front of me that we were losing both speed and elevation.

The pilot whipped out a map and studied it intently. Then he tossed the map at me and announced, "Forget Woodlake. We're going all the way to Visalia."

I thought about that for a moment. "I suppose that makes sense. They'll have a mechanic there who can work on the engine, right?"

"No," the pilot said, shaking his head. "Visalia is the nearest airport that can have a fire engine waiting on the runway. And there's a major hospital just a couple miles away."

As we glided over the fire lookout tower at Milk Ranch, just west of Mineral King, we were flying so low that the female lookout sunbathing nude on the tin roof had to jump up and cover herself with a towel. I waved longingly as we passed, not knowing if I'd ever see her again, but hoping that I would.

We descended into the San Joaquin Valley, where the smog was so thick, it felt like we were flying through a toxic orange soup. Heaven to hell in fifteen minutes. I couldn't have found the Visalia airport in that haze, but the pilot somehow managed it. And waiting there below us, alongside the runway, was a neon green fire engine with a full crew in Nomex suits.

The pilot pulled off the landing calmly and smoothly. It wasn't until we were out of the plane and he knelt down to kiss the ground that I realized what a close call we'd just had.

***

There have been so many plane crashes in the southern Sierra Nevada, it's difficult to understand why pilots of small planes continue to fly over it. Sequoia and Kings Canyon alone has had at least twenty-three crashes, and ten of those have been in the upper Bubbs Creek area. If you were flying from the San Joaquin Valley and your destination was Las Vegas or perhaps the ski resorts of Utah, it would be tempting to choose that route because it's shorter than flying south and then crossing the Sierra crest where the elevation begins to drop off, around Olancha Peak and the southern Kern River. But flying up Bubbs Creek is tricky—I know because I've done it many times. I always had several advantages, though: I was flying in perfect summer weather, I was flying with experienced pilots, and I'd hiked the terrain myself many times. I understood very well why so many planes had crashed there and I insisted the pilots listen to me when I explained the dangers to them.

Lower Bubbs Creek flows through a narrow, V-shaped, nearly straight canyon, with a gradual incline beginning at around 5,000 feet at Cedar Grove. At Vidette Meadow, elevation 9,500 feet, the canyon veers to the south, and from a small plane, that appears to be the logical route. But the correct route is to continue flying east, toward Kearsarge Pass, which, at 12,598 feet, is the lowest point in that area to cross the Sierra crest. If the pilot chooses to continue flying up Vidette Creek, he soon arrives at Center Basin, which is surrounded by higher peaks, including Mount Bradley at 13,270 feet, Mount Keith at 13,982 feet, and Junction Peak at 13,888 feet. At that point, the pilot has no choice but to try to circle back, which is difficult to do because the canyon has narrowed considerably. Center Basin is like a giant fly trap, and over the years it has caught a lot of flies.

I don't mean to be disrespectful of those who have lost their lives in plane crashes in the southern Sierra, but once the dust settles, plane crashes leave a big mess, and somebody has to clean it up. I was called upon to do that once in the early seventies with my friend Mike Palmer and our band of Navajos.

The crash was near Vidette Meadow, in a stand of lodgepole pines. The bodies had been removed from the cabin of the small Cessna, though blood and other signs of trauma still remained. Because the plane's engine had salvage value, it had already been removed from the site by helicopter. But the rest of the plane was just an ugly snarl of twisted aluminum.

We backpacked into the crash site from the east side, over

Kearsarge Pass. Slim Knutsen packed in our gear from Cedar Grove and met us at Vidette Meadow, where we set up camp. Then Slim wished us luck and left us on our own. Even after examining the wreck, we still weren't sure how to go about dismantling it. For such a small plane, the job seemed large. We'd never dismantled an airplane before and really had no idea how to go about it. Nobody in the park service had any advice for us either. Like so many assignments given to my crew over the years, this was a job nobody else wanted—which suited us just fine. We were too young to fear failure and even relished the chance to make fools of ourselves.

The ideal tool for that job might have been a reciprocating saw with metal cutting blades, but that would have required a gas-powered generator. Because we were working inside a national park, we couldn't use power tools, except for a chainsaw, which was useless to us. We hadn't even heard of rotary carbide blades for chainsaws, if such a thing even existed then. We did have hacksaws, tin snips, and dikes (diagonal pliers for cutting wire), so we went to work gnawing away at the wings and frame. But we'd only been at that for a couple of hours when we realized it would take us weeks to break apart a plane that way. Even with gloves on, the sharp metal was cutting our hands and forearms. What we wanted to do, what our instinct told us to do, was to crush the thing up in a ball like an empty beer can and be done with it. But we couldn't do that either, so we had to come up with a better plan.

Curtis Cohoe threw his hacksaw down on the ground in disgust, said maybe he had a better idea, and slinked off back to camp. A few minutes later he returned carrying our eight-pound maul that we used for splitting firewood. On one side of the maul's head was a flat hammer, but on the other side was a blade like an ax, except thicker and stronger. Curtis went to work hacking at one of the tail wings, and with each blow he sliced through three or four inches of the aluminum sheeting.

By avoiding the thicker frame, he was able to nearly sever the wing from the plane in about thirty minutes. There were cables that had to be sawed through by hand, and electrical wires that had to be cut with dikes, but that was easy. In some places we had no choice but to use our hacksaws to cut through the thick frame, which was slow and tedious. Dismantling a plane that way was still hard work, and because we only had the one maul, we had to take turns at it. But little by little, over a few days, we broke that plane up into two-foot sections and tied them into bundles with rope so Slim Knutsen, and other park packers, could haul them out over the summer.

After we'd finished that job, we hiked out over Kearsarge Pass, where our six-passenger truck was waiting for us at the trailhead parking lot. Rather than camp that night at Onion Valley, we chose to drive down to Lone Pine and spend the night at Portagee Joe's, the Inyo County campground some 10,000 feet below the summit of Mount Whitney. We all wanted a night on the town, and we thought we deserved it. So we washed up in the cold ditch than ran through the campground, put on our cleanest shirts, and walked two blocks into town for cheeseburgers and cold beer.

That night the powerful down-canyon wind the Owens Valley is known for began howling through Portagee Joe's. But we didn't mind, all snuggled up in our down sleeping bags. Around two in the morning, with all that beer sloshing around in his bladder, Mike Palmer decided he had to relieve himself. I heard him get up and, with one eye cracked barely open, saw him tiptoeing barefoot and naked into the desert. Just then a powerful gust of wind rose up and blew his sleeping bag away. As I fell back to sleep, I heard Palmer cursing and howling as he hopped across the Owens Valley in pursuit.

In 1974, I started doing winter snow surveys all over the southern Sierra Nevada, but mostly in Sequoia National Park. Snow surveys have been an important part of water management in California since the 1920s. Farmers in the San Joaquin and Sacramento valleys need to know how much irrigation water they can expect for the coming summer, and that depends on how much snow has fallen in the high country during the winter. For many years, the only way to get that information was to send skiers into the backcountry to measure the accumulation of snow by hand. By the 1970s, though, many of the snow surveys were being handled by automated stations placed in strategic locations throughout the backcountry—no humans required. Sequoia, Kings Canyon, and Yosemite National Parks had resisted the conversion to automated surveys, and the surveys there were still done the old-fashioned way, mostly by park service employees, but sometimes by state employees, as well. Many of the backcountry cabins used by rangers in the summer had been built by the State of California and were stocked with food and fuel every fall for the use of snow surveyors in January, February, March, and April.

I first started doing the surveys as a volunteer when the permanent rangers assigned to that duty asked me to give a helping hand. Later, after I'd learned the job well enough, I asked to be paid. Aside from the winter mountaineering skills needed to survive avalanches, blizzards, and sub-zero temperatures, plus the skiing ability necessary to negotiate ten or fifteen miles a day at high elevation over rugged terrain carrying a pack, the job was easy, and I loved it. Any idiot could have managed the actual surveys. Basically, you jammed a hollow aluminum pole into the snow until you hit dirt, then you pulled the pole back out, weighed it, measured the depth of the snow, and with those two factors you could calculate the water content of the snow. With hundreds of readings like that from all over the Sierra Nevada, the computer whizzes up in Sacramento could plan the coming year's water allotments for California farmers.

In those days, all we had for backcountry skis were light but narrow Nordic skis that glided well over flat terrain, if we used the right wax, but were terrible for skiing downhill. The great thing about a snow surveyor's job, aside from seeing all that magnificent country in winter, was that if everything went the way it was supposed to, we arrived at a warm cabin every night, with a blazing-hot wood stove, a shot of brandy, and a dinner of baked ham and potatoes. It was a backcountry skier's dream.

One of the snow surveys we did four times a year was the Pear Lake survey, in Sequoia. We would stay at the Pear Lake ski hut, which is a handsome stone structure that looks like an enchanted cottage from a Nordic fairy tale. It was built by the CCC between 1939 and 1941, and it's the only backcountry cabin in Sequoia available in the winter for public use, on a reservation basis. It's quite popular with cross-country skiers, and it has visitors nearly every night during the winter months, but there are plenty of bunks at the cabin, plus a loft upstairs, so the snow surveyors always found room there, as well.

A pleasant feature of the Pear Lake cabin is its indoor john, which is convenient when you have to go at four in the morning and there's a howling blizzard outside. Standard plumbing, with a flush toilet and a septic tank, wasn't feasible there because the cabin is at 9,200 feet, where winter nighttime temperatures are sometimes below zero. The pipes would be frozen all winter long. The cabin's designers foresaw this problem and created a clever system in which the toilet waste fell into fiberglass tubs, known as honey buckets, in the basement. When one tub filled up, it was capped by whoever happened to be staying at the cabin at the time, wheeled aside, and an empty tub was wheeled into place. The full tubs stayed nicely frozen all winter and spring, and in June they were packed out by park service mules.

Early one summer, my backcountry crew was sent to work on a small meadow restoration project in the Tablelands area, and our plan was to stay at the Pear Lake cabin. The park service dispatched a private packer to ride into Pear Lake with a string of mules and remove the full fiberglass tubs, and we were assigned the job of helping the packer load the heavy tubs onto his mules.

Before we could get into the basement, a snow drift that had frozen into a block of ice in front of the basement doors had to be removed with axes and shovels. As we were completing that job, we saw that a corner of the wooden door had been chewed away by some animal. When we were finally able to open the door, we saw that a family of marmots had been living in the basement all winter. All the fiberglass tubs, we saw, were missing their lids. Either the lids hadn't been properly fastened that winter, or the marmots, which can be devilishly clever with their nimble little hands, had managed to pull them off. And all the fiberglass tubs were empty—licked perfectly clean.

Our first reaction was the same as anybody's—revulsion. But the more we thought about it, we began to wonder why human digestion is so inefficient that everything we defecate was considered edible by marmots. Because we dug latrines at all our backcountry camps, we had a better opportunity than most people to observe the outcome of our previous day's consumption, and it was disheartening to see how little of it our bodies had digested. One day Mike Palmer came back from the latrine grumbling, "I'm going to quit eating corn. What's the point? It comes out looking almost exactly like it does going in!"

One of the first symptoms of altitude sickness is the loss

of appetite. We coped with it every year when we first camped above 8,000 feet or so. We usually recovered our appetites pretty quickly and went on to consume at least twice our normal daily calories. But at high altitude, we digested food poorly. All of us lost weight while living at high elevation, no matter how much we ate. Mike Palmer and Jimmy Castro lost as much as thirty pounds every summer. And for humans, that isn't at all unusual. Except for the Quechuas in the Andes, and the Tibetans in the Himalayas, and a few other populations around the world, it's rare for humans to live at elevations above 7,000 feet. Not only does the lack of adequate oxygen make every task more difficult than it would be at a lower elevation, requiring more calories, but the growing season at high elevation is too short for farmers to produce enough food. But the biggest problem might be that, even if you have an adequate food supply at high elevation, it's difficult for human bodies to digest it.

So we had to give those Pear Lake marmots some grudging respect for being able to do something we couldn't do. They weren't just seasonal visitors, like us. They had the ability to survive, and even grow fat, at high elevation. But I must admit that I've never been able to look at a sleek backcountry marmot again without wondering how it got so plump.

Fortunately, that obsolete system for storing human waste at the Pear Lake cabin was later replaced by a solar-assisted composting toilet.

∿∿
∿∿

In the late seventies, Sequoia National Park hired a meadow specialist named Steve DeBenedetti, a bright young man with a master's degree from UC Berkeley. The first time I met DeBenedetti, he was hiking out of the backcountry on the High Sierra Trail. He was heavyset, with a shaggy mane of sun-bleached hair and a big red beard, carrying a paperback book—a crime novel, I believe. The High Sierra Trail is one of the most beautiful routes in the Sierra, leading from the Giant Forest grove of sequoias, over the Great Western Divide, across the Kern River, and ending at the summit of Mount Whitney. People come from all over the world to hike that trail. But DeBenedetti, who had a study project at Sky Parlor Meadow, had hiked the route so many times he'd stopped seeing it and had grown bored with it. He solved the problem by reading a book while he walked—a solution I'd never seen before. We had a good laugh about that, and then DeBenedetti told me, "I know you're foreman of the backcountry resource management crew. When you get a chance, maybe in September when you come out of the backcountry, I'd like to sit down and talk with you."

"What about?" I asked.

"Meadows."

DeBenedetti had been working on a meadow grazing plan for backcountry stock users. For years there'd been confusing, or nonexistent, regulations on where or when horses and mules could be grazed in the backcountry. A few delicate places were forbidden to stock, but enforcement was spotty. Part of the problem had been that grazing animals, when turned loose, went where they liked, and it had been virtually impossible to confine them to acceptable grazing areas. But my crew had spent several summers rebuilding the entire system of drift fences throughout Sequoia and Kings Canyon. We'd been criticized for it by some purists who thought pack stock should be banned from the backcountry—something we knew was never going to happen.

DeBenedetti put our hard work to use by writing a comprehensive grazing plan for virtually every meadow in the park. For each location, there was a prescribed range of dates when stock would be allowed to graze there, and the prescriptions varied for wet years (when the meadows were boggy and vulnerable to damage), average years, and dry years. What made the plan feasible was that stock users could easily understand the plan and follow the guidelines, plus they could rely on our new system of drift fences to confine their animals to a defined area. But in my opinion, what really made that plan work was the power of Steve DeBenedetti's personality. Somehow that calm, modest, unassuming man was able to convince environmentalists, private packers, and park packers too, that the plan was practical and reasonable. I think that was a remarkable achievement.

That fall, when DeBenedetti and I finally had a chance to sit down and talk about backcountry meadows, we came to the conclusion that the greatest danger to backcountry meadows was no longer stock grazing; it was the damage caused by trails. The damage wasn't intentional or even the result of mismanagement. It was the result of basic human nature. Historically, trails followed the shortest route from one point to another. In the Sierra Nevada, most trails follow ancient animal paths, which always take the route that requires the least amount of energy. Native Americans followed the same paths, and when American cattlemen, miners, and sheepherders began exploring the backcountry, they used the same routes, especially when those routes crossed a meadow.

In the southern Sierra Nevada, flatland is nearly nonexistent, except for the meadows. That alone makes them unique. In that rugged and often vertical landscape, plush meadows create a sharp but pleasant relief. Their brilliant green vegetation creates a contrast to the blue skies and white granite, and if the wildflowers are in bloom, they provide a splash of color—orange, purple, scarlet—seen nowhere else in the mountains. Because meadows are open, without trees, the views open to distant snow-covered peaks or granite spires. And because meadow vegetation is so lush, deer and bear are often seen grazing near meadow perimeters. Meadows are almost a metaphor for paradise, a place of beauty and abundance, and for many people like Steve DeBenedetti and me, meadows are the backcountry's most precious resource.

What holds a high-country meadow together is a fine sedge named *Carex exerta*. It has short hairs above ground, but dense, tenacious roots below that form a compact sod that extends a couple feet below ground. It's not a grass (as the old mnemonic goes: "sedges have edges, rushes are round, but grasses are hollow from top to ground"). Sedges are so common in the high Sierra that I would guess they make up at least fifty percent of the ground cover above 9,000 feet. Everybody appreciates the splendor of giant sequoias or is charmed by the graceful limbs of a sugar pine, but for me, the tiny *Carex exerta* is the most beautiful plant in the Sierra. It changes color with the seasons, from bright green in the spring to golden-yellow in the fall; from many miles away, steep stringer meadows of sedge add a slice of color to a dark mountainside. And in an alpine world, where soil is shallow and scarce, sedges are the fabric that keeps that precious resource in place. Sedges have a grain head an inch or so in length that grazing animals, as well as rodents and birds, find irresistible. I've eaten it myself, and I believe Native Americans did, too, because it's abundant, nutritious, and could easily be harvested in large quantities. Horses and mules love it. If you happen to be a wrangler out searching for your stray animals, the smartest thing you can do is go where the sedges grow. You'll likely find your animals there, if not grazing, then rolling on their backs for the sheer pleasure of it.

But meadows are also very fragile. In the fall or late summer, when meadows are usually dry, sedges form a surface so hard it can break a shovel. In the spring and early summer, though, when the meadows are wet, a horse's hoof, or even a human's Vibram sole, can easily punch a hole into the turf six or eight inches deep. A path across a wet meadow quickly becomes a muddy mire, and then the water, which had been a uniform sheet across the meadow, begins to flow down the path, effectively draining the meadow dry. Large meadows have been destroyed this way.

It's easy to blame cattle or horses and mules. But cattle haven't been allowed in most of Kings Canyon since the 1930s, or in Sequoia since the 1890s. Horse and mules, of course, are still used in the backcountry by commercial and private packers, as well as by the park service, which mostly uses them to supply trail crews. But I believe the great popularity of backpacking has done more to damage backcountry meadows than all the horses and mules in the park's short history. That's a hard fact for some environmentalists to accept, but I believe it's true. The numbers alone make this apparent. On the John Muir Trail, hikers outnumber pack animals by at least a hundred to one. Also, mules are tied in strings and go where the packer leads them, in single file; when crossing a wet meadow, they don't worry about getting their feet wet. But when hikers see a muddy trail, they step out of the rut and start a new trail parallel to the old one. I've seen places where there were a dozen or more parallel trails crossing a meadow, and the meadow was so heavily impacted that its survival was in jeopardy. In addition, at the end of the day, when pack animals are turned loose, they disperse, sometimes traveling many miles in one night, much of it well off trail. Backpackers, though, congregate in camps, often at the very edge of meadows.

The solution isn't to ban either backpackers or pack stock. Neither of those options will ever be politically acceptable. The idea DeBenedetti proposed to me was that trails that cross delicate meadows could be rerouted, the trail scars could be rehabilitated, and with time a damaged meadow could be restored to a healthy condition. Over the next several years, he and I began that long, complicated process.

Today many large mountainous parks have crews trained in restoration work. But in the 1970s, there weren't many people in the parks or anywhere else who knew how to go about that work. Some people in the parks didn't even *want* to go about it. Building trails and bridges was something maintenance chiefs and district rangers could understand and appreciate, but unbuilding things implied that maybe park managers had made mistakes in the past. Undoing something was almost an admission of failure. It was regress, not progress. And trying to restore a wilderness area to a natural condition was seen as something only God or another ice age could do. The idea rankled some people—even wilderness purists, who couldn't imagine anything good coming from more of man's meddling.

With a little investigation, we learned that Yosemite National Park, just to the north of us, had also been trying to cope with this same problem, especially at Tuolumne Meadows, where there were several miles of trail through alpine meadow vegetation. A trail crew foreman named Jim Snyder had been developing techniques to deal with it. Snyder, who had a master's degree in history and later became Yosemite's official park historian, had been applying his knowledge of ancient Roman roads to wilderness trail work. To protect eroded creek crossings, he and his crew had built handsome, arched bridges of rock using the classic Roman techniques; they had rerouted trails where possible, and built raised rock and earthen causeways where it was not. Their efforts so for had been focused on relocating the trails and bridges where they would do the least harm, but they'd begun experimenting with techniques for restoring the damaged meadow vegetation as well. That fall our park's chief forester, Tom Warner, and I drove to Yosemite to see Snyder's work, and we came away determined to try similar projects ourselves.

One of the first places where we decided to try our hand at meadow restoration was Granite Basin, in Kings Canyon, where multiple trails about a half mile in length crossed an otherwise pristine meadow. We explained our plans to that area's trail crew foreman, John Gross, and he almost immediately had his crew build a new trail around the meadow.

The first day we arrived at Granite Meadow to begin the restoration project, I watched as a large party of Sierra Club backpackers reached the point where the new trail diverged. The local ranger had put up a sign there that read "Meadow Restoration Project—Do Not Cross!" I figured if anybody would understand our intent and obey that sign, it would be a Sierra Club party. But the hike from the trailhead at Cedar Grove to Granite Meadow is one of the most difficult single-day hikes I know of, including an elevation gain of about 6,000 feet over ten miles. The clearly exhausted Sierra Club party looked at the warning sign, took in the slightly longer route of the new trail, then trudged one after another across the damaged meadow.

That's what I mean when I say the Vibram sole has done more damage to backcountry meadows than cattle or pack stock. The many improvements to backpacking equipment, like the aluminum-framed pack, dome tent, polyester sleeping bag, Gore-Tex rain jacket—brilliant ideas invented by people like my climbing teacher Doug Tompkins—have allowed millions of people to enjoy the beauty of wilderness with a level of comfort never known before. But by the 1970s, it had become clear that if we want to pass our wilderness heritage on to future generations, we'd better learn how to apply some of that human ingenuity to protecting, and even restoring, some of it.

The first thing I did on that project at Granite Meadow was use our chainsaw to fall two large, dead, red firs along the edge of the meadow, effectively blocking the old route for good.

In those days, there wasn't much information available on the subject of meadow restoration. Steve DeBenedetti, who was after all a meadow specialist, suggested that we conduct this first project as an experiment. Instead of trying one technique, we should try several, then decide later which was most promising. And that's what we did, varying our technique in hundred-foot sections. Sand was plentiful in the creek bottom, but good soil was rare, and we couldn't justify stealing it from some other place. So we tried using sand alone as fill, then sand with organic material added, sand mixed with mule dung, and so on, in effect making our own soil. We tried breaking up the impacted trail scar, or not. We tried using sod plugs of *Carex exerta* on the surface, and we tried gathering seed by hand and sowing it just like planting a lawn.

The biggest problem we faced was how to move that much dirt and sand. We didn't have the luxury of a backhoe, or even a little Bobcat mini excavator. But we did have mules. Our packer Slim Knutsen recalled the days when large quantities of dirt had been moved by mules using pack boxes with a hinged bottom—dirt boxes, they were called. Nobody we knew had seen one in thirty years. Not even the park's oldest warehouse at Sycamore, where we could usually find stuff like a hundred-pound chainsaw that probably belonged in the Smithsonian Institution, had even one old dirt box lying around. So Slim drew the design for one from memory, took it to the park's carpentry shop at Ash Mountain, and there they made us six matching sets of dirt boxes.

The idea behind a dirt box is that you place a tarp over the mule's saddle and back to protect it from the abrasive dirt, sling a pair of the boxes over the saddle forks, then shovel the dirt into the boxes in equal amounts so the load will be balanced. Normally a mule carries 160 pounds, 80 pounds on each side. Two boxes of dirt weigh more like 200 pounds, but that was an acceptable load considering the mule would only be carrying that weight for a short distance, perhaps 300 yards.

We found a bend in Granite Creek, not far from our work

site, where a large volume of fine sand had been deposited by the creek during floods. We loaded the mules there one by one, then led them in a string to the trail scar. With a little effort, Slim was able to train the mules to step across the rut with their front legs and stand still while workers on each side prepared to dump the load. The trickiest part of the whole process was dumping both boxes at the same time—otherwise the weight on the heavy side might pull the pack saddle askew, or even pull the mule over. We started by having one worker counting "one, two, three," but with a little practice, we found we could synchronize the dump with just eye contact and a nod of the head. There was a clasp holding the bottom of each box in place, and when it was released, the bottom of the boxes hinged inward, dumping the entire load at once.

I estimated that each dirt box held about three cubic feet; therefore each mule carried six cubic feet, and a string of mules carried thirty-six cubic feet. That happened to be almost the exact volume of one backhoe bucket—but without the tread damage, soil compaction, and diesel fuel contamination of heavy equipment. Using mules to haul dirt took a bit longer than a backhoe would have, but we weren't in any hurry, and neither were the mules.

We found a site not far away where there was an accumulation of old pine duff, almost like mulch that had built up over the years. Fresh pine needles would have been too acidic, but the old duff had been leached by snowmelt and rain. By mixing the duff with our fill, we were able to add organic matter, increase the volume, and improve moisture retention. Also, the duff was so light, we were able to move it to the job site by wheelbarrow rather than mule. In some places we inserted log checks perpendicular to the trail scar so the fill wouldn't move when it became saturated in the spring. Finally, we took plugs of *Carex exerta* from the meadow by driving a post-hole digger eight inches into the ground and lifting out a column of sedge stem and root. The hole was then filled with dirt, and the plugs were transplanted to the newly filled rut.

We worked hard on that Granite Meadow project almost all summer long. In late September, Steve DeBenedetti hiked in to see what we'd been up to. I showed him around the site, explained what we'd done, and tried to justify our reasoning behind each action.

"Steve," I said, "honestly, we're just making this stuff up. I think we're on the right track, but sometimes I worry it could all be a big waste of time."

DeBenedetti smiled and said, "I think what you've done here is state of the art for backcountry meadow restoration. Let's start planning more projects to work on."

〜

The next spring, before the snow on the passes had melted enough that we could go to work in the backcountry, I was hiking by myself along the North Fork of the Kaweah, on my day off. It had been a good winter for rainfall, and the foothills were thick with grass such a radiant green that you almost had to wear sunglasses just to look at it. The day was warm, and I noticed that the poison oak, which grows in abundance in the foothills, was just starting to leaf out with shiny red twists of foliage. Poison oak is a beautiful plant in its way, I suppose, but one I hate seeing because I'm so sensitive to it.

The first time I had a really bad reaction to poison oak, I'd been cutting a fence line through a thick stand of the stuff, using a small chainsaw. I was wearing a long-sleeved shirt, jeans, gloves, and a baseball cap, and I figured that since it was the blade of the chainsaw making contact with the plant, not my skin, I'd be okay. The chain easily cut through the soft wood of the plant, but it splattered my clothing with the pulpy residue.

Still, I reasoned that as long as I didn't let it make contact with my skin, I was safe. That evening I had oozing, itching blisters covering almost my entire body. I learned then that calamine lotion, the most commonly recommended remedy for poison oak, is useless, and hydrocortisone cream only works up to a point. The only relief for a poison oak rash I've ever found, I discovered that night. I got in the shower and turned up the hot water as high as I could stand it. The relief was so immediate and overwhelming, it was almost orgasmic, and I don't care to describe it any further.

Sensitivity to poison oak varies from person to person. I knew of one firefighter at Sequoia who had to be hospitalized after inhaling poison oak smoke from a fire. On the other hand, my friend Kirk Stiltz, who grew up in Three Rivers, has no sensitivity to poison oak at all. Kirk had been an avid hunter and fisherman all his life, and his sensitivity to the plant had been put to the test a thousand times. He could go crashing through a thicket of poison oak and wouldn't develop so much as a tiny blister between his fingers. I was envious of him for having that superhuman ability, and I wondered how I might acquire it myself.

I'd read somewhere that Native Americans had immunized themselves to poison oak by eating the leaves in the spring. I asked Charlie Castro, but he said he didn't know anything about it. I asked the Navajos working on my crew about it, too, but they didn't know what I was talking about. Poison oak is less common in desert areas, and perhaps their people hadn't come in contact with it. So I figured the only way to find out if it was possible to acquire an immunity to poison oak by ingesting it was to ingest it. That beautiful spring day on the North Fork, I ate two small, shiny leaves.

Immunity to bacteria can be acquired by introducing weakened or dead strains of the bacteria so the body can develop antibodies. But the poison oak toxin, urushiol, isn't a bacteria. With a plant toxin, it's the body's response that causes the severe reaction, and generally the more you are exposed to the toxin, the worse the response is. In people like Kirk, who have no response to poison oak, the urushiol itself does no damage.

That night around midnight, I developed severe abdominal cramps, mostly on my right side below the navel. By dawn I was in severe pain. I dragged myself out of bed, got dressed, and drove to Kaweah Delta Hospital, forty miles away in Visalia. It took the emergency room physician about a minute to determine that I had an inflamed appendix. (The key symptom is rebound pain. If you press on the area where it hurts, there's a sharp pain when the pressure is released.) I didn't tell the physician why my appendix was likely inflamed because by then it didn't matter, and I didn't want him to laugh at my stupidity.

The appendectomy was quick and easy, but there was one unusual after-effect. Waking up from the anesthesia and still groggy, I had a vivid and disturbing memory of seeing a coyote leap onto the operating table, snatch my appendix from the surgeon's hands just as he'd removed it from my belly, and flee with it into the dark. I didn't know what to make of it at the time, but I realize now that the strange vision was my first attack of ghost sickness, something my Paiute and Navajo friends knew quite well.

# Chapter Four: Chubasco a Cappella

The spring of 1975, after one of the older trail crew packers retired, Slim Knutsen left our crew and went to work for the trails division. Everyone was sorry to see him go, but it was a good move for Slim because he could work more weeks a year. To fill his position on my crew, the park hired a new packer, Norman Jefferson, a Paiute from Lone Pine, California, on the east side of the Sierra Nevada.

The first time I met Norm in the parking lot at Ash Mountain, he looked nervous and uncomfortable, like he might get back in his truck and drive home to Lone Pine. He was about six feet, broad-shouldered and a bit baby-faced, and wore his hair long. Norm was only twenty-one at the time, and I wondered if he had enough experience to be our packer. I soon learned that he'd been packing mules his whole life, yet I still couldn't imagine how he, or anybody else, could replace Slim. It wasn't long before I found out how wrong I was.

After the usual Monday morning safety talk, we were loading the bed of a pickup truck with our crew's gear, getting ready to drive to Mineral King and pack into the backcountry. Somehow the valve on a five-gallon propane tank had been nudged open, and propane began gushing out. Another worker was smoking a cigarette close by, and before we knew what had happened, a flame three feet long roared out of the propane tank. My first thought was to get as far away from there as possible before the tank exploded. But almost before I could move, Norm slipped off his T-shirt and threw it on the flame, extinguishing it immediately. I stood there speechless, while Norm looked at me sheepishly and laughed.

Later that morning, we met up with Slim Knutsen in Mineral King Valley. Slim knew about Norm's background growing up on the east side of the mountains, and, curious, he stopped to watch Norm work. Packers on opposite sides of the Sierra go about their work a bit differently, and they can be stubborn about insisting their way is the only way. But Slim, besides being an expert packer, was a student of western lore, and he knew there were different styles of packing all over the West. He watched Norm tie a diamond hitch in a way that looked backward to a packer from the west side, but rather than trying to correct him, he slapped Norm on the shoulder and said he'd just learned something new.

Though Norm always tended to be reserved around people he didn't know, little by little he opened up and told me about himself. His father, Thomas Jefferson (everybody called him Tommy), had been part owner of Mount Whitney Pack Trains and was one of the most respected people in the Owens Valley. He was a handsome, broad-shouldered, mahogany-skinned man, known for his skill training horses, his fairness in dealing with people, and his humor. Norm told me that one of his earliest memories was standing at the trailhead at Whitney Portal, crying because his father was riding into the mountains and he couldn't go with him. Norm said that as Tommy rode away, he raised one arm and called back to those waiting at the trailhead, "See you in the fall if I see you at all!" It was an old western farewell, meant as a grim joke about the danger and uncertainty of life, but Norm thought his father meant it literally.

Norm's mother, a white woman, had died when he was only fourteen, and in the years I knew him, he only spoke of her once—and even then obliquely, without using her name.

By the time Norm became a teenager, he was already a respected rider, roper, and packer in the Owens Valley. Every spring he'd participate in the annual cattle roundup and branding on the Olivas Ranch, where horsemanship was taken so seriously that when a rider's mount grew tired, a fresh horse was brought to him and he switched from one to the other without his feet touching ground. Norm spent every summer in the backcountry, mostly on the Kern Plateau, helping his father with the family business. Even in those days, there were thousands of people every year who wanted to stand on top of Mount Whitney, and Mount Whitney Pack Trains could place them at Trail Crest, just nine hundred feet below the summit. Mount Whitney Pack Trains became one of the most successful pack stations in the country until 1973, when the US Forest Service banned stock use on the Mount Whitney trail, citing what it called conflicts between hikers and stock users. It was a blow to Tommy Jefferson and his family, and that experience left Norm forever suspicious of the federal government.

The Lone Pine Reservation, which is only 237 acres, had been created in the 1930s as a land exchange between the Department of the Interior (which oversees the Bureau of Indian Affairs) and the City of Los Angeles, which had already bought or stolen most of the land and water rights in the Owens Valley so it could funnel the water of the Owens River into the LA Aqueduct and fuel the growth of the San Fernando Valley. What had once been a thriving agricultural district in the Owens Valley became a desert, though in my mind still a strikingly beautiful one. Like most people in the Owens Valley, Norm was bitter about what the City of Los Angeles had done to his home. Every time he crossed the LA Aqueduct, he would stop his pickup truck in the middle of the road, get out, and urinate into the water flowing south. "I guess they want it all," he would say. "So here, let 'em have a little more."

Norm attended Lone Pine High, which was so small the football team had only seven players. On Saturday night he and his buddies would buy a twelve-pack of beer and raise hell up and down the Owens Valley, often covering a hundred miles or more before dawn. Sometimes after midnight, they'd drive their trucks out onto the dry Owens Lake bed. In the old days, Norm's ancestors had caught trout three feet long in that lake, and hunted ducks and geese that flocked there by the thousands. But after LA diverted the river, the lake remained dry most of the year. When the wind blew from the south, arsenic dust that had been collecting on the lake bottom for thousands of years would rise up and cast a pink storm over the town of Lone Pine and the reservation. The lake bottom was mined for soda ash and other minerals, and one night the mining company left their heavy equipment with the keys in the ignition. Norm and his buddies started a couple of big earth loaders and raced them around the lake bed until they managed to get them bogged down in the mud. Then they left the loaders there and slogged back to their trucks just before the sun came up.

Besides being a skilled packer, roper, farrier, hunter, trapper, and fisherman, Norm was also a good rock climber and a fair tennis player, too. He also took his tribal ancestry, and his people's teachings, very seriously. Once I showed him a quartz arrowhead I'd found near the Saline Valley (in the desert east of the Inyo Mountains), where I'd been poking around a talus cave just above a dry water course. The cave was the only natural shelter for miles around, and I was sure it had been used by humans in the past. I was mostly interested in finding pictographs, or petroglyphs, which are even more rare, but when I reached up to a ledge and ran my fingers along its deepest recess, I found an arrowhead that had been left there perhaps hundreds of years ago. When I pulled the arrowhead out, I was surprised to see that it was made of pure white

# Chubasco a Cappella

quartz, and flawlessly shaped, with small, uniform facets. Most arrowheads in California and Nevada were made from black obsidian, which could be found in abundance at the Inyo and Mono craters north of Mammoth Lakes. Obsidian is a form of natural glass that is perfect for shaping arrowheads or spear points. Sometimes chert was used, too. But it's very rare to find arrowheads made of quartz because it's brittle and difficult to shape, and would likely shatter on impact with flesh. The only purpose for a quartz arrowhead that I could imagine was ceremonial. But I was curious to hear what Norm had to say about it. The Native Americans who had lived in that desert had been Paiutes and were therefore likely his ancestors. When I handed the arrowhead to Norm, told him where I'd found it, and asked him what he thought of it, he turned it over once in his hand, then gave it back to me.

"If I were you," he said, "I'd drive out to the Saline Valley right now and put that back exactly where you found it. It isn't the sort of thing you should be messing around with."

Often at suppertime in the backcountry, Norm would take his plate of food and disappear into the woods for a few minutes. Once I happened to see him take a small portion of the food off his plate and place it at the base of a tree. I apologized, feeling I'd intruded on something private, but he said, "That's okay. It's just something my people do. It's a way of giving thanks to the Earth."

I saw then that Norm considered his religion real and alive, not a dead carcass like my own, and that impressed me very much.

Norm told me that when he was still in high school, he'd been an avid deer hunter, and every fall he hunted to help put meat on the family table. But one deer didn't go very far feeding a family of five. He'd been watching with great interest as the population of tule elk in the Owens Valley increased year after year. Tule elk aren't native to the Owens Valley; they were transplanted there after they were nearly hunted to extinction in central California during the Gold Rush. The tule elk did well in the Owens Valley, though, and their population grew until ranchers there considered them pests. The elk not only ate the natural forage in the valley, which was scarce now that most of the water went to LA, but they also ate the alfalfa the ranchers grew to feed their cattle during the winter. At that time the elk were protected—no hunting allowed—but like most residents of the valley, Norm didn't think that policy made any sense. So one cold October evening, right before dark, Norm went down to the Owens River, not far from his house, where the elk were grazing, and he shot a big bull at least twice the size of any deer. He cut its throat, bled it, and gutted it, but then he lost his nerve and left it where it lay. He went home for supper, where the topic of conversation happened to be tule elk—how there were too many of them, how they were taking all the grazing, how the damn government stole most of their land and water, and now the government told them they couldn't hunt the elk that were standing right outside their door.

"Maybe we should just go ahead and hunt them anyway," Norm suggested.

Tommy Jefferson was already angry at the government for banning stock use on the Mount Whitney trail. He and his partners had sold the pack station, and to earn a living he'd started making western saddles there at home. But that hadn't replaced the prosperous business he'd once had. "Maybe you're right," his father said. "Maybe we should go ahead and hunt those elk."

"But that would be against the law," Norm pointed out.

"Law or no law, it's still the right thing to do," Tommy said.

"Do you really believe that?" Norm asked.

"Of course, I believe it!" Tommy replied, becoming more irritated the more he thought about it.

"You mean, if I told you I'd killed an elk, you'd think that was okay?"

"Absolutely," Tommy replied.

"Well then, you better get the truck because I shot an elk down by the river about an hour ago."

♒

Although I'd learned a few things about packing from Slim Knutsen, Norm taught me a lot more; for example, how to shoe horses and mules—and not just back at the shed with an anvil and sledge, but out on the trail, using nothing but a hammer and a granite rock. Norm taught me to get up before first light to go wrangle the loose animals, how to track, and how to train the animals to come to you so you don't have to walk all over the wilderness looking for them. And he taught me something about saddles.

The park service had a supply of old saddles that looked like they might have been surplus from the Civil War. They were almost black with age, shiny as steel and nearly as hard, and, worst of all, they had narrow trees, as if they'd been intended for skinny-assed congressmen and superintendents, not for real men who used their rear ends for something other than perching on a chair. Norm rode a beautiful western saddle his father had made for him, and it had a broad tree. He let me use it now and then, and I never forgot the difference between that and a government saddle.

One Monday morning at Ash Mountain, after I figured I'd learned enough about packing to call myself a packer, I showed up for work wearing a white straw cowboy hat that Norm and I had bought at the western wear supply in Visalia that weekend.

Norm wore a gray felt Resistol himself, maybe the best cowboy hat made, but he advised me not to get too cocky and to settle for the white straw for now. I hadn't even walked across the parking lot when other park employees, just showing up for work, started making fun of me. "Hey there, midnight cowboy!" they called out. "You wasn't walkin' that bowlegged when you left here on Friday!" Cowboy hats weren't really an official part of the park service uniform, but packers somehow got away with it. For me to show up wearing a white straw cowboy hat was a statement of defiance, and it must have looked awfully funny. When a district ranger challenged me on my credentials right there in the parking lot in front of everybody else, I held my chin up and said, "I'm an official graduate of the Norman Jefferson school of animal packing. I have every right to wear this hat."

The ranger looked at me, glanced at Norm, who nodded back, and the ranger said, "Well, hell, why didn't you say so?"

That Friday after work, Norm and I changed shirts and drove down to the Gateway Inn, just below the park entrance, to have a beer and celebrate my first full week as a half-assed cowboy. Three Rivers had a reputation in those days for being a honky-tonk town. On the weekends young women came from all over the San Joaquin Valley hoping to meet a cowboy, and plenty of young men in town who worked at construction five days a week did their best to oblige them by becoming cowboys on Friday night. I figured it was a role I could play now, too. Norm, though, didn't have to play at anything. He was the real deal, and somehow women knew it.

I'm not sure why those farmers' daughters from the valley had such a fascination with cowboys. Cowboying is one of the lowest-paying jobs in the country, and for about half the year, it doesn't pay anything at all. Cowboys I have known tend to be irresponsible, inarticulate, emotionally immature, and impractical. They're terrified of permanent relationships and permanent jobs, they drink too much, and their trucks only run on weekends. It's true, though, that they have a talent for living their lives in a tragically poetic way, and maybe that's the attraction women have for them. I don't really know.

It wasn't just the women who were fascinated with the cowboy way of life, though. The San Joaquin Valley had hundreds of wealthy farmers who'd made a fortune growing cotton (or at least collecting a government subsidy for *not* growing cotton). Yet they'd buy a cattle ranch in the foothills and spend their weekends pretending they were cowboys, even though the ranch never earned a dime, while the dirt farm grew nothing but money.

Norm understood all this much better than I did. He called wannabe cowboys "gunzles," a derogatory word with many obscene definitions, but used in the Owens Valley to describe fake or inept cowboys. I never saw Norm make fun of gunzles, exactly, but he understood that America had turned cowboys into caricatures of themselves, both idealizing and ridiculing them at the same time. He still cherished the western tradition and was proud that he came from a place where horsemen were still authentic. Whenever Norm saw someone or something that fulfilled his idea of the real West, he took satisfaction in pointing it out—a cowboy who let his dog sleep in the same bed with him, an old wrangler who scraped the mouse turds off a slab of butter before applying it to his biscuits, or a cowgirl who beat up her brother when he came home drunk one night and tried to crawl into bed with her.

"Now that," Norm would say, "is pretty damn western."

But Norm was the most authentically western guy I ever met in my life. When he washed his clothes at the laundromat every weekend, the dirty clothes came out of his duffle bag, into the washer and dryer, and then the clean clothes went right back into the duffle bag—I never saw him fold anything. Norm wouldn't cook, ever—if food wasn't put before him, he drank beer or went hungry. One of Norm's girlfriends told me she could always tell when he forgot to take toilet paper on his hunting trips because he'd come back with his shirt tails cut off. It seems odd, but there are a lot of women who find that sort of thing endearing.

That evening at the Gateway, several women approached Norm, just hoping to meet an obviously authentic cowboy and have a drink with him. They were enchanted by his warm eyes, his honesty, and his easy sense of humor. A few of the men there that night resented Norm for the attention the women paid him. And some of them hated him just for the color of his skin. As we were getting ready to leave and heading for the door, a fellow I knew from Three Rivers staggered up to me. He was a construction worker, six foot four, and he said with whiskey breath, "Tell your greasy Indian friend I don't want to ever see him in here again."

I'd been a high school wrestler and still enjoyed a good fight. I knew that size doesn't mean all that much in a bar scuffle, and it means nothing at all if your opponent is drunk.

"If I ever hear anything like that come out of your ignorant mouth again, I'll slap you silly," I said.

Out in the parking lot, Norm asked, "What was that all about?"

"Nothing."

"Listen," Norm said. "You don't have to look out for me. I can take care of myself."

"I know you can."

Not long after that, a beautiful young woman from the valley fell in love with Norm. She was tall and blonde and could have had any man she wanted. And Norm liked her, too. They dated awhile, but when she took him home to meet her redneck father, and her father saw that Norm was Native American, he forbade her to ever see him again. They met on the sly for a while, then Norm told the young woman it wasn't right for her to disobey her father, that in the long run it would only make her unhappy. He bowed out of the relationship, and it broke that poor girl's heart. I couldn't believe Norm would do that, but then I hadn't seen what he'd seen, I didn't know what he knew, and maybe I just didn't understand.

〜〜
〜〜

Later that fall I was back working on the hazardous tree crew again. One Monday morning our plan was to drive from Ash Mountain to Cedar Grove, where we'd spend the week removing trees in the campgrounds. We were all in a hurry to get out of Ash Mountain as quickly as possible, but it was a struggle. There were the usual Monday meetings, with safety talks, and bureaucratic indoctrination. But eventually we finished loading our six-passenger truck with the fuel, food, and gear we'd need to last us the week, and we made our escape.

Along the way, we stopped at Dorst Creek Campground to buck up a large red fir that had fallen across the road by the entrance booth. We ate a late lunch at Stony Creek, then continued driving on through Grant Grove, past Converse Basin, and began the long, steep, winding descent into Kings Canyon.

The highway reached the bottom of the canyon and crossed the Kings River at Boyden Cave, where there was a large parking lot. Rising straight up from the river are 2,000-foot blue marble cliffs known as the Portals to the Kings. Those marble cliffs, though grand in their way, always seemed odd and out of place to me in a land of granite. But it's a fact that on the western slope of the Sierra Nevada there's a long swath of marble much older than the granite mountains above them.

Although the most beautiful sculptures in the world have been carved from marble, for me it doesn't have the purity of granite. The problem is that marble is metamorphosed limestone, and limestone is just the remains of dead sea organisms. When I look at marble, I see millions of years of death congealed on the ocean floor. Marble was already old before granite—the real backbone of the Sierra Nevada—forced its way up through the Earth's crust. Rock climbers know that marble doesn't have the strength and integrity of granite because it's so brittle. Entire columns of marble that might appear stable can peel off from just the weight of a human body.

We'd just crossed the bridge over the Kings River when we saw a forest service truck in the parking lot with its red light flashing. A forest service employee wearing a yellow Nomex jacket waved us into the parking lot. I rolled down my window, and the young man said, "There's been a climbing accident on Windy Cliffs. Are any of you climbers?"

"I am," I said, "but I don't have any gear with me. And I'm not an EMT."

"That's okay. Our rescue crew has already started up the trail. They might need you to assist them."

The rest of our crew stayed in the truck. They weren't rock climbers and they didn't want anything to do with a rescue. As I passed by the ticket booth for the cave, I recognized the man who leased the concession there. He looked ghastly pale. "What's going on?" I asked.

"All I know is there's been a terrible climbing accident," he said. "When I saw those climbers heading up the trail, I told them it wasn't safe up there."

I started up the Windy Cliffs Trail by myself, but I had only hiked a quarter mile when I met the rescue crew running back down the trail toward me. "What's going on?" I asked again. "Do you need help?" But they kept running right on by me. "We don't have the right gear!" one of them called back. "We have to go back to the truck!"

I stood there wondering what I should do—go back with them, wait, or continue up the trail by myself. The narrow canyon was already dark with shadows, and gusty winds were blowing dirt and oak leaves in swirls along the trail. The whole situation gave me a very bad feeling, but I felt I needed to push on. Maybe somebody up there in the canyon desperately needed help.

It only took me another two or three minutes to reach the scene of the accident. A party of young rock climbers from a nearby summer camp had been trying to scale the marble cliffs. One of the climbers above had dislodged a slab of rock the size of a trash can, and it had struck a young woman below on the head. She was lying there alone, wearing shorts and a T-shirt, and I knew as soon as I saw her there was nothing I could do to help. This was a beautiful young woman who had been alive just minutes earlier.

I could see two more climbers on the cliff above. They looked agitated and didn't seem to know what to do next. Were they stuck in place, unable to move? I knew firsthand how fear could erode self-confidence, so I called up to them, "There's a safer route over there!" And I pointed up canyon to a spot where they could have descended easily.

The lead climber, a thin young man with shoulder-length hair, called down to me. "I know what I'm doing! I don't need your help!"

There was nothing I could do then but wait for the forest service crew to return with a rescue litter so we could carry the body down the trail.

What I saw that horrible afternoon on Windy Cliffs haunted me for years. I couldn't see how the loss of that young woman's life could be justified by anything like the pursuit of sport or adventure. It was a terrible, unexplainable tragedy, and it changed my attitude about rock climbing, and risk taking in general. I still enjoyed climbing, backcountry skiing, surfing, and other extreme sports, but I approached them with a degree of caution and forethought I didn't have before. While I'd once been the most careless person on our crew, often working with a foolish sense of invincibility, I became the most cautious person, sometimes to the extent that my coworkers considered me a nag about safety.

Not long after that incident at Windy Cliffs, I had the opportunity to take a course provided by the park service in emergency medical training. I completed the course and became a certified EMT. I knew that no amount of training would have helped that young woman, but I encountered injured people in the backcountry all the time, and I felt it would be irresponsible not to be prepared to help them if I could.

In the spring of 1978, I reported for work at Ash Mountain to learn that the budget for all the national parks had been cut significantly. At Sequoia and Kings Canyon, a lot of seasonal employees weren't hired back. I was told that the park service wanted to continue my meadow restoration projects in the future, when our funding was restored, but for now they were on hold. I could continue to work on the hazardous tree crew (that work was essential for visitor safety), but for the time being, I had no backcountry crew. I had to call up my old friend Mike Palmer, who'd worked beside me for eight years, and tell him there wouldn't be a job for him that summer. And except for Curtis Cohoe, who was hired by the park service to work on the hazardous tree crew, I never saw my Navajo friends again.

The really odd thing was that the park service didn't fire me, too. After all, what good is a foreman without a crew? But by 1978 I'd qualified as a line boss and falling boss on wildfires, which meant I might come in handy one day. Fire management was funded separately, and the government wouldn't have dared cut that budget. I was also qualified to conduct my own prescribed burns in the parks, and those projects were becoming a high priority. So it really wasn't costing the park all that much to keep me around in case they needed me.

Still, I was angry and resentful. That winter the park superintendent had spent $10,000 of government money to raise the ceiling in the bathroom of his Spanish-style mansion at Ash Mountain because his wife found it oppressively low. That was more money than I needed to fund my meadow restoration projects for the whole summer. I'd been a government employee long enough to know that all bureaucracies are mindless and chaotic, but I also knew it was sometimes possible to put that chaos to good use. So I proposed to my supervisors that I spend eight weeks that summer categorizing and ranking all the backcountry meadow restoration projects in Sequoia and Kings so that when our funding was renewed we'd know where to begin again. To my surprise, my proposal was approved on condition that I produce a written report at the end of the summer, and that I be ready to go back to work on the hazardous tree crew by September.

Another odd thing, though, was that the funding for our horse and six mules survived the budget cuts too. It wasn't a lot of money, but it did cost something to keep a working pack train intact. And that meant Norm Jefferson's job as packer survived. What it eventually came down to was that Norm and I had about sixty days to ride throughout the backcountry of

Sequoia and Kings Canyon, going just about any place we liked. One park old-timer told me he'd never heard of a better assignment in his entire career.

Sequoia and Kings Canyon is not only a large park, but the terrain is extremely rugged, which means it's just about impossible to see it all in one summer. Yet that's what Norm and I set out to do. We started from Mineral King and headed for the Hockett Plateau, where I already knew there was a pretty bad erosion scar through Sand Meadow. Neither of us wore our park uniforms, so to backpackers we looked like just a couple of cowboys out on a summer lark, which was sort of true.

The horse Norm rode that summer was a good-looking chestnut gelding called Skip, which we didn't think was a fitting name for any horse, let alone the leader of a pack train. Norm suggested we give him another name, just for the summer, and I agreed. "Any ideas? I asked.

"Well," Norm said, "last winter I saw this movie with Rex Harrison, *A Man Called Horse*."

"Oh, that movie's like eight years old."

"Hey, that's how long it takes movies to find their way to Lone Pine!"

"Okay, no need to get mad about it. . . . Did you like it?"

"Not really," Norm said. "No offense, but I don't think white people should make movies about Indians. They never get it right. I mean, how would white people like it if Indians made movies about white people and we just invented all kinds of stuff about their history and religion?"

"Good point," I said.

"But I thought it was interesting that the Indians in that movie named the white guy Horse."

# Chubasco a Cappella

"Um. . . . Don't tell me you want to name your horse Horse!"

"No," Norm said. "I want to name him Man."

And that's what we did. For the rest of that summer, Norm rode a horse called Man.

Since we only had one horse, I had to ride one of the six mules, and only one of them had been broke for riding, an old swaybacked male named Chub. Actually, I don't know for sure that Chub had ever been broke for riding either, but he'd arrived at a stage in life where he accepted whatever indignities came his way, as long as he got a nose bag of oats every morning and was turned loose to wander with the other mules every night. At heart Chub was a good-natured old boy who liked to stand around in the warm sunlight with his eyes half closed, advertising his virility, which, even at his advanced age, was quite impressive. He never chafed under a heavy load or caused trouble with the other mules. He reminded me of a lot of old park service employees who were counting their days to retirement, and he even had the NPS (for National Park Service) brand on his flank.

Because he was a bit small, Chub could have been mistaken for a burro, and one day Norm said to me, "You know, riding Chub, you look almost like one of those Franciscan priests, maybe Junípero Serra, riding through California two hundred years ago."

He was just trying to tease me, I suppose, but I liked the comparison. Sometimes when we saw backpackers coming the other way, I'd take off my cowboy hat, slip the hood of my gray sweatshirt over my head, make the sign of the cross, and say, "*Vaya con Dios*, my children."

From the Hockett Plateau, we continued on to the Quinn patrol cabin, which is one of the oldest structures in Sequoia.

Built in 1907, the cabin dates back to the days when Sequoia was administered by the US Army. The Quinn cabin is also one of the many places in Sequoia hopelessly haunted. In fact, I'd venture to say it has the largest population of ghosts in the parks. I'd learned that a few years earlier when John Kraushaar, Tim Stubbs, and I had spent a fitful night there during a February snow survey. The next day, even with a stinging blizzard, we were eager to beat our way ten miles back to the Hockett cabin, which only has ghosts in the rear bedroom and maybe a few in the tack shed.

Norm, who was even more sensitive to ghosts than I was, refused to sleep inside the Quinn cabin, so we both slept under the stars that night. We left early the next morning, crossed over Coyote Pass, and descended to Kern Ranger Station, the southernmost point in the park.

Kern Ranger Station is the only station in Sequoia where the backcountry ranger travels by stock. (Kings Canyon also has a stock station at Roaring River.) There are fenced pastures and corrals at Kern ranger station, making it a convenient place to keep pack animals, and the entire Kern River area has many meadows separated by drift fences, making it an ideal place to travel by stock. The whole setup at Kern Ranger Station was a cowboy's dream, with a comfortable cabin, a river full of trout, and miles of open trails in every direction. The odd thing was that the new ranger there, Bruce Flom, wasn't an experienced packer or horseman at all. In fact, he was a real greenhorn. Bruce was about average height, with a receding hairline, and one brown eye and one green. He'd been selected for his job through a process that makes no sense to anyone but a government personnel officer. Still, Norm and I liked his easygoing way. Most rangers we'd known took themselves too seriously, but Bruce seemed like he'd been waiting all summer to raise a little hell and figured we were the guys to help him do it. On Bruce's invitation, Norm and I turned our animals loose in his pasture and accepted his invitation to have supper at the ranger station that night.

First, though, Bruce said he had something he wanted to show us. He led us to a large bend in the river, not far from the ranger station, and, after stripping down to his underwear, showed us how he could float downstream on his back a couple hundred yards, get out and walk across the neck of the bend, re-enter the river, and do it again, sort of like riding the slide at a water park over and over. Norm and I stripped down to our underwear, too, and the three of us spent the rest of that evening, until it was nearly too dark to see, enjoying that soothing pastime.

Bruce, who was a good cook, put on a white apron and made clam linguine for us that night. We stayed up late, sitting around a fire outside the ranger station, sipping whiskey and getting acquainted. But in the morning, when we went to the pasture to separate our animals from Bruce's, Bruce began chasing his ill-mannered horse around in the enclosure until all the horses and mules were galloping in a circle, having a wonderful time misbehaving. That infuriated Norm—one of the few times I ever saw him angry.

"Good god, what a goat rope!" Norm groaned. "I hate it when a gunzle like that works the stock into a frenzy." He waved Bruce off—practically ordered him out of his own pasture. Norm saddled and mounted Man, then quickly lassoed Bruce's unruly horse and forced it into submission. The horse, once it gave up, seemed almost relieved that somebody with a firm hand had finally put an end to his bad behavior. After that, the mules calmed down too and came to us meekly when we offered them oats.

Later that morning, Norm took Bruce aside and gave him a talking-to. I don't know what was said, but my guess is that Bruce knew he was in over his head with that job, and Norm came along at exactly the right time to help him out. Bruce wasn't too proud to accept instruction, and by watching Norm that day he learned a lot about how to manage pack stock.

Norm and I continued on up the Kern River, with Bruce, reluctant to see us go, following along behind. At Junction Meadow, Bruce turned back to his ranger station, while Norm and I kept riding as far as Lake South America. There we turned south, riding past Diamond Mesa, Tyndall Creek, and Wallace Creek. That area, all in the shadow of the highest peaks in the Sierra Nevada, is known as the Kern Plateau. It was Norm's home territory; he'd practically grown up there, and he knew every peak, gully, creek, and ridge. As we rode through it, memories from his youth came to life and he told me stories relating to each place.

"One time we brought in this big Sierra Club group, probably forty people, over Trailcrest," he said. "A lot of them were older folks who couldn't have made that trip without pack stock, and most of them only carried a daypack. But there was this big lunkhead in their party, a young guy who kept saying that real men always carry their own gear. He insisted that everybody lift his pack to see how heavy it was. So one morning, just before we started off, he went to use the latrine, and while he was gone we opened his pack and put about twenty-five pounds of rocks in the bottom. He was the last guy in camp that night. He straggled in after dark, dead tired. He didn't even figure out what had happened to him until the next day."

As much as Norm loved that Kern Plateau, being there made him a bit sad. It had been part of the ancestral homeland of his people, and his father had once made his living there. Norm was pleased that it remained wilderness, but in some ways, at least for his people, the land had been preserved as an artifact, like obsidian spearheads in a glass case. They couldn't hunt there, build a summer home, or bury their dead there. For Norm the park represented a loss his people had suffered.

Perhaps even worse, being there prompted memories of his childhood and people he would never see again, like his mother.

Sitting around a campfire at Crabtree Meadow, I asked Norm about his mother, who I knew had died when he was fourteen. I didn't want to pry, it was just that I'd never heard Norm say anything about her, and I didn't understand why.

"It's not a good idea to talk about the dead," he said. "Better to let them go."

I learned later that many Native Americans, not just Paiutes, believe it's dangerous to speak the name of the dead after the customary mourning period of one year has passed. The dead don't want to leave this world, and they'll return to it if they can through the dreams of their friends and relatives who go on clinging to their memories. The penalty for not letting go of the dead is what the Paiutes call ghost sickness, something I'd learn more about in years to come.

In the morning, I told Norm I wanted to look at an erosion scar I'd heard about near Guitar Lake, and since we were so close to Mount Whitney, we might as well make a quick detour to the summit. Like everybody else who has seen that mountain, I wanted to stand on top. I invited Norm to go with me, but he declined, saying he'd already been there plenty of times and didn't need to go again. He moved the stock to a small meadow just below Crabtree Lakes, and I rejoined him there that evening.

Next morning before dawn, Norm shook me awake and said, "Get your fishing pole." Without breakfast or even coffee, we hiked up to the lakes, where we caught some of the biggest golden trout I've ever seen. Their flesh was as pink as salmon and, fried with bacon, tasted even better.

At upper Rock Creek, we found what turned out to be the worst meadow erosion I'd ever seen in Sequoia and Kings

Canyon. I'd already heard about it from Bruce Flom and others, but I was surprised to see how bad it truly was. There were two miles of multiple trails through a fragile stringer meadow, all over 10,000 feet in elevation, which meant the growing season there was short and recovery would be difficult. And less than a mile away, on the Siberian Pass trail, there was another erosion scar almost as bad. We spent a couple of days there taking measurements and drawing maps. By the time we'd finished, I was certain my crew, if I ever had one again, would be working there for a long time.

Norm had brought along a set of tossing horseshoes, so next to our camp we measured off forty feet and drove the steel stakes into the ground, and every evening after dinner we played several rounds. Backpackers, hearing the sound of clinking steel, and our laughter echoing off the canyon sides, came and joined in. We'd play until it was too dark to see, slapping at the mosquitoes, boasting of our own prowess, and cursing our rival's good luck.

We'd been twelve days on the trail by then. Our work schedule was still ten days on and four days off, but since we couldn't tell the difference between work and play, we'd mostly ignored that schedule. Still, we were getting short on food, and because the Cottonwood trailhead was only a few hours away and Lone Pine was only an hour's drive from there, we figured now would be as good a time as any to resupply.

Saturday morning we packed up early and rode over Cottonwood Pass, and by noon we were at Cottonwood Pack Station. Norm knew the owner there, and we quickly made him a deal: We'd pay for the hay out of our own pockets if he would hold and feed our stock in his corral overnight. He'd just received a delivery of hay, and the truck was heading back down to the Owens Valley right away. So we stuffed our sleeping bags into our duffles, stashed the rest of our camp gear behind the pack station, and hauled ourselves up on the bed of the truck like a couple of cow hicks.

As we drove down the long switchbacks to the valley floor, we had a discussion about our plans.

"We're only here one night, right?" Norm asked.

"I'd like to get back on the trail as soon as possible," I said. "We've got a lot of miles to cover yet. Also, the longer we stay in town, the more likely we are to get ourselves into trouble."

"I was thinking the same thing," Norm admitted. And then he added, "I don't mean to be inhospitable, but if this is going to be the kind of Saturday night I think it is, maybe it's best if we don't even stop by my dad's place."

"Yeah, you're probably right," I agreed.

Just before reaching Lone Pine, we passed through the Alabama Hills, a jumble of gigantic boulders the color of burnt sugar that stood in stark contrast to the white granite of the Sierra above them. It felt like we were passing through an old childhood dream come to life in vivid color, and that was because those hills had been the location for more than a hundred cowboy movies. Tom Mix, Roy Rogers, Gene Autry, Hopalong Cassidy—I'd seen them all galloping through those hills, chasing or being chased by Indians, outlaws, sheriffs, or angry wives. I couldn't recall even a single plot of those movies, but I recognized the settings of many desperate shootouts as if I'd fought them myself. And now I had an odd feeling that I was about to walk into one of those old movies, too.

The flatbed truck dropped us off on Main Street at the only stoplight in town. From there we could look north and see one half of Lone Pine, or turn around and see the other half. The whole town only amounted to a grocery store, barber shop, a couple of restaurants, the Dow Villa Hotel, the forest service station, and way too many bars. Looking west, practically looming over the town, was Lone Pine Peak, which still had plenty of snow on it. At nearly 13,000 feet, it's a big mountain, though just behind it stands the biggest, Mount Whitney, at 14,505 feet. But because Lone Pine Peak is much closer to the town, the smaller peak nearly blocks from view the taller peak. Tourists driving through town on Highway 395, on their way to Yosemite or the gambling casinos of Reno and Lake Tahoe, usually have no interest whatsoever in Lone Pine, but they do want to say later that they at least saw Mount Whitney. The residents of Lone Pine had become tired of explaining the geographical peculiarities a long time ago, so when tourists stopped to ask them if the snow-covered peak in the foreground was Mount Whitney, they'd just reply, "You're looking at it!"

It's odd how you can spend two weeks in the backcountry with nothing but cold baths in the creek and still feel clean. But the minute you hit civilization, you're immediately aware of your own stench.

"Do I smell as bad as I think?" I asked.

"You smell like an old saddle blanket dried over a smoky fire," Norm said. "Let's go get a shower."

The barber shop in town sold hot showers by the minute, and it also offered a few coin-operated washing machines and dryers. We stripped down to our gym shorts, tossed our smoky clothes into the laundry, then fed quarters into the showers for twenty or thirty minutes. While we waited for our clothes to dry, we each had our hair cut.

Stepping out onto Main Street wearing clean clothes and smelling like talcum powder, we saw that the sun had already gone down behind Lone Pine Peak. The only problem now was that we were still lugging along our duffle bags, like cattle bums. I glanced at Norm and saw that he was thinking the same thing. "I got an idea," he said. "Come on."

We crossed the street to the Last Chance Saloon, an old place with swinging doors and creaky wooden floors that looked as if it had barely survived the 1872 earthquake. (Next door was a used-clothing store named Next to the Last Chance.) The bartender was a friend of Norm's—I soon discovered that everybody in town was a friend of Norm's—and Norm asked if we could stash our duffle bags behind the bar.

"We'll be back later to pick them up," he said.

The bartender just nodded.

So now we were free, two young drifters on a Saturday night, with money in our pockets and nobody to tell us what to do. I'd have been content to just stay there at the Last Chance Saloon, but Norm seemed to know exactly how he wanted the night to work out, almost as if he was sticking to a script.

As it turned out, Lone Pine had one bar hidden from public view, and that was where Norm wanted to start. The place, in fact, was a mobile home, one block west and two blocks south. When I saw that it belonged to a chapter of the VFW, I said, "Norm, I'm no vet. Hell, I didn't even like the Boy Scouts."

"Don't worry," Norm said. "They'll let anybody in, even you. And the best part is the drinks are only a buck."

He was right. I asked for Jim Beam, but the bartender just laughed and set us up with a cheaper brand of whiskey. As I looked around the small room, I saw it was an odd mix of World War II vets proudly wearing bits and pieces of their ancient uniforms, and glassy-eyed Vietnam vets who wreaked of pot. A baseball game was playing on a black-and-white TV.

A Paiute mule packer, maybe fifty years old and more than half drunk, sat down next to Norm and began berating us for being so young.

"You guys think you're some kinda studs," he said. "But I

feel sorry for your girlfriends. You go maybe two, three times in one night. But an old guy like me? I go nine times!"

Maybe it was a Paiute joke, I don't know, but Norm thought it was hilarious.

By the time we left the VFW, it was completely dark outside. We hadn't eaten anything since before dawn back at Rock Creek, so we walked to a steakhouse on Main Street and ordered their biggest steak dinner. It seemed like everybody in town passed by our table, and they all wanted to sit down and have a chat with Norm.

"Norman! I drove by your dad's place the other day and saw his pasture is all overgrown with nettles. Ask him if he wants me to bring my goats over to chew it all down."

"You gonna be around tomorrow morning, Norm? Let's play tennis before all the Bible thumpers get outta church."

"Norm, I got a coyote messin' with my chickens again. When you get a chance, will you stop by one day and shoot that sumbitch?"

After supper we worked our way north, hitting the bars one by one. One place we stopped at had a jukebox and a wooden dance floor with only room enough for four couples. Somehow I managed to get drunk enough to dance, which is a rare Saturday night for me. I was wearing cowboy boots, though, which always make dancing easier. I can't recall anything about my partners, except they were all old enough to be my aunt.

And then sometime after midnight, we were back at the Last Chance Saloon, just like Norm knew we would. There wasn't a single female of any age in the place. I'd been thinking all night long that we'd eventually meet up with some young Lone Pine cowgirls wearing tight Wranglers and pearl-button shirts with the top two buttons undone. But it never happened. Like most small western towns, Lone Pine either didn't have single women, or they kept them under lock and key. Having been a fan of the great fifties TV serial *Gunsmoke*, I kept thinking we might see Miss Kitty come slinking down the stairs wearing a silk negligee, but the Last Chance Saloon didn't have a stairway and Miss Kitty must have been occupied someplace else. The only thing left for a cowboy to do on a Saturday night was fight.

Somehow I managed to get into a heated discussion with a fellow there at the bar who claimed he'd been a professional wrestler. "You weren't no damn wrestler!" I told him.

"The hell I wasn't!"

"You wasn't, and I can prove it!"

"How?"

"By whipping your sorry ass right now!"

This guy was taller than me and weighed about 210 pounds, but in my cowboy boots I could look him in the eye. He lumbered toward me, I grabbed his right elbow in my right hand, jerked hard, and he spun around like he was my dance partner. I grabbed him around the waist, locked hands, leaned back, and he came clear off his feet. Then I slammed him on the floor and collapsed on top of him.

"That's it!" the bartender hollered, as he came running around the corner of the bar. "You two are outta here!"

Norm collected our duffle bags and met me out on the street.

All he said was, "What the hell do you care if he wants to be a wrestler? It's Saturday night. He can be any damn thing he wants."

I didn't have an answer but it didn't matter. It had been a respectable ending to one of the best Saturday nights I'd had in a while.

Norm and I stumbled by moonlight two blocks to Portagee Joe's, the county campground, pulled our sleeping bags out of our duffles, and collapsed on top of them.

Then the next thing I knew, the morning sunlight was shining in my eyes. We splashed some cold water from the ditch onto our faces, then crammed all our gear into one of the duffle bags. I took the empty duffle, walked back to Joseph's Bi-Rite, and bought enough groceries to last us at least two more weeks. Then we stood out on the road in the shade of a big cottonwood, and in less than ten minutes a forest service truck picked us up and drove us all the way back to Cottonwood Pack Station.

And by the way, those are the two most important uses for Texas-style cowboy boots: to let you slide easy across a dance floor and stand tall in a fight. Norm Jefferson, a real cowboy, wore a lace-up packer's boot with a wide toe and a more sensible heel.

♒

Two weeks later, Norm and I were up on the Big Arroyo, near the old patrol cabin, where we were taking measurements on another large meadow restoration project we'd found. Once again, there were multiple trail scars through a long stringer meadow, and I estimated it would take a large crew an entire summer to repair it.

Tom Warner, the park's chief forester, had asked me to look at something else while we were in Big Arroyo. A year earlier, while flying over the area on a fire reconnaissance, I'd spotted a swath of dead lodgepole pines, about a mile long and perhaps a quarter mile wide. I'd never seen anything quite like it before. I knew the trees had died recently because their needles hadn't yet fallen. It looked as if somebody had taken a giant paintbrush and slashed an orange stripe across the canyon floor.

Back at Ash Mountain, I'd asked Tom, "Hey, what's with all those dead lodgepole pines up in Big Arroyo?"

"I don't know," Tom said. "This is the first I've heard of it."

Tom hitched a ride on the park's helicopter to Big Arroyo and spent a day there on the ground. He concluded that I'd found a large infestation of needle miner.

Needle miner is a moth that lays its eggs in pine needles, which the pupae later devour, killing the tree. It had never been a problem in Sequoia or Kings Canyon, but Yosemite had lost 40,000 acres of lodgepole pines to needle miner. When I asked Tom what the park should do about it, he surprised me by saying, "Nothing. We might not like it, but sometimes needle miner infestations are just a natural part of the cycle in lodgepole pine forests."

Since I was passing through Big Arroyo anyway, Tom asked me to walk through the infestation and see if it was getting any bigger. I quickly saw that it wasn't, but after seeing that swath of forest close up, I saw that the real cause of the infestation wasn't the needle miner moth, it was that almost nothing grew there *except* lodgepole pines. The forest was dark and dense, the lodgepoles had crowded everything else out, and the forest floor was littered with dead wood to the extent that you could scarcely walk through it. It was a monoculture. To humans it was ugly, but to a needle miner moth it was a thing of beauty.

Like Tom Warner and other professional foresters who knew a lot more than I did, I was worried that we had contributed to the monoculture by suppressing wildfires over the previous hundred years. Sometimes we sounded like pyromaniacs, but a lot of us in the park service looked forward to the day when diseased corners of the forest, like that one in Big Arroyo, could burn freely.

That evening Bruce Flom joined Norm and me at our camp. Bruce, as a roving stock ranger, had the freedom to ride just about anywhere he liked, and like a lot of rangers, he got lonely. We stayed up late that night, sharing a bottle of Jim Beam. Bruce liked to spend his winters in Mexico, mostly lower Baja, and he told us tales of fishing in the Gulf of California and four-wheeling in the rugged Sierra de la Giganta. Bruce said he'd paid for his last trip by smuggling a pickup load of Levis into Mexico, where he sold them at a profit, and when he came back he brought a load of illegal fireworks into the US. It seemed an odd business for someone wearing a law enforcement badge, but Norm and I had to admire his enterprise. I finally went to bed, though Bruce and Norm were just getting started.

About midnight I was awakened by the sound of a loud explosion. I thought I must have been dreaming, so I just lay there for a while on my back, wide awake. And then I saw a white starburst that nearly filled the night sky, followed by another explosion and bursts of drunken laughter. The ranger and my packer were firing off bottle rockets in what was supposed to be a federal wilderness. Yeah, I wanted to see the park burn freely, but not like that.

The next morning, Bruce, looking a bit sheepish, packed up early and moved on. After working two weeks straight, I figured we deserved another day off, so over breakfast I said to Norm, "I've always wanted to climb Black Kaweah. I think today's the day. You wanna come along?"

Norm declined. "I hate to leave the stock alone," he said. "Besides, Pot and Mandy both need new shoes. I think I'll just stay here."

Black Kaweah is the most rugged peak in the Kaweah

Range. At 13,686 feet, it isn't the highest, but there was something about the way it stood off by itself, dark and sulking, that had always attracted my interest. Like most of the Kaweah range, it's old, fractured metamorphic rock, not the solid young granite most of the southern Sierra Nevada is made of. I knew it was rated Class 4, which meant I should have taken a rope and climbed with somebody else in case the route required a belay. Norman Clyde, the greatest of the early Sierra mountaineers, called it one of the most difficult and dangerous peaks of the Sierra. In fact, the year he climbed it, 1927, a Stanford graduate student was killed trying to climb it solo. But I was determined to do it. I was already camped at Big Arroyo, the perfect place to begin, I'd spent weeks at high elevation getting acclimated, and I didn't mind at all doing the climb alone.

The route I took, a chute on the south face, was the shortest and most direct, and also one of the steepest. But it wasn't any steeper or more dangerous than the climbs I had done in Yosemite with Doug Tompkins the summer of 1968, and as I worked my way up Black Kaweah that day, I found myself thinking about him, about how kind he'd been to me, and wondering where he was now. It's odd, but climbing alone often makes me feel nostalgic. I think about people I haven't seen in years and suddenly I feel their absence in a painful way. I don't know why this happens.

To stand on the absolute summit of Black Kaweah, I was going to have to make what old-fashioned climbing guidebooks used to call an "airy leap" from one pinnacle to another. It was only a few feet and wouldn't have been anything on flat ground, but with so much exposure below, it made me think twice. Without a climbing partner or even a rope, a belay was not possible. I wasn't wearing climbing boots with a Vibram sole, either. I was wearing my old, slick-soled farmer boots that were perfect for wrangling stock every morning but weren't made for climbing. I leaped as airily as I could and landed firmly, but for only the third time in my life I felt that wobbly sensation called sewing machine knee.

What I recall most vividly about that climb, though, was the descent. I took a different route down, following a broad snowfield I'd spotted from the summit. In my slick-bottomed boots, I was able to glissade rapidly down the slope, almost like skiing. About halfway to the bottom, I passed through an area with the largest suncups I have ever seen. Suncups are depressions formed by the melting of old snow. Usually, they're round-bottomed, and on a steep slope they become much higher on one side than the other. Normally suncups are only one or two feet deep, but these were at least ten feet deep, and they were linked one after the other. Perched at the top of one suncup, I could glissade to the bottom, and my momentum carried me up the short lip to the top of the next. It was like playing in a gigantic skate park, and it went on like that for 400 yards.

Later that summer, Norm and I made another loop through Kings Canyon in search of more damaged meadows. We found a large trail scar in the Woods Creek area, measured it, and made an estimate of the time required to repair it. You could say I was obsessed with finding meadow restoration projects by that time. In fact, the more I saw of that vast wilderness, the more I wanted to fix everything man had screwed up there in the past hundred years. Norm had little interest in my obsession, though. He appreciated wilderness even more than I did, but he was doubtful that we could fix anything without taking a long, hard look at how the wilderness had been damaged in the first place. His ancestors had used the wilderness for centuries without leaving much more than a few obsidian flakes. He was more philosophical than I was, and wiser.

Late one afternoon, Norm and I got into camp, pulled the loads off our animals, and turned them loose. Norm had taught me that if you leave a can of beer out at night to get cold, then roll it up in canvas first thing the next morning, that evening it will still be as cold as if it had been on ice all day. So Norm handed me a cold beer from one of the pack boxes, then popped one open for himself and lay down in a pile of pine needles under a big lodgepole. But as usual, I couldn't relax. The previous residents at the site had dug a fire pit and surrounded it by a heap of rocks two feet high—an inefficient design because the fire, deprived of air, burned poorly, and because the rocks blocked the heat radiating from it. So I went to work removing the rocks and filling in the pit. Somebody had dragged in logs for sitting on, but they were arranged in a way that made moving around the camp awkward, so I started putting them in order, too. After thirty minutes of this, I was sweaty and black with soot.

Norm crumpled his empty beer can and lobbed it at me. "You're such a white guy," he said.

"What's that supposed to mean?" I asked.

"Instead of moving the damn logs, why don't you just walk around them? Why do you always think you can make everything better, instead of just living with things the way they are?"

"It *is* better," I said. "We can stand close to the fire now and warm ourselves."

"If you wanted to be warm, you should have stayed home."

"I don't wanna be home. I wanna be out here in the wilderness!"

"Then why are you trying to make the wilderness just like home?"

I sat down to drink my beer and think that through, and I soon came to the conclusion that Norm was right. Most of us, including me, are compulsive builders and doers, with a powerful need to think we are making things better. That's how we ended up with cities and suburbs so depressingly ugly, we can't bear to live in them. Without wilderness, I was afraid the whole human race might lose its sanity, and following that conviction, I had set out on a mission to erase the sign of man on backcountry meadows, if I could. I justified that with scientific reasoning, but mostly I just needed to know there were places as free as possible from the meddlings of man. Yet I couldn't control my own meddling.

Then, in late August, our time finally ran out. I was supposed to go back on the hazardous tree crew, while Norm's services would be needed on the annual "sore-ass trip," caddying political deities and park service nabobs on a tour of the backcountry. We hadn't completed our survey of northern Kings Canyon, but I figured that could wait. We'd already identified enough meadow restoration projects to occupy a large crew several summers.

On our return to Cedar Grove, we stayed one night at Simpson Meadow with the most unusual trail crew I had ever encountered up to that point. It was composed entirely of women. When I started working for the park service, there were no women at all in backcountry positions—no rangers, laborers, sawyers, foresters, or technicians. Women worked in office positions, or perhaps as naturalists in the visitor centers. The thinking up to then had been that delicate female bodies wouldn't hold up under strenuous labor, and it wouldn't be proper to submit innocent women to the barbaric behavior that was part of trail crew life. How could the men on those crews be expected to refrain from at least trying to get cozy with the women? And if one of them succeeded, wouldn't that be grossly unfair to the other men who weren't as fortunate? Back in those days, most of the men in management positions in the park service came from a military background, and they ran things the way they'd been taught to run things—the old way.

The all-female trail crew at Simpson Meadow was an experiment, and for the park service, I thought, a daring one. Norm and I didn't know any of the women ourselves, but we'd heard stories about them from other trail crews, mostly in regard to their sexual preferences, and we wondered if maybe we were riding into a web of black widows. Before we arrived at their camp, though, we decided we'd be on our best behavior. And I'm glad we did. The young women on that crew washed the grit and chainsaw grease from their hands and faces, tied their hair back with colorful bandannas, and put on their cleanest work shirts. Still, until that evening I'd never known that women in their natural element, undeodorized and unshampooed, smell differently than men in the same circumstances—not bad, you understand, just different. The women made a large spaghetti dinner in our honor, served it on a checkered tablecloth, and that evening Norm and I had as fine a time as two young men on their best behavior can be expected to have.

After dinner the women brought out guitars, harmonicas, and a mandolin to play around the campfire. They weren't putting on a show for us—they played music every night—but I must say I was impressed. On all the crews I'd worked on, I'd never seen or heard a musical instrument played. We usually just sat around the fire, farting and spitting, telling lies about our sexual prowess, or staring sullenly into the flames without a thought in our heads. But those young women played and sang for each other, mostly folk songs and blues, but country-western songs too. They asked Norm and me to join in with them. I hadn't sung in public since I'd quit going to church twenty years earlier, and I had no intention of starting again. I was surprised, though, to see Norm mumble along on the songs he knew. He was too self-conscious to really let himself go, but at least he tried, in a painful sort of way.

The next morning, we wrangled our stock early and rode out of camp before the women were even out of bed, the way true men are supposed to.

We crossed the bridges at Horseshoe Creek and started up the long, steep trail to Granite Pass. Somewhere along the way, just to pass the time, I said to Norm, "I didn't know you could sing."

At first Norm figured I was just trying to bait him, which I was, and he refused to answer. But after a while he said, "That's part of it too, you know."

I thought that over for a half mile or so. "Part of what?" I finally asked.

"The whole western thing. It's not just riding and roping and drinking whiskey and all that. A guy should know how to sing and play something. Best cowboys I know can play at least some guitar. My father can. Otherwise, you're just letting other people entertain you, and that's no good."

"Well, it seems to me that if a guy doesn't want to sing in public, that's his business. Plenty of singers in the world. What difference does it make if there's one less?"

"You don't understand the tradition," Norm insisted, even getting a little worked up about it. "My father told me once that he doesn't know half of what his father knew, and I know I don't know half of what my father knows. So it doesn't matter whether I want to sing or not. I have a responsibility to at least try to carry on the tradition, if I can."

After I'd thought about that awhile, I asked, "Why don't you do it then?"

It took Norm a couple of switchbacks to mull that over. "I *can* play guitar a little bit," he finally admitted. "I practice it some in the winter, when I don't have anything else to do. But the truth is, I've always been afraid to sing in public."

"Why's that?" I wondered, seeing him squirm.

Norm fell silent for a ways. "No excuse," he finally concluded. "It's just plain cowardice."

By the time we passed the cutoff to Lake of the Fallen Moon, there were black cumulus clouds rolling and swirling over the Monarch Divide, and we were getting hit with gusts of wind. Our plan had been to spend the night at Granite Meadow, letting the animals graze all night on the dry sedges there, but as we crossed over Granite Pass, we got pounded with a driving rain that splattered into our faces so hard, it was difficult to see. If we passed Granite Meadow, it would be another eleven miles to Cedar Grove, and then three more miles to the park service corrals. It was all downhill, but once we passed Granite Basin there'd be no good place to make camp along the way, and we'd have to keep going, which meant we wouldn't get to the pack station until after dark.

"What do you think?" I shouted back to Norm. "You wanna try and set up camp in this storm?"

Norm thought it over. "The mules aren't carrying much weight, and they sure as hell don't mind moving in the rain. I'd rather try to keep on moving."

"How about stopping just long enough for the worst of this to blow over?" I called.

"What if it doesn't blow over? Then we have to finish it with a wet saddle and a soggy butt. Besides, I hate to see the mules stand around with a load on—even a light one."

Norm told me once that he'd seen his father fire a packer for stopping to eat dinner while his mules were fully loaded.

The rule was, if you stopped for any reason, the pack loads should come off. To Norm's way of thinking, the animals always came first.

We untied our yellow slickers from the back of our saddles and slipped them on, pulled our hats low so the rain streamed over our collars, and we kept riding.

Traveling from Granite Basin to Cedar Grove requires a 6,000-foot descent, with one long switchback after another. The storm was a full-on *chubasco* by now. The swirling wind whipped at us from every direction, and the rain came down in pulsing torrents. But once we'd crossed over the lip of the basin, the animals knew they were going home and they picked up their pace. On the south-facing slope, descending into Kings Canyon, the timber thinned out and we were riding through dense stands of manzanita and buck brush, with no protection from the rain at all. Water was flowing over the trail in a muddy stream, and we could hear lightning clanging into the granite cliffs above, like a hammer striking steel.

One good thing about riding in such a violent storm was that I got a chance to see how water behaves. Though I was supposed to be an erosion expert, nobody had ever taught me anything about it. Everything I knew I'd learned by observation and by talking with old trail crew foremen who had built and maintained hundreds of miles of backcountry trails. There were only a few basic design tools to control water flow in the backcountry. While modern roads are built sloping into the hillside, where the water is collected in channels and sent to culverts buried beneath the road, trails use the opposite approach; they're built with their shoulders sloping down the hill so the water can flow off directly. To divert any water flowing down the trail, angled water bars of either logs or rock are installed every few yards. If the trail is in a place where water can't be diverted, then checks, like mini dams, are placed to slow the flow. When I later had a chance to hike part of the Inca

# Chubasco a Cappella

Trail in Peru, I saw that the Incas had used these same basic tools long before they'd had any contact with Europeans.

By the time Norm and I reached Lower Tent Meadow, about halfway down, the rain had eased, and to our surprise, the storm began to lift. Overhead the clouds were still thick, but before long we could see the golden haze of the sun, already low in the sky, glowing through the gray clouds to the west. And below that was a strip of blue. The entire canyon had become quiet and calm. Chub, always eager to get back to the barn where he knew there would be oats and hay, stepped out nearly a hundred yards ahead of the others.

And then I heard something that at first startled me because I couldn't place what it was or where it was coming from. I reined in Chub and stopped there in the trail for a moment so I could listen better. When I knew for sure what I was hearing, I nudged Chub in the ribs and kept on moving. It was Norm, singing a cappella except for the accompaniment of mules' hooves clomping rhythmically down that soggy trail. And before long I could make out *what* he was singing: Willie Nelson's version of the Irving Berlin classic "Blue Skies."

> *Blue days, all of them gone*
> *Nothing but blue skies from now on.*
> *Blue skies smiling at me,*
> *Nothing but blue skies do I see.*

Norm sang in a modest voice, not loud or showy, but not shy either. It was a confident, masculine voice, the voice of a cowboy who didn't care if I or the whole damn world heard him. And he kept singing for a mile or so, the same song over and over, getting a little better each time.

It would have been easy to tease Norm about his singing, and it might have been fun, too. But for once I kept my mouth shut and never said a word about it.

~~~

By the time we reached the trailhead at Roads End, the blanket of clouds overhead was blocking even starlight from reaching the valley floor. As Norm liked to say, it was dark as the inside of a cow. We had flashlights, but the batteries had run out days before. The pack station was just three miles away, but that was an enormous distance to somebody blind, which is what we were. "Maybe we should just unload the animals and spend the night right here," I suggested. "I can't see a thing."

"Neither can I," Norm replied. "But the animals can."

"You really think they can follow the trail in this pitch black?"

"I *know* they can. How do you think they find their way around the backcountry every night?"

I figured Norm was probably right. He didn't just understand the animals, he could think like them, too. But to allow an animal to carry me through total darkness required a degree of faith I just didn't have. Unwilling to take the lead, I nudged Chub aside so Norm and the mules could slip past. Then Chub and I fell in behind them.

Even though I'd pruned that trail of all low-hanging branches by horseback that very spring, I rode with my arms held out in front of my face, as if they would protect me. Once, I saw the headlights from a car over on the highway, but then the night was completely dark again. Those headlights, though, had allowed me to see that Man was leading us right down the middle of the trail. When I heard an odd clomping sound ahead of me, I ducked low and grabbed onto the saddle horn, before realizing that the animals ahead were crossing the wooden bridge at Granite Creek—the same creek we'd crossed eleven miles, 6,000 feet in elevation, and five hours ago. All summer long we'd been asking these animals to trust us when we led them up the ramp of the stock truck, when we rode them over an unknown river crossing, when we tacked a metal shoe onto their feet, and when we hung awkward loads onto their backs. But this was the first time I'd had to completely trust them. It was unnerving, at least at first, but by the time we saw the porch lights of the pack station ahead of us, I'd made my peace with it and was beginning to understand what Norm meant when he said, "I can't trust them if they can't trust me. It has to work both ways."

When the other packers and trail crew workers staying at the pack station heard us ride in, they came out with bright flashlights and helped us unload at the dock, saying things like, "Jeez, if you guys would get out of bed before noon, maybe you wouldn't get in after dark." When we told them we'd ridden all the way from Simpson Meadow, they granted us a little respect. Then they started saying things like, "Consider yourselves lucky, boys. The last guys that stayed with that all-woman trail crew in Simpson Meadow were never seen again!"

We gave our animals hay and an extra handful of oats in their nose bags, then we turned them in with the other park stock in the corrals. They all knew each other from wintering together down in the San Joaquin Valley every winter, and in the dark we could hear them biting and kicking as they settled old grudges and rekindled unfinished love affairs.

As we ambled stiff and bowlegged toward the packer's dorm, I said to Norm, "Feels good to be walking on my own two feet again."

As it turned out, we had arrived at the park service corrals the night before the farewell party for John Gross, one of the most respected trail crew foremen in the parks. He'd announced that he was quitting the park service and going back home to St. Louis to begin a new career as a welder. Saturday morning, when I asked John why he'd do such a crazy thing, he spit a long line of black chew off the front porch and said, "Because I've worked for the goddamn gov'ment for ten years now, and I've about had a bellyful of it."

The park service has always had a hard time retaining its best seasonal employees, though it doesn't really care. The government knows that outdoor jobs are highly valued by many young people, and if the seasonal employees don't like living in rat-infested shacks, being supervised by arrogant jackasses who don't know half what they claim to know, or being paid half of what it takes to raise a family, there are many more applicants waiting in line behind them. Although much of the work is physical and dangerous, and takes a heavy toll on the body, seasonals have no medical or retirement benefits. The divorce rate among all park employees is high, the rate of alcoholism is well beyond the norm, and it's no wonder that the best workers often end up finding opportunities elsewhere.

In a few more years I would come to the same conclusion as John Gross, but at that time I thought he was making a big mistake. "I'll be sorry to see you go, John," I told him. "I hope you find what you're looking for."

"Well, you can't get rid of me just yet," John said. "Because tonight we're gonna have one helluva party."

Park service employees call the corrals and dorm at Cedar Grove Hole in the Wall. It's probably the best place in all of Sequoia and Kings Canyon to throw a blowout party. The place is modeled after the old western bunkhouse, with a kitchen at one end, and a big open room at the other with metal cots. Out front is the corral, hay shed, and loading dock, and just beyond that runs the Middle Fork of the Kings River, where we sometimes caught big German browns after work. Directly behind the bunkhouse looms a 3,000-foot granite cliff. At a time when ranches all over the West were being bought by millionaires for their weekend playgrounds, and their old ranch houses were being remodeled by their dilettante wives, Hole in the Wall still looked and felt like something out of the true Wild West. Better yet, the place was so isolated that tourists never found it, and even the park rangers usually left it alone.

That Saturday morning, one of the trail crew workers announced that he was going to make the seventy-five-mile drive into Fresno for supplies, and he'd be taking our orders. Norm and I each asked for a case of beer and a fifth of Jim Beam. Everybody else placed similar orders, too. Later that day, we pulled the worn shoes off our stock, washed our clothes, showered and shaved, and took a long nap.

Before supper, I went for a walk, following the cliff behind the corrals. There were obsidian flakes in every clearing, which meant Native Americans had spent a lot of time there. The south-facing exposure would have made it a cozy place to stay, even in winter. Next to the cliff lay a jumble of granite boulders that had broken off and tumbled down over the years. I crawled into a tiny talus cave—really just a shelter large enough for one person to get out of the rain—and I found an obsidian spear point nearly three inches long. It must have been a few hundred years old because the exposed side was coated with a gray layer of mineral deposits that had dripped down from the cave ceiling—that was the reason it had stayed hidden so long. It was a powerful object, and the temptation to pocket it was great. But remembering Norm's warning, I dug a pit with my hands and buried the spear point deep enough that it might stay hidden there for a hundred years more.

Back at the corrals, people were beginning to arrive: workers from all over the park, friends from Three Rivers and the San Joaquin Valley, and packers from the private Kings Canyon Pack Station just down the road. Word had gotten out that this wasn't a party to be missed. Somebody had rigged up a sound system so we could hear music outdoors, and we started playing Ernest Tubb, Hank Williams, and Emmylou Harris, with the volume cranked up loud. The party couldn't start without beer and whiskey, though, so we tried to get something to eat—just a sandwich or a bowl of soup. And then, just before dark, the truck finally arrived. We put out big galvanized tubs, tossed all the beer in there together, then topped the tubs off with ice. The whiskey we put aside for later.

There was an older packer there, Maxie Cheshire, whom Norm and I always enjoyed seeing. Maxie was originally from Montana, where back in the fifties he'd been working on a cattle ranch. One day another ranch hand told Maxie he'd heard there were government jobs out in California for cowboys who knew how to pack mules; he was going out to see for himself, and he asked Maxie if he'd like to go along. Maxie, who spoke in a voice so garbled you could barely understand him, said, "I believe I will!" Maxie had never really worked as a backcountry packer before, but like most cowboys he'd packed salt blocks and rolls of fence wire around ranches, and that experience was enough to get him hired at Yosemite National Park. He later transferred to Kings Canyon, and he stayed on there for many years.

Maxie wasn't the most accomplished packer we'd ever seen. He was an alcoholic who drank on the job, was in poor physical condition, and had begun taking shortcuts to ease the work strain. For example, in the backcountry he didn't like to get up at dawn to wrangle his stock, so if he couldn't keep his animals within drift fences, he'd turn them loose up canyon, lay his saddle and bed in the trail, and spend the night propped up there drinking and listening to his transistor radio. If he heard the lead mare's bell approaching, he'd get out of bed and shoo her back up canyon. Once, near Charlotte Creek, Norm and I had ridden by Maxie early in the morning, sound asleep, with his stock quietly gathered around him, waiting patiently for him to wake up so they could have their morning oats. We rode on by as quietly as we could.

I don't know if Maxie was ever married, but he was single as long as I knew him. Years before the movie *Brokeback Mountain* came out, he told hilarious stories about cowboys in love with cowboys. I doubt that he favored men, but the winter nights are long and cold in Montana, and who knows what went on. For some reason I never understood, Maxie could sleep with his eyes open. I don't know if that was a god-given talent or if it was a survival trait he'd learned from sleeping in Montana bunkhouses. But in the dorm at Cedar Grove, it was just plain creepy to roll over in the middle of the night and see Maxie staring at you, even when you knew he was sound asleep.

I suppose it was female companionship Maxie longed for most. He satisfied that desire every weekend by driving down to Kings Canyon Avenue, on the eastern edge of Fresno, where there was a strip of honky-tonks, cheap motels, liquor stores, and women who offered their services to lonely men. Maxie's favorite place was a topless bar called the Chi-Chi Club. Because Maxie drank too much, it was easy for the women who worked there to take advantage of him. One Monday morning, Maxie came to work with his pants practically falling down.

"Maxie, what happened to your belt?" we asked him.

"Nothing happened to my belt!" he said. "But those goddamn hookers stole my silver belt buckle!"

That evening at Hole in the Wall, just as our party was

getting started, I watched Maxie do an interesting thing. Before it was dark out, he went into the kitchen and cracked the seal on a bottle of Old Granddad. But rather than take a drink right away, as I expected, he took a clean glass, filled it with whiskey, opened the cupboard, reached up, and placed the glass as far back on the top shelf as he could reach.

Lots of other interesting things happened later that night. One ranger's wife, a fine-looking woman twenty years older than most of us, showed up by herself and danced with just about every man in cowboy boots before disappearing with one of them into the dark. Another park employee gave his car keys to his girlfriend so he wouldn't try to drive home drunk; when he left with another woman, his girlfriend threw his keys into the Kings River. The biggest fool of the night might have been me. I made several passes at a lovely young woman everyone but me knew preferred the company of other women. She wasn't offended, though, and later we had a good laugh about it.

Sometime, perhaps around one in the morning, a ranger still on duty stopped by in his patrol truck. He was an earnest young fellow, from back East somewhere, though we didn't hold that against him. He asked when we planned on shutting the party down, and someone said, "Probably around sunrise, but it's still too soon to call!" The ranger left quietly but returned half an hour later in his civilian clothes.

Next morning, like several other people, I woke up on a hay bale out by the loading dock, with the bright sun in my eyes. I gathered myself together as best as I could and, on my way to the kitchen, passed by the galvanized buckets hoping to find one last cold beer to smooth out the start of the day. But I was too late—the ice had melted and all the beer was gone. Whiskey bottles were lying everywhere, but they were empty. In the kitchen, somebody who'd had the good sense to stay sober—I don't remember who—had started a big batch of scrambled eggs and sausage, and was handing out burritos to people as they walked in the door.

And before long, Maxie wandered in, too, looking better than most of us, but not by much. He refused the burrito but went directly to the kitchen cabinet, reached up to the top shelf, retrieved his glass of Old Granddad from the very back, and downed it in one shot.

〰︎

That blowout party we had at Hole in the Wall began a tradition of fall rendezvous in the parks. The idea was based on the drunken and riotous gatherings held each year by the old Rocky Mountain fur trappers in the early nineteenth century, a tradition we'd read about and admired. Most often our rendezvous were never really planned—somehow they just came together when the time was right. Sometimes they happened Labor Day weekend, when most of us had three days off. Sometimes they coalesced during a fall *chubasco*, when the heavy tropical rain made work impossible and forced crews to hole up somewhere and wait for the unstable weather to pass. And then sometimes they didn't happen until the so-called "fall project," when backcountry crews in Sequoia or Kings Canyon assembled in one place, usually a lower-elevation site, to work on one large task together, say, the repair of a log bridge or the construction of a new section of trail.

Our rendezvous were a way for us to meet up with other backcountry workers we hadn't seen all summer and share stories of our adventures. Working in the backcountry can be a form of social deprivation, and by September many of us felt the need to mingle with people other than those we'd spent all summer with. One trail crew foreman and his packer sometimes grew so sick of each other that they spent the last half of each season not speaking to one another. Like an old married couple, they couldn't be civil to each other unless they were in company. Because very few women worked on backcountry crews in those days, many men were starved for female companionship. Some of the married men had their wives visit them in the backcountry, almost like a conjugal visit for prison inmates. Sometimes the married men had girlfriends visit them, too, as if what happened three days from civilization wasn't bound by the flatland rules of fidelity. And sometimes wives and girlfriends passed each other on the trail without even suspecting they had something in common.

## Chapter Five: God's Gardener

Next spring, 1979, the park service budget problems weren't any better, and my boss told me he could no longer afford to hire a packer for my crew. As soon as the trails division heard that Norm Jefferson was available, they snatched him up. When I ran into Norm in the parking lot at Ash Mountain, he admitted to feeling a bit guilty about going to work for another division, almost as if he'd abandoned me when I needed him most. But I told him I knew it hadn't been his choice, and in the end, the trails division could offer him a better deal, including more months of work each year and a pathway to a permanent job with full benefits.

Also that spring I ran into Curtis Cohoe, my Navajo friend who now worked for the hazardous tree crew. He told me that Jerry Martine, the Navajo who had advised me to wear a sack of corn pollen around my neck to protect me from witchcraft and ghosts, had been killed in an auto accident on the reservation that winter.

Although my backcountry crew was never funded in the old manner again, it did survive in a new form, and stronger than ever. The parks had begun to experiment with backcountry crews provided by the California Conservation Corps, or CCC. The CCC had been started when Ronald Reagan was governor as an alternative service for conscientious objectors during the Vietnam War, and it was modeled after the old Civilian Conservation Corps of the Depression era. The CCC members, who were between the ages of eighteen and twenty-five, worked as wildland firefighters, responded to floods and other emergencies, planted trees, and assisted the National Forest Service and National Park Service with trail construction projects. Their motto was "Hard work, low pay, miserable conditions," which, for some reason, attracted more prospects than they could hire.

At first I was skeptical about using CCC workers for my restoration projects because I was worried I'd end up babysitting a bunch of spoiled city kids. But I soon changed my mind. Most of them were bright young people who belonged in college but for whatever reason weren't ready for that yet. Some lacked the money for school, some hadn't decided yet what they wanted to study, but others, like me at their age, just felt an overpowering need to be outdoors. And they turned out to be some of the hardest workers I'd ever seen. Any slackers were weeded out or, more often, pressured by their coworkers to carry their own load. But what surprised me most about those CCC workers was that they really cared about learning how to sharpen a chainsaw, build a rock retaining wall, or cook a pot of beans over an open fire. And they cared about my restoration projects, too.

We started out using just a handful of CCC workers on a project at Tokopah Valley that June. The job was to build a series of rock causeways on the trail from Lodgepole Campground to Tokopah Falls. Tokopah Valley is like a mini Yosemite, with steep granite walls, lush meadows, a river flowing through it, and a waterfall at the end of the trail. It makes a beautiful short hike, and because it's so close to a large campground, the trail gets a lot of traffic. In several places, though, it had become a boggy quagmire and the delicate meadow vegetation had taken a terrible beating. Our biggest problem was that because the canyon is so narrow, there was no way to reroute the trail around the meadows. So our solution was to build rock causeways across the meadows, a method we knew had been successful in other places. Rock causeways are elevated trails that work like this: Large rocks are placed loosely along the old trail, creating a firm bed above the boggy sections;

because the rocks are not too close together, the moisture from the meadow can continue to flow through the rocks in an almost natural way; smaller and smaller rocks are added until the top surface, perhaps eighteen inches above ground level, is fine gravel. Although rock causeways are not truly natural, they're built from native materials, and if done correctly, with time they look as if they belong in a wilderness environment.

At that time, my rock-working skills didn't amount to much, but luckily the CCC supervisor, Pete Lewis, had worked several years on trail crews in Yosemite and had done a lot of rock work there. I let Pete worry about the rock gathering and placement, while I focused on protecting the meadow.

Pete was an interesting guy, deeply loved and respected by the members of his crew. Originally from Rochester, New York, he'd spent a few years in Gambia and Ghana, working for Crossroads Africa, and he'd brought home with him a long, flowing dashiki robe. Sometimes on the weekends, Pete liked to wear it around in remembrance of the friends he'd made in Africa.

One Saturday morning, Pete and I were hanging around Wolverton Corrals, where the private pack station kept its horses and mules. The park service had corrals there, too, and a hay shed which the CCC crew used as their residence while we worked on the Tokopah project. Together Pete and I strolled over to the corrals to watch a redneck farrier from the valley, a burly man named Shaver, put new shoes on some mules. Pete was wearing his dashiki, with a little round pillbox hat that matched, spitting tobacco juice into an empty beer can, with some of the juice running down his beard. After Shaver had finished with one mule's hind foot, he stood up straight, cracked his aching back, wiped the sweat from his eyes, took one look at Pete, and asked, "Son, what in the world are you high on?"

I didn't mind rednecks in general—the only reason my neck

wasn't red too was that my long hair covered it—but I couldn't tolerate ignorant bullies. I still enjoyed a good fight, and I was about to get in Shaver's face. Pete, though, was a pacifist, and to his great credit he just spit in his empty can, looked Shaver straight in the eye, and said, "Nothing but Copenhagen and clean mountain air."

～
～

When we moved into the backcountry that summer, to work on a meadow restoration project at Hockett Meadow, my biggest problem was that I no longer had a mule packer. Thanks to the oddities of government budgeting, though, I still had a horse and six mules. So, in effect, I had to become my own packer. It was an impossible workload, trying to run a crew and be its packer at the same time, and, looking back on it today, I wonder why I didn't quit. I'd crawl out of my sleeping bag every morning long before the sun came up, track my stock sometimes for miles before I found them, lead them back to camp, groom them and feed them oats, have a quick breakfast with the crew, spend eight hours of hard labor on restoration projects, limp back to camp, maybe put a new shoe on one of the mules or care for a saddle sore, eat supper, then try to stay awake for radio check at eight that evening. The next day I'd start the whole grind over again.

That was the hardest work I ever had to do in my life, and I was doing it without any of my old friends for support. Mike Palmer, Jimmy Castro, Curtis Cohoe, and Norm Jefferson had all either left the park service or were working on other crews. I was ten years older than most of those CCC workers, which doesn't seem like much now but felt like a lot at the time. All my life until then, I'd thumbed my nose at authority, and now I'd become a sort of authority figure myself, and I didn't like it much. The meadow restoration projects are what kept me going, and I didn't want to leave the park service until I saw some of them through.

Later that summer, after my CCC workers were assigned to other projects, my crew of three moved to upper Rattlesnake Creek to take on a new erosion scar that had appeared that spring. It was at the base of the switchbacks coming down from Franklin Pass, where the trail first meets meadow vegetation. Because of a few failed water bars on the trail, a large volume of runoff during the spring thaw had eroded a rut into the meadow that was twelve feet deep in some places, and about 200 feet long. To fill a scar that deep would have required far more dirt than we could have moved using mules and dirt boxes. Instead, using the natural slope, we were able to re-sculpt a portion of the meadow, moving soil and sod already there, as well as adding new soil where it was needed. It bothered me at first that we weren't restoring the meadow exactly to its previous condition, and I wondered if my sleight of hand was violating some ethical issue. I suppose it's still an open question, but we successfully restored the correct water flow, preserved as much vegetation as possible, and left the area looking almost natural.

One Friday afternoon in September, after I'd gone back to work on the hazardous tree crew, my supervisor, Larry Bancroft, called me into his office. And he looked mad. "I thought you told me you spent two weeks on a meadow restoration project on upper Rattlesnake Creek, right where the switchbacks start."

I nodded.

"Well, I just rode through there on the annual sore ass trip. I wanted to show everybody what one of my crews had been working on."

"What'd they think of it?" I asked.

"They didn't think anything of it because I couldn't find it!"

I laughed out loud, which only made Bancroft more angry. He'd been an officer in the Air Force and didn't like being trifled with by his inferiors. "Would you mind telling me what's so damn funny?" he asked.

"That's the best compliment anybody could have given me," I said. "You just made my whole summer."

Bancroft didn't calm down until I showed him the photos I'd taken of that project before, in process, and after. Bancroft made copies of them and passed them around with the report I'd written for that project. From then on, I never again had to stand before a superintendent, assistant superintendent, or chief ranger, and explain to them with diagrams on a chalkboard what I was trying to accomplish in the backcountry. And I never had to fight for funding for any of my projects again, either. Though I never received a single word of encouragement from any of those sore asses, I guess they figured I was up to something worthwhile.

༄

When I ran into Norm Jefferson back at Ash Mountain that October, he told me that the previous winter he'd been hanging out with some skilled rock climbers in the Owens Valley, bouldering in the Alabama Hills, and practicing on some of the rock faces at the base of the eastern escarpment. He said he'd been thinking about climbing Mount Whitney by way of the old classic mountaineer's route, rather than using the modern trail, which we both considered cheating. He asked me if I'd be interested in doing that with him. I told him to count me in. Norm mentioned that he was still a bit light on gear, so I said I'd take care of it. That weekend I drove to Royal Robbins's climbing shop in Fresno, on the north end of town, just off

Highway 41, where a lot of Yosemite rock climbers bought their gear.

When I saw the variety of new climbing hardware on the shelves there, I was confused and a bit intimidated. Climbing had changed so much in recent years, I didn't even know what some of that gear was used for. When Doug Tompkins had taught me the basics of rock climbing ten years earlier, we still used manila rope and steel pitons. Now climbers were using high-quality nylon ropes, and pitons had been replaced by a perplexing variety of chocks that could be placed in cracks without the need for a hammer. Because I'd been climbing mostly by myself in the backcountry and avoided routes I couldn't climb without protection, I was ignorant of the latest technology. So with a little advice from some other climbers there, I selected a nylon climbing harness, a variety of nylon webbing, a new nylon rope, and an assortment of aluminum chocks.

As I was shopping for more gear, a group of young men entered the shop. They were all lean, tanned and bearded, with scabbed arms and elbows, wearing shabby clothes, and laughing irreverently—obviously Yosemite climbers. And one of them looked vaguely familiar to me. He was thin but extremely fit, had long blond hair and a red beard, and his face showed the lines of somebody who'd spent a lot of time outdoors. He was clearly the leader of the group, showing confidence and grace in the way he moved, but his ironic smile and the laughter in his eyes showed he didn't take himself all that seriously. He and his friends quickly found what they'd come for and left. As I was paying for my purchases, I asked the young man behind the counter, "Was that Doug Wiens?"

The man smiled and nodded. "That was Doug. Do you know him?"

"I did a long time ago," I said. "We worked as busboys

together at the Yosemite Lodge cafeteria back in the summer of 1967. I barely recognized him now."

I hung around at the climbing shop while the young man behind the counter filled me in on what Doug Wiens had been up to. Wiens had not only become a very accomplished rock climber, eventually scaling El Capitan, but had become an instructor at the Yosemite Mountaineering School. On a 200-mile winter ski trek along the crest of the Sierra Nevada, his ski partners had nicknamed him "the Piston" because of his relentless stamina and determination. Wiens later worked as a cross-country ski instructor at the Trapp Family Lodge in Stowe, Vermont, where he met Maria von Trapp, who wrote the book that the movie *Sound of Music* was based on. The irrepressible Maria took a liking to Wiens and asked him to teach her how to ski. Wiens refused, saying she was too old and would certainly fall and break something. Later, though, he relented, and sometimes in the late afternoon, Wiens would escort the elderly Maria around the lodge's ski trails.

The director of the ski school at the Trapp Family Lodge, Ned Gillette, had been a member of the 1968 US Olympic ski team and later became a world-class adventurer in his own right. In 1977, Wiens, Gillette, and two others set out on a 450-mile ski trip around the northern tip of Ellesmere Island, which is in Canada 600 miles below the Arctic Circle. There were no food caches or air drops supporting the trip, and each man had to pull a fiberglass sled containing 240 pounds of provisions. While on Ellesmere, they climbed six mountains with elevations up to 7,000 feet.

In 1978, Wiens kayaked 1,200 miles from Seattle to Juneau, and while in Alaska he and three others (Ned Gillette, Alan Bard, and Galen Rowell) completed the first circumnavigation of Mount McKinley (now known as Denali) by skis, carrying eighty-pound packs. That adventure was featured in the July 1979 issue of *National Geographic*. Galen Rowell, the famous nature photographer and mountaineer, later made a lecture tour describing the trip. I'd attended one of those lectures in San Diego and heard him describe how their smallest teammate had a peculiar talent for finding crevasses on the glaciers by being the first to fall into them. I didn't realize until later that Rowell was describing my shy Yosemite tent mate from the summer of 1967.

※

Later that month, just before going back to my writing job in San Diego, I met Norm in Lone Pine, and we set off to climb Mount Whitney the honest way.

The approach from Whitney Portal up Lone Pine Creek required a full day of hard cross-country hiking. We were traveling as light as possible, without tents or even a cook stove, and our camp that night at Iceberg Lake was minimal. The night was cold, so we made a small fire of foxtail pine branches, then hunkered down close to the fire to stay warm.

Norm told me about some of the guys he'd been climbing with the previous winter. "I don't know," Norm said. "Sometimes it seems like those guys don't care if they live or die. I enjoy climbing with them, but I don't know if I'll ever be as dedicated as they are. Lots of other ways to get yourself killed, if that's what you want to do." Then he asked me, "Did I ever tell you about the time my dad climbed Mount Brewer?"

"No. I didn't even know your dad *was* a climber."

"He isn't, but back in the fifties he rode a horse to the top."

I'd been to the top of Mount Brewer myself, and though it's a fine-looking mountain that can be seen for many miles in every direction, I would hardly consider it a climb, really, just a scramble.

"On one side of Brewer there's a bunch of big boulders stacked like blocks. The whole deal was finding a route a horse could manage, then convincing the horse to do it."

"That's pretty damn western," I said.

Next morning we had perfect fall weather, and we completed our climb of Whitney before noon. On the last pitch to the summit, we used the gear I'd bought in Fresno. Norm led and I followed. After two days without seeing another person, it felt odd to emerge onto that big flat summit where at least a hundred people were celebrating their arrival by way of the trail from Whitney Portal. It felt like we'd wandered out of the wilderness and stumbled into somebody's garden party.

※

The following June, the park service gave me the go-ahead to begin my dream restoration project at Rock Creek, and they gave me a crew of twenty CCC workers. Working on a backcountry crew was considered the best assignment you could get in the CCC, the selection process was highly competitive, and my crew consisted of some tough, smart, highly motivated young people. The crew came with their own leader, plus I was given a full-time park service cook and a new packer.

As soon as the snow on Cottonwood Pass melted, we loaded our trucks and vans, and drove around the southern end of the mountains to Lone Pine. Although all the CCC workers were in great physical condition, some had never actually been in the backcountry before. Just to make sure they would all arrive in camp safely, I wanted to hike in with them. But I was told by my supervisors that wouldn't be possible. The tools, food, and equipment for a crew that big were far too much for a single mule train, and park management had decided that the cheapest way to get our camp situated in Rock Creek was to fly most of it in by helicopter. The helicopter pilot had no idea where to drop the equipment, so it was decided that I would fly in with him on the first trip. The CCC leader, a woman about my age named Judy, would have to see that the crew arrived safely.

We all spent that night at Portagee Joe's, thinking we'd get up early the next day, our cook and I would jump into the helicopter, and the crew would hike in from the Cottonwood trailhead. By the time they arrived at Rock Creek that afternoon, I'd have the kitchen set up, the cook would have a nice dinner prepared, and we'd celebrate our first night together in the backcountry. But early the next morning there were unusually strong winds over the passes along the Sierra crest, and by ten o'clock the helicopter pilot had decided he couldn't fly that day.

So I was stuck with twenty California state employees who had nothing to do. I ordered them to clean up Portagee Joe's while I drove over to the forest service office in Lone Pine and explained my situation, practically begging them for work. But the forest service people just figured I was dumping my problem on them. "If you'd given us a day's notice, we might have been able to come up with something," they said. "But we've got nothing for you now."

I walked over to the Dow Villa Hotel, where I sometimes stayed when I was in Lone Pine. It had creaky wooden floors, lion claw bathtubs instead of showers, and restless ghosts that prowled up and down the stairways all night long. But it also had a big swimming pool out front. I spoke with the young manager at the desk, seeing if I could work out a deal. "Would you mind very much if I brought twenty very well behaved young men and women to swim in your pool this afternoon?"

"Are you currently staying at the Dow Villa?" the manager asked, knowing I wasn't.

"Not at this very moment, but I've been a loyal customer of the Dow Villa many times in the past," I replied.

"Well, all I can tell you is that guests staying at the Dow Villa are welcome to invite their friends to the pool," he said. "But if you aren't staying here, I can't help you."

I took out my wallet and paid for the cheapest room he had.

Back at Portagee Joe's, I found all the weeds had been pulled, the trees pruned, the bathrooms cleaned, and the trash picked up. The place, normally a dump, had never looked so good. Our cook had made everybody sandwiches, and we ate lunch together in the shade of the big old cottonwoods. Then I said, "This afternoon we'll be taking advantage of this break in our schedule to conduct water safety training. Is there anybody here who can't swim?"

A few hands went up.

"Is there anybody here who's ever taught swimming?" I asked.

A few hands went up again. "Okay, you swimmers will be teaching the non-swimmers. You can get into your swimsuits now."

That afternoon, around four o'clock, a car with official California state markings and plates pulled up to the curb in front of the Dow Villa pool. Out stepped Dave Muraki, assistant to the director of the California Conservation Corps (and later director himself). Muraki had visited Ash Mountain a few times, so I recognized him. He'd been driving back to Sacramento from a meeting in Los Angeles, on Highway 395, with the intention of passing through Yosemite to visit one of his crews working there. When he saw our blue CCC van parked in front of the Dow Villa, and then saw twenty of his corpsmembers frolicking in the pool, he pulled over immediately to see what in the hell was going on.

I was reclining in a lounge chair when Muraki strode up. Shielding my eyes from the bright afternoon sun, I looked up and saw that he was mad. "Oh, hi, Dave," I said. "Good timing. We're just about ready to knock off for the day."

After I'd explained the situation, Muraki calmed down and said, "At least you could've parked the van in the alley out back."

I sent one of the corpsmembers to move the van. Muraki pulled off his shirt and sat in a lounge chair next to me, taking in that magnificent view of the Sierra crest. "Isn't that Mount Whitney?" he asked, pointing at Lone Pine Peak.

"You're looking at it," I replied.

〰︎
〰︎

Next morning at dawn, the wind was calm enough for the helicopter to make it over Cottonwood Pass, so I flew into Rock Creek on the first flight with Lisa, our cook. After circling a couple times in the helicopter, I selected the campsite I wanted, we landed, and I looked it over again on the ground. We were going to be there all summer, and I needed to make sure the site would be right for such a large crew. Then Lisa and I waited on the ground while the helicopter made two more trips with sling loads of our food and gear. I felt a bit guilty, almost like a candy-ass lieutenant flying to the battle site while his troops slogged through the jungle below, but there was no doubt that this was the best way to get such a large camp established quickly. Lisa and I went to work setting up the kitchen, then she started preparing dinner while I used the chainsaw to cut a supply of firewood.

The only thing that worried me now was the possibility of my CCC crew getting lost on their way into Rock Creek. Their supervisor Judy (a permanent California state employee) insisted there would be no problem, that she had lots of backcountry experience, was skilled at reading a topographic map, and would be at Rock Creek with the whole crew by early afternoon. But I knew she actually had little backcountry experience and was unable to admit it. Though it wasn't a difficult route or a very long hike, I still went over it with her several times: Cottonwood Trailhead to Cottonwood Pass, where they'd pick up the Pacific Crest Trail, follow it to Siberian Pass, then continue on to our camp at Rock Creek. I knew that some of the younger workers on the crew had backcountry experience, so I went over the route with them, too. Also, I did make sure Judy had a park service radio, she knew how to use it, and the battery was good.

I tried to make contact with Judy throughout the day to check on the crew's progress, but the park's repeaters weren't situated to reach areas outside the park, and most of the crew's route was south of the park boundary. So I didn't worry too much on that account. By suppertime, though, I was starting to get nervous. I got a radio call from the park dispatcher saying she'd received a broken transmission from the CCC crew on another channel, but she couldn't understand the message. A short time later, I got a call from one of my supervisors, who had stayed late at Ash Mountain to monitor the situation. He was concerned and a bit annoyed. "You're responsible for their safety," he said. "If they aren't there by now, they're obviously lost. I don't want to have to call for a search-and-rescue for your crew on their very first day in the backcountry."

I gathered up my radio and binoculars, told Lisa I'd be back soon, and started moving slowly toward Siberian Pass. After ten years working as a backcountry crew leader, I'd never had anybody on my crew injured or lost. Now I was beginning to wonder if I'd lost an entire crew. By the time I got to the top of Siberian Pass, the late afternoon light was turning golden and I knew I only had about an hour or so to find my crew and herd them back to camp.

I had a pretty good idea where they were. Even though most of their route was outside the park, in the Golden Trout Wilderness, I'd skied through that area several times on winter snow surveys and I had a hunch how Judy's map reading had gone wrong. I sat down at the base of a foxtail pine and glassed the area below the pass with my binoculars. After a couple minutes, I spotted them, about three miles away by trail but less than two miles by line of sight.

What Judy had done was make a wrong turn at Cottonwood Pass. Instead of turning north on the Pacific Crest Trail, she had turned west down Stokes Stringer. Somewhere out on Big Whitney Meadow, she'd realized her mistake, turned around, and started marching the crew back up to Cottonwood Pass. They might have been able to reach the pass an hour or so after dark, but then they'd have had to spend a night out on the trail.

As soon as I could see that the crew was okay, I decided to have a little fun. I switched my radio to channel one, which meant I was broadcasting in direct line of sight and my voice wouldn't be picked up on the park's repeaters. I lowered my voice a notch, pressed the key, and said, "Judy."

After a moment I heard Judy's breathless voice. "This is Judy. Who's this?"

"Judy, this is God speaking on Channel 1."

"Who?"

"You knew in your heart this day of judgment would come, didn't you?"

"Look, I don't have time to play games right now!"

"Switch to Channel 1, do exactly as I say, and I will deliver you from this predicament you find yourself in."

There was a long pause. I could see Judy waving her arms angrily. "Okay, dammit, I'm on Channel 1!"

"Good. Now I want you to turn around and walk due west."

"But that's the wrong way! We need to get back up to Cottonwood Pass where I know damn well I screwed up in the first place!"

"Judy!" I said in a firmer voice. "I've been watching over you all this time, and I'm watching over you now. Do as I say and turn around."

Of course, Judy knew I was just having fun, but she couldn't figure out where I was or how I could see her, and she wasn't in the mood for my foolishness. But she had no choice except to do as I said. She thought about it for a moment, threw her arms up in frustration, and turned the crew around.

After they had walked west for a few minutes, it was time to really test Judy's faith. "Judy," I said. "I want you to leave the trail now and turn due north. Do you know which way is north?"

All I heard was a garbled "Goddammit!"

By sending the crew across Big Whitney Meadow, I had saved them at least a mile of walking to the next junction. In a few more minutes, they'd intersected the trail to Siberian Pass and were headed directly toward me.

It's a pretty good pull from Big Whitney Meadow up to Siberian Pass, and those poor CCC workers had been wandering around in the wilderness with heavy packs all day long. But I knew they were all strong and could take it. When they were just below the pass, I could see a couple of stragglers falling behind. I went down and greeted Judy, who was both furious and relieved to see me at the same time. "How in the hell did you do that?" she sputtered.

I continued down the trail and greeted my crewmembers one by one with a smile and a pat on the back. The last person was a delightfully determined but tiny young woman whose pack was so long it banged her on the back of her legs with every step. I asked if I could carry her pack, and she gratefully nodded that I could.

Thirty minutes later, right at dusk, we were all in camp enjoying a spaghetti dinner by firelight.

༄

The camp we set up there on Rock Creek was one of the finest backcountry camps I've ever had. It was just below Mount Langley, at about 10,000 feet in elevation, and situated on a large flat just above the creek, with good morning sun and a fine view of the Kaweahs far to the west. With so many workers eager to learn every aspect of backcountry life, I delegated the jobs I'd done myself a thousand times in the past, which meant at Rock Creek I never cooked a meal, never washed a dish, never hauled a bucket of water, and never dug a latrine. Life was easy in some ways, yet I dearly missed my old crewmembers.

I put all my energy into the restoration project, and it went well. I knew what I wanted to accomplish now, and I knew how to go about it. Using what I'd learned in Rattlesnake Creek about re-sculpting a sloped meadow, I tried to find ways to repair the old erosion scars by doing the least amount of damage to the surrounding landscape. Because the canyon had been scoured by glaciers during the last ice age, soil was scarce in places. But there were other places where the flanks of the glaciers had heaped up mounds of dirt that had been waiting there for 10,000 years. We could steal a bit off the top or sides and nobody would ever know. I found, too, that by removing an island of turf between two deep ruts, we could cut the turf into fist-sized pieces and use them for sod plugs, thereby making a little turf go a long way. The work was interesting and challenging, and at the end of every day I could look back on perhaps a thousand square feet of restored meadow and take satisfaction in what we'd done.

Little by little, though, I was learning that for humans to re-create wilderness is nearly impossible. We have a compulsion to establish order that is almost the exact opposite of wild. It's so basic to human nature, we don't even know we're doing it. For example, when I'd tell the CCC workers I wanted sod plugs planted across a section of refilled ruts, I'd come back later to find a checkerboard pattern. When I'd tell them to scatter boulders across a drier section of restored meadow to simulate the surrounding glacial rubble, I'd come back to find boulders of similar size equally spaced. So I'd gather my twenty workers together and we would talk about chaos. "Nature doesn't have the same compulsion we have to arrange everything in perfect order," I said.

"But we're not trying to arrange anything," they would say. "It just happens."

"Exactly. It's an unconscious thing. You have to resist it," I'd explain.

"How?"

"Well, one way," I told them, "is to decide where you would like to put that sod plug, then put it someplace else. Put it where it doesn't go."

That made sense to some of them, and for days after I'd hear them reminding each other, "Bossman says put it where it doesn't go!"

The problem with trying to imitate the chaos of nature, though, is that nature also creates order in the most surprising fashion: the way different species of wildflowers will arrange themselves on a gravelly slope according to their requirements for moisture and light, like strokes of a paintbrush; the way a dry creek bed leaves deposits of sand and gravel in perfectly graded scrolls; the way a snowpack melts on a hillside year after year, leaving pine needles arranged in triangular patterns above every rock; the way an old lightning strike burns out the roots of a foxtail pine, leaving an elegant octopus pattern. With time I came to see that in wilderness there are infinite layers of chaos and order too complex for us to ever replicate. While we might be able to destroy the patterns of man, we can never truly re-create the patterns of nature.

Sometimes I'd go to work in the morning filled with doubts. Maybe the freedom I'd been given to do this work was only a bureaucratic mistake, and once some government auditors figured out what I was really up to, they would take away my mules and my crew, and put me back to work doing something useful, like painting stripes on the Generals Highway. Sometimes I wondered if it was even possible to restore wilderness to a natural condition, as if we were playing God. And other times I couldn't even figure out what wilderness was.

White settlers arriving in California 200 years ago might have thought of the Sierra Nevada as wilderness. But Native Americans had already been there for thousands of years. They'd lived and prospered by using large portions of it, and they'd left their mark on it. In North America some game animals had been hunted to extinction by people using nothing but arrows and spears. In the Sierra Nevada, Native Americans had burned large tracts of land to make it more accessible and perhaps more suitable for the animals they were hunting. Obsidian flakes that came from the Mono and Inyo craters in the eastern Sierra can be found littered throughout the backcountry, almost like discarded bottle tops. The land had already been altered by the time we got here, which makes it difficult to think of wilderness as a place untouched by the hand of man.

I didn't want to become some misanthropic crank raging about the horrors of mankind. And I didn't want to sound like a thumb-sucking academic fretting over the precise definition of wilderness. But through another blend of chaos and order, the federal government had given me the remarkable task of trying to re-create wilderness. It was the only challenge I could have taken seriously at that time in my life. The work mattered, at least to me, and I wanted to get it right if I could. To do that I had to try to understand what wilderness was.

With time I came to think of wilderness as a place where the interests of man are secondary, and nature has been allowed to do what nature always does. It's pointless to talk about preserving wilderness with the intent of preventing all change. Change is what created wilderness and change is essential for its survival. Wilderness is a process that continues even in places so horribly damaged by man that their original character can't even be recognized, like the center divider along a southern California freeway. Any place left alone long enough will revert to wilderness, though perhaps in a period of time that seems unreasonable to humans—thousands of years, or after the next ice age. Humans, I believe, should try to speed up that process of recovery in a place as special as the Sierra Nevada backcountry. It's an obligation we have to future generations, to give them the opportunity to enjoy the beauty that has enriched our lives. But I must admit that in the long run perhaps it doesn't matter what we do. Nature will have its way in the end, with or without us.

Some of the young men on my crew chafed at that sort of work. Like most males, they wanted to be building big, impressive structures out of rock and wood, monuments to their manliness, not getting down on their knees to do God's gardening. But the women took to it in a wonderful way. They would plant every sod plug with tenderness and love, cooing encouragement and motherly advice, adding handfuls of water from buckets they'd carried from the creek. I don't mean to say they were soft in any way. Some of those women had broad shoulders and brawny arms, and they could do anything any man on the crew could do.

One day a group of older backpackers, men and women, passed through our work site. They looked like educated city folk, sporting new clothing and gear, as if they'd hiked straight out of an Eddie Bauer catalog. They approved of our project after I explained what we were doing, but one of the older women took my elbow and drew me aside. She looked indignant. "I suppose it's none of my business," she said, "but I'm concerned about these young women doing such hard physical labor. You know, men and women aren't the same. There are important anatomical differences."

"I've noticed that," I said.

"These women could be doing great harm to their bodies trying to prove they can do anything a man can do."

"Well, you know, a couple of years ago I might have shared your concern," I said. "But lately I've changed my mind."

Her eyes narrowed with skepticism. "And what made you change your mind?"

"I've come to the conclusion that in most ways females aren't that much different from males. You work them hard and feed them well, and they get stronger. Some of them even end up stronger than some of the males."

"You'd have to prove it to me," she replied.

Just then our string of mules was coming over the hill with a load of dirt fill. I pointed to them and said, "Look at those six animals and tell me which one you think is the strongest."

She studied the mules for a moment, then pointed at a long-legged bay with glistening flanks and a neck rippling with muscles.

"Good choice," I said. "Her name is Mandy."

One morning there at Rock Creek, just after first light, I got a call on the backcountry radio from the park dispatcher. "9-2-8, what's your location?"

"This is 9-2-8. I'm in bed."

"At Rock Creek?"

"That's right."

"Helicopter 5-2 will be there in fifteen minutes to pick you up. Can you be ready?"

"I suppose so. What's this about?"

"The pilot will explain."

The helicopter landed just outside our camp, and I tumbled into the passenger seat. I looked at the pilot, but the engine noise made it too loud for us to talk, so he just smiled and pointed skyward. All my crewmembers were crawling out of their tents now, half dressed, wondering what was so important that the park service urgently needed their bossman at this hour of the morning.

The helicopter, a Hughes 500, lifted off, circled several times to gain elevation, then turned north, following the crest of the Sierra. By the time we were over Mount Whitney, I had a pretty good idea what this was about.

In the summer, something like 150 people a day hike to the top of Mount Whitney, and most of them take a crap on the summit, probably for the same reason coyotes like to leave their scat on a high rock. Most high peaks in the Sierra have a register climbers can sign in order to prove they were there, but somehow the old fecal system still prevails. To accommodate that much human waste, the government had installed an outhouse with a fiberglass collection bin that had to be swapped out for an empty bin every few days. The full bin, known as the honey bucket, like the one at Pear Lake, was then flown out by helicopter. But somebody had to be on the ground to attach the steel cable from the honey bucket to the helicopter—supposedly, the pilot can't get out and do it himself. Normally the honey bucket detail was handled by backcountry trail crews or the area ranger, but for whatever reason, this time the task fell to me. The park service had turned me into a sanitation engineer, just like old Mac McCool, with his dented hardhat.

The helicopter landed on the summit of Whitney, I hopped out, snapped the heavy-duty cable into place, then crawled back in. We dropped the honey bucket off at the Lone Pine airport for the forest service boys to deal with, and we flew back to Rock Creek.

Everybody in camp was still eating breakfast when we landed, and after the helicopter had flown off again, they demanded that I explain where I'd been. They were like puppies who get nervous the first time their master leaves them alone. I had to worry about maintaining my mystique of the silent but all-knowing foreman, and I wasn't about to tell them I'd been on the honey bucket detail. I shut off the park radio so there wouldn't be any chatter from the other trail crews teasing me about my morning assignment.

"You've heard about the Coso Range?" I asked.

They all shook their heads no.

"It's south of the Owens Valley, just a few minutes from here by helicopter. You can see it from up on the crest."

"So?"

"Well, the Cosos are sacred ground to the Paiutes, you know, or at least they used to be. That's all part of the China Lake Naval Weapons Range now, and there are some very spooky things going on up there."

"Like what?"

"I'm really not at liberty to talk about it," I shrugged. "Everything that happens in the Cosos is top secret."

※

I was mostly satisfied with how things were going—the work, the camp, the crew—except for one thing: the packer. I can't recall his name now, so I'll just call him Carl. He was about fifty, retired military, alcoholic, from some desert town, maybe Barstow. The problem was that he couldn't pack. I mean he knew almost nothing about horses or mules, and couldn't have thrown a simple box hitch if he had a diagram of it in his shirt pocket. It might seem odd that a guy like that could be hired as an animal packer by the National Park Service, but anybody who has worked for the government knows things like that happen all the time. Applicants routinely exaggerate their qualifications, and because of the preference given veterans, less qualified people are often hired ahead of more qualified people. The park's personnel department probably knew Carl wasn't a packer, but as long as they followed the rules handed down to them, Carl was my problem, not theirs.

You might think it would be easy to find plenty of people for a job that required you to spend eight hours a day riding a horse through the most glorious landscape on the planet. Every small-town bar west of the Missouri has at least one guy in a cowboy shirt, sitting on a stool spitting Copenhagen drool into an empty beer can, admiring his image in the mirror, thinking he's pretty western. If you gave him a park uniform and a good wage, you'd hope he could stay sober enough hours in a day to deliver groceries by horse and mule. But you'd probably be wrong, because the country has changed. During the Civil War, almost anybody in either army could have packed a mule. Before World War II, about twenty-five percent of the US population lived on farms and knew their way around livestock well enough to avoid getting kicked. But by the 1980s, only about two percent of Americans lived on farms, which meant ninety-eight percent of Americans couldn't tell the difference between a jack and a jenny. Pickup trucks and tractors had replaced stock on most farms, so even farmers had lost the ability to work with animals. The truth is, good mule packers are hard to find, they're tenaciously independent, and if the park service doesn't treat them well, they quit.

Our plan that summer was to resupply the crew from Lone Pine, which was much closer than Three Rivers. Normally, the horse and mules would have been trucked around from the west side, but the truck and driver weren't available when we needed them. So I suggested to my supervisor, by radio, that Carl ride the stock over empty. It was about forty miles, but that was only a three-day trip, and I figured maybe he'd learn something about packing along the way. My plan was approved, but on one condition. When the helicopter came to resupply us the first week, I'd have to fly back to Ash Mountain so I could accompany Carl and our stock on the trip across the Sierra. In other words, I had to teach my gunzle how to pack.

Before flying back to Ash Mountain by helicopter, I lined out a few days' work I thought my crew could handle without me, and I scribbled out a long list of dos and don'ts, like a single parent leaving his teenage kids alone for the weekend. I worried about them, naturally, but Judy ran the crew with a firm hand, they had my backcountry radio in case of an emergency, and I figured they'd be okay without me.

After just one night at Ash Mountain, Carl and I got up early and drove to Mineral King, where our animals were waiting for us. That same day we rode over Franklin Pass, Coyote Pass, and down to the Kern River—something like twenty-five miles. It was farther than I wanted to go our first day out, but I began to realize right away that Carl was not only green, he stayed so drunk he could hardly hold onto his saddle horn. I hadn't given up on him yet, but I figured the sooner we got to Rock Creek the better.

I would have loved to quit my job as crew leader and take over as animal packer. Then I wouldn't have to supervise anybody or tend to the endless frustrations of looking out for the well-being of twenty other people in the backcountry. I could spend most of my time riding alone through the backcountry. The only problem was that I'd started thinking I could actually restore damaged meadows to something like a natural condition. In addition, I had an obligation to Steve DeBenedetti and a few other people who'd expressed confidence in me. I knew the park service, and maybe all government, was hopelessly screwed up and would probably always be that way. But they had allowed me to go about this work however I saw fit. Those meadow restoration projects were my ambition, not theirs, and I knew I'd never forgive myself if I didn't see at least some of those projects through.

As we rode across the Sierra together, I tried to teach Carl everything I knew about packing, but I can't say I made much progress. Most of the time he wasn't in any condition to learn anything. Maybe I should have put more thought into what would happen with our stock in the days to come, but as soon as Carl and I got back to Rock Creek, I refocused on my restoration projects again and didn't pay much attention to him.

The drift fences throughout Sequoia and Kings Canyon work best in narrow canyons like Rattlesnake Creek or the Kern River, where a fence can span the width of the canyon, from one talus slope to the other. Packers love that system because they can turn their horse and mules loose, and the animals can roam free all night long while eating their fill. The next morning it's easy to track the animals down, catch the horse with a nose bag of oats, and lead all the animals back to camp. But not every area in the park is suitable for drift fences, and Rock Creek is one of them. There the animals still have to be turned loose every night—that's a rule no respectable packer would violate, except in the most unusual circumstances—but in Rock Creek, sometimes trying to catch the animals the next morning can be challenging. Ill-behaved stock with a taste for freedom can travel for thirty miles or more in one night. They might return to Mineral King, head east to Cottonwood, venture up the Kern River, or god knows where. The sorry truth, which most packers would be embarrassed to admit, is that in a place without fences, packers sometimes walk more miles before the sun comes up than backpackers walk in a day.

After a few days, I asked Carl if he was having any trouble catching his stock in the morning. "None at all," he said. But I didn't believe him. I saw him lead the animals away from camp every night before turning them loose, though that wasn't unusual. If a packer can lead his stock to a good meadow for grazing, and maybe throw out a salt block to keep them interested in the place, he has a chance of finding them close by the next morning. But I was suspicious because I'd never actually seen Carl turn the stock loose. So that night, after Carl came back to camp, I followed the stock tracks a mile or so below our camp, where I found them all tied to a tautline in the trees. I immediately turned them loose, then went back to camp and told Carl what I'd done. "If you ever tie those animals up at night again, you'll be walking out of here with my boot print on your ass," I said.

Tying your stock up at night isn't good for the animals' health because they aren't getting the nutrition they need. But also it just isn't fair. Those animals do everything we ask them to do, carrying heavy loads up steep mountain trails where the air is thin and the temperature can be over a hundred degrees. All they get out of it, other than a handful of oats every morning, is the right to run free with their own kind every night.

To deny them that freedom is contemptible, and no good packer I ever knew would tolerate it.

The next day, while the rest of us were out working on the restoration project, Carl was out tracking our stock. Or at least he was pretending to. As a general rule, if you haven't caught your animals by midmorning, your chances of catching them that day go down considerably. The horse gets a whiff of freedom, takes note of the packer's incompetence, and decides it will go anywhere it feels like, taking the mules with it. If you don't catch them within twenty-four hours, you might not catch them at all. As Norm once told me, "We like to think we have these animals trained and they'll always do what we ask them to do. But the truth is, they can come untrained, too."

Once, on the first trip of the season, Norm and I rode twelve miles from Mineral King to Hockett Meadow. That night all the animals returned to Mineral King. Norm tracked them the whole way, then turned them around and rode the horse bareback to Hockett Meadow, with the mules following behind. And to teach them a lesson, he drove them hard, arriving back at our camp just after noon. "If you let them win even once," he told me, "you're screwed for the rest of the summer. As far as they're concerned, you're just some dumb hick."

I'd explained all this to Carl already, but the lesson didn't take. After one day of tracking his stock, he returned to camp just in time for dinner and admitted defeat. "I don't know where they went," he told me.

I've heard that alcoholics favor vodka because it doesn't have much odor. Maybe that's true in a smoky barroom, but in that clean mountain air, Carl's breath reeked of alcohol.

I went to my tent and put on my slick-bottomed farmer's boots, then rolled up a GI blanket and slung it over my shoulder hobo style. I filled a nose bag halfway with oats, added Skip's halter and lead rope, and flung that over my shoulder too. Then

I handed my radio to Judy and said, "Tomorrow just keep on doing what we did today. You know how it goes by now."

"When will you be back?" she asked.

"Tonight, if I find the stock. Maybe a week or so if I don't."

※

The way I learned to track stock is the way Norm taught me, which was the way his dad taught him. You start by making a circle around the area where they were last seen. That's called cutting tracks. I've heard old timers say Tommy Jefferson was the best tracker in the Owens Valley, and that search-and-rescue parties would often call him when they were stumped. Years ago an Inyo County sheriff's deputy went missing out on some ranch in the valley. After the other deputies had exhausted their tracking abilities, they called Tommy Jefferson, who began by cutting tracks at the deputy's vehicle. Tommy followed the faint boot trail to the Owens River, where he soon found the overweight and exhausted deputy bogged down to his knees in mud.

Horses and mules are easier to follow than sheriff's deputies because they make a lot more tracks. My biggest problem was that these animals had been running free for a while, and their tracks went in every direction possible. It didn't take me long, though, to see that the freshest tracks went down canyon. That was neither good nor bad, but it did eliminate the Owens Valley, Nevada, Utah, and all points east. So I started moving down Rock Creek.

When I say tracking horses and mules, what I really mean is tracking the horse. The horse, whether a gelding or mare, is the boss, and the mules will almost always go wherever the horse leads them. In this case it was Skip, the gelding Norm and I had called Man for one summer. It was easy to make out his tracks because a horse has a large, rounded hoof, while a mule has a smaller, U-shaped hoof. But it didn't really matter. Because horses are the boss, wherever the horse track went, the other tracks followed.

It was a beautiful warm night, with a nearly full moon that reflected light off the granite cliffs. In a way I was happy to be out there wandering around in the moonlight by myself, free from my other responsibilities. But I also felt like the park service had let me down, and it was a feeling I'd been having more and more lately.

I followed the stock tracks past the Rock Creek ranger station, which was unmanned that year, another casualty of the budget cuts. The thinking was that with my large crew in the area, there was no need for additional park service presence. In case of an emergency, hikers who needed help would eventually find me. So in a way, I was expected to do a ranger's job, too.

From there the trail turned north, leaving Rock Creek Canyon. The creek itself continued on to Kern River, but that route was impassable. In fact, between Golden Trout Creek to the south and Wallace Creek to the north, there's no trail that descends from the Kern Plateau to Kern River. It's a rugged, 4,000-foot plunge that only the foolhardy would attempt, and I knew Skip well enough to know he would never lead the mules that way. So I had eliminated everything to the south. Now I knew our stock would likely be somewhere between Rock Creek, the Pacific Ocean, and Canada. My guess was they'd seen enough of Carl, didn't want to risk being tied up by him another night, and had simply run away in protest. They could be retracing our route all the way back to Mineral King, or they could spend all summer grazing the stringer meadows along Wallace Creek, Tyndall Creek, and the Bighorn Plateau. In fact, the more I thought about it, wandering around all summer on the Kern Plateau sounded pretty good. Maybe I would join them.

# God's Gardener

By the time I got to Guyot Flat, I'd walked about eight miles. It must have been around ten o'clock by then, but with the moon higher in the sky, the night was even brighter, and all that white gravel practically glowed in the moonlight. And then, to my surprise, I saw the tracks leaving the trail and turning west. That eliminated Canada and points north. In fact, with their route west blocked by the steep descent into Kern Canyon, the only place the stock could be now was Guyot Flat between Whitney Creek and Mount Guyot. That was still an area of about twenty square miles, but it was a big improvement over the entire American West.

I followed the tracks for a mile or so when I faintly heard Skip's bell. Of course, it wasn't really Skip's bell at all—I'm sure he hated the damn thing. But when the halter came off at the end of every day, the bell went on, like a criminal's ankle bracelet. It was like saying, "Here's your freedom, but we both know you aren't really free." Standing right next to Skip, the bell would have been loud and deep, but what I was hearing was just a tinkle, maybe two miles away. Because much of Guyot Flat was densely wooded, with lodgepole pines filtering out much of the moonlight, the tracks were getting harder and harder to see. But with the sound of the bell, I now had a direction I could go without looking for tracks.

I followed the faint clanging of the bell west for a mile or so. It sounded like Skip was just ambling along, stopping to take in a mouthful of sedges when the opportunity arrived, then moving on again. I had no reason to think he knew I was tracking him, but every time I thought I was getting closer, he moved away. Skip turned south, and I followed him another mile. Then he turned east, and I followed him almost back to the trail again, never getting close enough to see him or the mules.

We went around in a big circle like that a couple more times. I was sure by now that Skip knew I was following him, and that he was staying just far enough ahead of me to make sure I had no chance of catching him. It was a game for him. Because Skip had spent so much of his life submitting to man's will, it was fun for him to be obstinate when he knew he could get away with it.

And then it occurred to me that maybe Skip and the mules didn't really know it was *me* following them. They might have assumed it was Carl, and there was no way they were going to surrender to that drunken fool again any time soon. It was around two in the morning by now, the moon had gone down behind the Kaweahs far to the west, the night was getting very dark, and I was tired. So I picked a spot beneath an old lodgepole where the accumulation of pine needles was sixteen inches deep. I burrowed out a spot the size of my body, lay down in it, put the nose bag of oats under my head for a pillow, and pulled my army blanket over the top of me. It was a fine bed, so blissful, and in a few seconds I fell asleep.

I don't know how long I slept in my snug little burrow, but what finally woke me was the sound of Skip's bell, which was loud and getting louder. Apparently, Skip and the mules wanted to know why I'd quit following them. They'd had a wonderful time leading me in circles, and now I'd spoiled their fun. Skip came within about fifteen feet of me, snorted once, then realized I wasn't Carl. I took the nose bag from under my head, pulled out the halter and lead rope, then shook the bag a couple of times so all the animals could hear and smell the oats.

Skip, thinking only of himself, hurried over to get a taste of the oats before the mules had a chance. Still lying on my back, I held the halter so he had to put his nose through it to get to the oats. Then I fastened the halter and let Skip mash down a few quick mouthfuls before I stood up. I led Skip to a smaller tree nearby, stroked him on the neck to let him know I wasn't mad, and tied him up.

All the other mules—Chub, Mandy, Pot, Ellis, Dory, and Troy—crowded in for their taste of oats too. I had no way to tie them up, but there was no need. They weren't going anywhere without Skip. The mules were happy to see me, though, needing reassurance and wanting me to understand they hadn't been responsible for this mutiny—it had all been Skip's fault.

"No hard feelings," I said. "Let's try to get a little rest before the sun comes up."

I slept hard until the sky began to brighten. I would have liked to sleep longer, but I was worried about my crew back at Rock Creek. What if somebody cut their foot splitting firewood, or tipped over the five-gallon bucket of hot water on the fire and scalded themselves, or sliced open their hand trying to sharpen the chainsaw? So I untied Skip, used the lead rope to fashion a hackamore—a crude bridle without a bit—hopped onto his back, and started the ten-mile ride to camp. The mules followed meekly with their heads down, dead tired after their two-day lawless spree.

What I was doing, leading a group of untied mules, is called "loose herding," and it's against the law in the parks, the idea being that uncontrolled animals are a danger to backpackers. (There are some exceptions, for example, untying a string of mules while crossing a steep pass so that if one mule trips and falls, he won't pull the others over the side with him.) I've known rangers who followed the rule book so closely, they would have written me a citation, but I was miles away from any ranger. Besides, by then I didn't really care. They could have my mules, my drunk packer, my whole crew, and we'd see what they could make of them.

We stopped when we reached Rock Creek so the stock could have their fill of cold water. As we were standing there, a fighter jet from one of the military bases out in the desert flew up Kern Canyon, maybe two miles to our west, screaming and howling like a banshee from hell. Skip and the mules had heard that sound many times before, yet it still made them skittish and they danced sideways on the banks of the creek to show their displeasure.

There are military bases all over southern California and Nevada: China Lake, Nellis, Fallon, Edwards. The military also has aerial gunnery ranges where they practice bombing or strafing artificial tanks and villages they construct out of plywood. Those fighter jets weren't supposed to fly over the national parks, but they did so anyway, with impunity. I always pictured some young pilot behind the controls of that $300 million hot rod, knowing very well he wasn't supposed to fly over park service air space but unable to resist the temptation to turn up Kern Canyon and fly just above the treetops at nearly the speed of sound, like he was playing some video game. The park service had complained to the military many times, but the base commanders always insisted it wasn't their boys doing the joy riding and if we'd show them a picture of the jets, maybe they could tell us who it really was. Once at Baxter Pass, which is supposed to be a zoological protection area, I'd watched a herd of thirteen bighorn sheep scatter wildly in all directions when a military jet flew overhead. Bighorn sheep were an endangered animal, and their numbers had declined dramatically in recent years. Because newborn lambs are very vulnerable to predators, the rams and ewes won't reproduce unless they feel their range is secure. The sound of a screaming monster swooping down out of the sky must have been horrifying to them. Though I couldn't prove it, I had a suspicion that the park service, with so many of its leaders coming from a military background, had little interest in stopping the jets from flying over park air space, and it made me angry.

After the fighter jet passed, I hopped on Skip's back again and we started up the trail toward camp, which was still about four miles away. Within half an hour, I began to smell bacon cooking. Ours was the only camp in the upper canyon at that time, so I knew the smell had to be coming from our kitchen. The sun still hadn't come up over the Sierra crest yet, and that delicious aroma was wafting toward me on the night breeze. Lisa, our cook, had already lit the fire and started the coffee, and now she was cooking bacon and pancakes for breakfast. Soon I could see wispy curls of campfire smoke above the treetops, and I could hear my workers laughing with each other as they got out of bed to start their day. As I crossed the last little creek before our camp, some of the workers heard the mules' hooves clomping over the loose stones. Through the trees, I could see them pointing excitedly toward me, while others ran closer for a better glimpse of their bossman returning triumphantly with the lost stock. One of the crewmembers raised a fist in victory, and the others cheered.

And then another military jet came screaming up out of the Kern in a long, blazing arc over Rock Creek. It was going so fast and flying so low, neither I nor the animals heard any sound at all until it was almost directly overhead, and then it was like an explosion that shook the trees and sent the mules scattering in all directions. Skip trembled in fear, then lurched sideways. I knew what he was going to do, and I couldn't blame him, really, but with just my simple hackamore I had no chance of controlling him. Skip reared back, lifting his front legs high in the air, and I was dumped into the creek.

One of the workers, a woman who had a talent with horses, grabbed Skip by the hackamore and led him into camp. The mules followed obediently. And I, tired and wet, went directly to my tent.

〰️〰️

One Sunday morning at Rock Creek, a few CCC workers

came over to my tent and asked if they could have a word with me. They looked nervous. "What's up?" I asked.

Their spokesperson was a bright young woman named Amy. "Well, yesterday was Marie's birthday, and we wanted to have a party for her," she said.

"Yeah, I heard a little hooting and hollering last night. That's what Saturday nights are for."

"The party was okay. But, see, it was her twenty-first birthday, and we planned on having a punch bowl."

"Oh, I see. You mean a *spiked* punch bowl." One of the strictest rules in the CCC was that there would be absolutely no consumption of alcohol.

"It was supposed to be just a pint of vodka for about two gallons of fruit punch," Amy said.

"Well, I can't imagine anybody getting too drunk on that. But even if they did, that's CCC business, not park service. And I couldn't care less."

Amy looked away nervously. "The problem is that we gave Carl some money when he rode out to Lone Pine last week so he'd buy the vodka for us."

I just shook my head, already imagining how that worked out.

"He brought us the bottle all right," Amy said. "But the seal was cracked. He drank all the vodka riding in and refilled the bottle with water."

So Carl had cheated them. They didn't want to let him get away with it, but they couldn't go to their supervisor because they'd broken the CCC rule by asking Carl to buy them the alcohol in the first place.

"How much money did you give him?" I asked.

"It was twelve dollars," Amy said, then added, "If Judy finds out about this, we could be fired."

"Okay," I said. "Let me take care of it."

I went looking for Carl and found him sprawled out in the shade of a foxtail pine, sipping Irish coffee. He slipped his quart bottle under a saddle blanket when he saw me coming. "Hey, Carl," I said. "You got twelve bucks?"

Carl looked up at me and saw the expression on my face. Then he reached for his wallet, took out twelve dollars, and handed it to over. "Those kids aren't supposed to be drinking alcohol," he said.

"Don't call them kids. Every single one of them does more work in a day than you do in a month. And if I hear one more word about this from anybody, I'll have you arrested for theft."

Later I sent a note out to my supervisors explaining the problems I was having with Carl, leaving out the part about the pint of vodka. I told them I was worried Carl would allow the stock to wander away again and I might not be able to find them, or even worse, he'd ride out to Lone Pine on a resupply, go on a bender, and we'd be without food for a week. My supervisors decided that from then on our crew would be resupplied by helicopter from Ash Mountain and our stock would only be used to move dirt for our meadow restoration project. So in a way, things turned out for the better.

※

Early on a Thursday morning, the day before we were supposed to be resupplied by helicopter, I got a call from the chief of maintenance, who was responsible for all trail work in Sequoia and Kings Canyon. "Hey, Steve," he said, "we've got a trail crew foreman up in Kings Canyon with a big CCC crew like yours."

"Yeah, that's Jerry Torres," I said. "How're they doing up there?"

"Well, they're doing great. They just rerouted a big section of trail out of a stringer meadow along Woods Creek and they want to try doing a restoration project like the one you're doing."

"I know that meadow scar at Woods Creek," I said. "I'm happy to hear they're going to fix it."

"The problem is Jerry's never done a restoration project before. Could you get on the radio this evening and explain to him what you've been doing?"

I didn't know Jerry Torres very well, but I knew he was a capable guy. I also knew I couldn't explain the kind of work we were doing to anybody over the radio. "I've got a better idea," I said. "Why don't I go up there to Woods Creek and show him myself?"

There was a long pause on the other end. "Uh, that's something like sixty miles by trail. Isn't that right?"

"Sure," I agreed, "by trail. But it's only fifteen minutes by air. The helicopter is coming here tomorrow morning to resupply us. What if I jumped on the return flight and we made a detour to Woods Creek?"

There was another long pause. "You know, that might work. We need to drop a few things off at Woods Creek anyway. But how would you get back to Rock Creek?"

I had an idea for that, too, but I didn't want to explain it yet. "I'll have all weekend to figure that out."

On Friday morning before breakfast, the helicopter dropped a sling load weighing several hundred pounds at our camp, then landed. My crew emptied the sling in a couple minutes, I tossed the empty sling and my backpack into the back of the helicopter, climbed in, and we took off. Twenty minutes later, I was having breakfast with Jerry Torres and his CCC crew at Woods Creek.

I spent that entire day with the Kings Canyon crew, showing them the techniques I'd learned over the past few years. Their project was much rockier than anything I'd worked on yet, and soil was scarce. But Jerry was experienced in rock work, and he knew better than I did how to control water flow using checks and water bars. I showed him how he could sculpt the terrain to make a bad scar look natural, and how he could make a little soil and vegetation go a long way. It meant a lot to me that he understood the need for that kind of work. He had a hard-working crew, and I knew they'd do a good job.

That night the cook at Jerry's camp made pizza in a Dutch oven—not easy when you're cooking for twenty hungry people—plus a fresh salad and chocolate brownies for dessert. A lot of the CCC workers on Jerry's crew knew the workers on my crew, and they wanted to hear how their friends down in Rock Creek were doing. So we stayed up late talking, and when I finally went to bed that night, I had a mail pouch full of letters and messages to take back with me.

Next morning I slipped away before daylight. The cook had already made me a couple of sandwiches for the trail, and right before I left, I downed a cup of lukewarm coffee from the pot that had been left on the fire overnight. It was a cold morning, with frost on the willows along Woods Creek, but it felt wonderful to be alone, high in the mountains, with no worries or responsibilities. As much as I appreciated riding horses and mules through the backcountry, there was nothing that could compare with the freedom of moving on foot, light and fast.

I soon left the Pacific Crest Trail and turned east toward Woods Lake, climbing rapidly, not seeing another soul out at that early hour. Norm Jefferson and I had passed this way a couple years earlier, so I was familiar with the route. I reached the top of Sawmill Pass, on the crest of the Sierra, before seven o'clock. As I was sitting there on the pass, eating one of my sandwiches, I saw something moving slowly across a talus slope far to the south. It was a tawny color, so I assumed it was a deer that had bedded down for the night in the protection of the rocks and was now heading lower for water. It was creeping toward a little patch of meadow that was still in shadow, and I could see there was another deer standing there, nibbling on the sedges. And then gradually I saw that the first animal had a tail as long and thick as my arm, and it wasn't a deer at all—it was a mountain lion, and it was stalking the deer below.

Because they are mostly nocturnal, shy of humans, and superbly gifted with a predator's stealth, mountain lions are rarely seen. But that doesn't mean they aren't there. Slim Knutsen told me that in his fifty years in the Sierra he'd only seen a mountain lion once. Although I saw their tracks quite often at muddy creek crossings, this was only the second mountain lion I'd actually seen, and I considered myself fortunate to have this sighting.

Like most people, I had a prejudice against predators that I didn't even know I had. Norm and I once came across a deer that had been disemboweled and partially eaten, with cat tracks as big as my hand all around it. I expressed sympathy for the deer, saying something like, "What a shame."

"Why's it a shame?" Norm asked.

"Well, the deer died."

"Yeah, but the lion lived."

This time I found myself silently cheering for the mountain lion, but things didn't work out in his favor. The deer caught his scent in the down-canyon breeze and easily bounded away over the rocks.

Sawmill Pass was over 11,000 feet in elevation. Owens Valley, where I needed to be, was 6,000 feet lower. So I had a long descent ahead of me. But my pack didn't weigh much and I was able to move swiftly, down the switchbacks above Sawmill Meadow, and then across the Hogsback. As soon as I could see a direct shortcut to Highway 395, I left the trail and headed over the lava beds that sprawl across that part of the Owens Valley.

It must have been nearly eleven o'clock when I finally reached the highway. The temperature was approaching ninety-five, I could feel heat radiating up off the asphalt, and cars were roaring by at seventy miles an hour. I drank the last swallow of water from my plastic bottle, then stuck my thumb out.

Only ten or twelve cars had gone by when a big old beige Lincoln Continental pulled over on the shoulder in front of me, swaying back and forth like a boat crossing its wake. The power window in front opened just a couple of inches, and a young man called out, "You a cop?"

I'd forgotten that I was wearing my uniform. "No," I said. "I work for the park service!"

"You mean like a game warden?"

"Something like that!"

He popped open the power locks and said, "Hop in back."

The windows on the Continental were darkly tinted, and it took a few seconds for my eyes to adjust to the light. As the Lincoln kicked up gravel and accelerated back onto the highway, I saw there were two men in front, and neither of them looked older than twenty-five. There was an ice chest next to me on the seat, and on the other side of that was a cute blonde wearing a neon pink bikini. She looked young, but when she smiled I saw she was missing her two front teeth and maybe she was a little older than I'd first thought. "You like to party?" she asked.

"I sure do," I replied.

She opened the ice chest and handed me a cold Coors.

"Where you headed?" the driver asked, checking me out in the rearview mirror.

"Lone Pine."

"Where's that?"

"Just down the road a ways. Maybe thirty miles."

"We're headed to Vegas for the weekend. You're welcome to come along."

"I'd like that," I said, "but I gotta work."

By the time we'd reached Lone Pine, I pretty much knew their whole situation. They were from Reno and needed to get out of town for a few days. In their line of business, that happened from time to time. There was a big heavyweight fight coming up in Las Vegas, and boxing fans were always looking for female company. If things didn't work out, they could lay around the pool and catch Wayne Newton's new show on Saturday night.

I had them drop me off in front of the forest service station in Lone Pine. As I closed the door of the Lincoln, the girl called after me, "I thought you said you was a partier!"

As it turned out, the forest service had a truck going to Cottonwood Campground in about an hour, and I was welcome to ride along. So I walked across the street to the restaurant and had a cheeseburger with fries and a chocolate shake. I also ordered a grilled tuna sandwich to go.

By three o'clock I was standing at the entrance to Cottonwood Campground, trying to decide what to do. I could spend the night at the campground and get started first thing in the morning, but I loathed forest service campgrounds, with their Lysol outhouses and chlorinated water. So I just started ambling up the trail, thinking I'd stop whenever I felt too tired to go on—maybe Horseshoe Meadow. By the time I got to Chicken Spring Lake, I still felt strong enough to keep shuffling along.

I finally reached our camp at Rock Creek around ten o'clock that night. There were still a few crewmembers hanging around the campfire, so I sneaked quietly into my tent before anybody saw me, ate my tuna sandwich, and went to bed.

Sunday morning I slept in until I smelled breakfast cooking. Then I put on a pair of shorts and flip-flops and sauntered into camp with the mail bag, handing out letters like I'd never gone anywhere but the corner mailbox.

〰︎
〰︎

Later that summer, in August, I was sound asleep in my tent when one of the crewmembers came and woke me. "Hey, bossman, there's somebody here who needs your help."

I looked at my watch and saw that it was three in the morning. I had placed my tent a hundred yards from camp just so I'd never be disturbed after hours, and now I was thinking maybe I needed to move it even further. I unzipped my tent and poked my head out. A middle-aged man with a flashlight was standing there. "Do you have a backcountry radio?" he asked. "We have a man at our camp who's going to die if we can't do something for him real soon."

I dressed as quickly as I could, grabbed my radio and EMT kit, and followed the man into the darkness.

Their camp was just a half mile downstream from ours. It was a stock party of perhaps a dozen people I'd seen come in that afternoon. A Coleman lantern hanging from a tree was blazing in the center of the camp, and beneath it was another middle-aged man reclining in an aluminum lounge chair. His face was purple.

I'd seen a few cases of pulmonary edema before, but never anything like this. Pulmonary edema is an accumulation of fluid in the lungs. It can happen to people at sea level with heart problems, but the type we see in the mountains is called high-altitude pulmonary edema. It's caused by an ascent so rapid that the body doesn't have time to adjust to the change in air pressure. It can be fatal, and the only effective remedy is immediate descent. My friend John Kraushaar came close to dying from it. John was the assistant district ranger for the backcountry of Sequoia and Kings Canyon, and he spent almost his entire summer at high elevation. I'd done many multiday backcountry snow surveys with him, and I considered him one of the strongest hikers and skiers I'd ever known. But one winter he took his family on a trip to Disneyland, spent two weeks at sea level, and then immediately left on a backcountry ski trip over Shepherd Pass. In that one day he'd gone from sea level to 12,000 feet, a greater ascent than climbing from base camp at Mount Everest to the summit. John developed pulmonary edema on his first night at high elevation and might have died had he not been able to return to lower elevation on his own. I knew if it could happen to somebody as strong as John, it could happen to anybody.

I soon learned that the purple man at Rock Creek had driven early that morning from southern California to Cottonwood Pack Station, then rode on a horse to Rock Creek, for a total elevation gain of about 10,000 feet in less than twelve hours. In ancient times it would have been impossible for a human to ascend 10,000 feet in one day, so in a sense, high-altitude pulmonary edema can be thought of as a modern illness.

The man had a rapid pulse. He was breathing with a lot of effort, I could see he wasn't getting enough air, and there was a crackling sound coming from his lungs. He wasn't able to speak, but I could tell by the look of distress in his eyes how uncomfortable he was. What worried me most was his color. If I hadn't seen it for myself, I wouldn't have believed it possible for a person with that color to still be alive. It gave me hope, though, that when I squeezed his hand, he looked me in the eye and squeezed my hand back.

I moved out of hearing range from the others and called the park dispatcher at Ash Mountain. She called an experienced paramedic, waking him up, and explained the situation to him. Then she called me back.

"We can have a flight leave here at first light," she said.

"That's good," I said. "But can anybody there give me some advice on what I might do to help this man right now?"

The dispatcher patched me through to the paramedic. "Do you have an oxygen bottle?" he asked.

"No."

"Have him sit up so he can breathe better. That's about it. I'll bring an oxygen bottle with me."

"Please come as soon as possible," I said. "This man is in a very dangerous situation."

Those were tense hours for all of us. I took the man's hand again and explained to him, "It's too dangerous for the park helicopter to try to make a landing here in the dark. The helicopter will leave Ash Mountain as soon as the pilot thinks it's safe. A very experienced paramedic, with an oxygen bottle, will be with him. I'll let you know as soon as they leave. After that it'll only take them about twenty minutes to get here."

I felt so frustrated knowing there was absolutely nothing else I could do for him.

The canyon was barely light when the helicopter landed in a clearing beside the creek, so I knew the pilot had left Ash Mountain in the dark. The paramedic immediately got the patient hooked up to an oxygen bottle, which made him feel better, though it did nothing to relieve the underlying problem. We put him in a down sleeping bag, then strapped him into the litter, which was outside the helicopter, above one skid. That must have been a terrifying experience for that poor man.

As I watched the helicopter lift off, I knew we'd done all we could. But there was one more thing that worried me. They were taking him to the hospital in Visalia, not Lone Pine. That meant they had to fly over Kaweah Gap, which was a few hundred feet higher than we were. He actually had to ascend even more before he could descend. Later that day, though, the dispatcher at Ash Mountain called to tell me the man had arrived safely at the hospital and was doing fine. I passed the good news on to his friends at their camp.

# Chapter Six: Ghost Sickness

By 1982, Jimmy Castro was no longer working for the park service. He wanted to be able to go home to his wife, Molly, and kids in Visalia every night, and that wasn't possible when we were working in remote areas of the park. But I still saw a lot of Jimmy on the weekends, when he'd invite me to family gatherings in Visalia or we had get-togethers in the park. Most of the time Jimmy seemed like the same happy-go-lucky guy, but I slowly began to see that something was troubling him. Besides his normal biting humor, there was a lot of unfocused anger and resentment. Before long I saw that he was having trouble with his marriage, too. On the weekends, he drove up to Three Rivers to drink in the bars, leaving Molly at home with their three kids. Sometimes I'd run into Jimmy on a Saturday night, he'd be drunk, and I'd say to him, "Jimmy, you're the one always lecturing me about the importance of family. Why don't you go home?"

But Jimmy's drinking only got worse. One night on a drinking binge, he stole a friend's car and drove it home, blind drunk. Soon he had a string of DUIs, each with heavy fines he couldn't afford, and eventually his driver's license was suspended. Still, he wouldn't stop driving, or drinking, until one night he got in a serious accident and was sent to jail.

Jimmy saw that if he wanted to keep his family together, he had to resolve the anger he still had about his father abandoning him when he was young, forget about the crushing poverty he'd known growing up, and make peace with the Anglo culture that often treated him like an outsider in the land where his ancestors had lived for hundreds of years. But most of all, he knew he had to stop drinking. While in jail, Jimmy joined

Alcoholics Anonymous. After he was released, he continued attending the AA meetings, and he found that by following the AA approach, not only could he control his own drinking, but he could use his understanding and insight to help other people with their drinking problems. Instead of being angry at the world all the time, he decided to try to change it. It was a huge leap of faith, and I've never seen anybody alter the direction of their life so quickly and dramatically as Jimmy Castro did.

Also while in prison, Jimmy, who was already a good cook, learned to be a baker, and when he got out he was hired by a bakery in downtown Visalia. Sometimes on my days off, I'd drive the forty miles from Three Rivers to see him. He worked late at night, but if I rapped on the front door of the bakery, he'd let me in, offer me coffee and a sweet roll, and we'd sit down together to talk.

"There was this doctor who started coming to AA a few months ago," Jimmy told me. "He said right up front that he wasn't sure about AA, that he didn't think there was any real science backing it up, and it probably wasn't going to be the right thing for him. But he said he'd give it a try. After a while, he said, 'Well, I haven't had a drink in three months now, and that's good. But I still have the *desire* to drink. What I'd like to know is, how long will it be before that desire goes away?'"

"What'd you tell him, Jimmy?"

"I told him, 'Doc, I wouldn't expect it to ever go away. You might have that desire to drink for the rest of your life.' And he was crushed. He was angry, too, and he didn't come back to AA for a while. But then one night, he slipped in after the meeting started, and when it was his turn to speak, he stood up and said, 'I'm a doctor of medicine, and some people think I'm a pretty smart guy. I've read all the literature about alcoholism now, and I'm supposed to know what I'm talking about. But it took a Mexican baker to tell me the truth!'"

I've always wished that Jimmy had been able to help more of those guys we worked with back in the seventies. Alcohol did a lot of damage to many of them, and to their families. Jimmy tried to help, but for most of them, it was already too late.

∼∼∼

In December 1982, I read in the *Los Angeles Times* about a terrible accident that took the life of Doug Wiens, the shy adventurer who'd been my tent mate in Yosemite back in the summer of 1967.

Wiens had been working as an avalanche control expert at the Helms Creek hydroelectric project in the Sierra Nevada, about eighty miles by road northeast of Fresno. He had valuable experience dealing with avalanches and was paid well by ski resorts, and sometimes by road and construction companies that had to work in areas where snow avalanches were a threat.

The project he'd been working on stored water at Courtwright Reservoir and, during hours of peak electricity use, released the water by way of pipelines and tunnels that fed into huge hydraulic turbines that generated electricity for the cities of California. The water then flowed into Wishon Reservoir, and when California had excess power, usually at night, the water was pumped back up to Courtwright. Back in 1977, a worker had been killed in a snow avalanche at that project. In September 1981, a pipeline had burst at an area called Lost Canyon, at an elevation of 8,200 feet, disrupting the delivery of water to the turbines. Pipeline workers had been busy all that winter trying to repair the damage, and the avalanche experts had been called in to make the area safe for them.

Wiens and his crew of ten had been using a rocket launcher

mounted in the back of a flatbed truck, which was considered a better method for setting off avalanches than using either dynamite or skis. The rocket launcher they were using that day was called an Avalauncher, built by Howitzer and customized just for that project. Wiens and his coworkers had been firing rounds into the mountainside when, apparently, on the last round, the breach to the artillery piece hadn't been properly closed. The gun exploded and Wiens, along with three other workers, was killed. The six other workers at the site weren't seriously injured. According to the article, Wiens died of massive trauma. He was only thirty-four.

Later I had a chance to speak with Doug's older brother, Delbert, and I told him how much I admired the young man I'd known briefly that summer of 1967. Delbert sent me a copy of a letter Doug had written to his mother following the famous circumnavigation of Denali that had been featured in *National Geographic*. I thought it was one of the finest descriptions of pure adventure I'd ever read: "It was difficult skiing as it got steeper and the snow was hard and windblown and very rough. Galen and Ned were in front when Alan fell. I waited for him to get up but quickly saw he was in pain. I tore off my skis and went to him and saw he had dislocated his shoulder. I screamed to Ned and Galen and they started back. Then I put my foot in his armpit and pulled his arm until his shoulder popped back in. Alan skied a little farther without his pack and we set up camp." And then later, after they'd finished their circumnavigation: "Ned and Galen wanted to attempt a one day ascent of McKinley.... About 6:30 we heard them return and thought they had given up because of deep snow, but Ned said Galen was hurt. They had fallen and Galen had cut his lower lip and knocked out 4 teeth and lost a lot of blood. Ned had bandaged him up with a bandanna so all I could see was a very pale Galen.... We quickly broke camp and skied down to the landing strip 8 miles away."

Delbert also sent me an article about Doug from a Mennonite magazine, *The Christian Leader*. I learned from that article that Doug had been a conscientious objector and had served two years alternative service. Like me, he'd quit several jobs that required him to work indoors. Doug was quoted in the article as saying, "I've learned certain forms of discipline, especially a high degree of cooperation. Living together for a couple weeks in a small tent is no small task. Many expeditions crack up because of it ... the way someone chews his food, blows his nose.... You have to give a lot.... You get close to someone when your life is literally in their hands."

Over the years, I've had a chance to speak with people who shared adventures with Doug Wiens and knew him well. They all say how unselfish he was, how kind and patient he was under trying circumstances, and that, in spite of being quiet and shy, how solid his character and determination were.

Call it a coincidence if you wish, but all three of Doug Wiens's partners on that famous circumnavigation of Denali died early and tragic deaths. Alan Bard was killed in a climbing accident in the Tetons; Ned Gillette was shot and killed in his tent during an attempted burglary, in the Karakoram range; and photographer Galen Rowell died in a small-plane crash near his home of Bishop, California. Taking risks is habit forming, like gambling, and the more successful you are at it, the more compulsive the habit becomes. But unlike simple games of chance that begin again with each shuffle of the cards, games of risk outdoors can end forever with one mistake.

∼∼
∼∼

The summer of 1983, I went back to Rock Creek with a crew of twenty CCC workers and finished the meadow restoration project there, as well as one at Siberian Outpost, just south of Rock Creek. It was gratifying to see that work completed, but I was mostly just going through the motions by then. I couldn't blame the park service entirely for my dissatisfaction. I had mentors who'd tried to talk me into switching to fire management, where I already had qualifications and might have had a long career with the parks. But it wasn't a career I wanted. If I couldn't work in the wilderness, I preferred doing something else. Also, I had a second career as a journalist waiting for me. *The San Diego Reader* was encouraging me to come work full time, offering me the freedom to write about anything I wished, and that offer was beginning to look attractive.

What finally forced me to make a choice, though, was the park service's decision that year to transfer all meadow restoration work to the trails division. Several people in the trails division understood the value of my restoration work, and some of them encouraged me to come work for them. It made perfectly good sense, too, because the trails division, which was much larger than resource management, could more easily manage the logistics of resupplying large crews at work in the backcountry. But I knew I was done.

Because seasonal employees are only hired for one term, then rehired the next year, all I had to do was not reapply and my career with the park service would be over.

That October, Norm invited me to go deer hunting with him in the Inyo National Forest, at a place called Summit Creek, north of Kennedy Meadows and south of Olancha Peak. Norm had hunted there with his father, cousins, and friends many times while growing up. He had a lot of memories there, and I was pleased that he would invite me to go along on a trip that had so much personal meaning for him and his family.

As the crow flies, Summit Creek was only about fifteen miles southwest from Lone Pine, but because it was on the other side of the Sierra crest, it took us a couple of hours to drive there. We took Norm's blue Chevy stakeside pickup, listening to his country-western tapes. I'd brought some of my own tapes along for the drive, too, but except for Bob Marley, whom Norm had never heard before but liked very much, he preferred his own music. We must have listened to every Hank Williams song ever recorded.

At Summit Creek, Norm's family kept a big canvas tent, a wood stove, and some other camping gear stashed in the cleft of a big rock. We hauled it all out, dusted it off, and set it up that first morning, then spent the afternoon gathering pinyon limbs for firewood. My habit in the mountains has always been to rinse off in the river or creek before going to bed, and that night was no exception. There was ice forming along the edge of Summit Creek by then, but because I'd been in the high country all summer and fall, and had become accustomed to cold water, I was still able to manage a quick rinse that night.

An hour before dawn, Norm and I crawled out of our down bags and hiked a mile or so to a saddle along the Sierra crest where the deer crossed over every morning. Their routine was to browse on the flats around Kennedy Meadows at night, then bed down during the day in the steep canyons on the east side of the crest, where they felt more secure. We took a position in the rocks and watched perhaps thirty deer file by in an hour. I finally saw a decent-sized buck, shot it, and then gutted it. But Norm wasn't satisfied with anything he saw. "These little bucks are all mama's boys, just hanging out with the does," he said. "The buck I'm looking for won't come to us, he'll be up in the rocks all by himself. Which means we'll have to go find him."

We hiked back to camp and borrowed a pack horse from some other Owens Valley hunters camped nearby. We retrieved my deer, skinned it, and covered it with a canvas tarp. After we'd washed our bloody hands in the creek, I cooked us a big breakfast of fried eggs, onions, bacon, and fresh deer liver. We loafed around in the morning sunlight awhile, then Norm stood up and said, "We better get moving. That big buck up there is getting restless, waiting around for us."

Since I wasn't hunting anymore, I led the pack horse on foot. Norm went ahead, cradling his rifle, a .270 Ruger, in his arms. We walked north a ways until we were directly beneath Olancha Peak, then we started climbing. We soon reached a height where we could see perhaps fifty miles to the south, across a mountainous landscape I knew almost nothing about. I'd always thought of the Sierra crest as ending with Mount Langley, the last 14,000-footer. It was a kind of snobbery I'd adopted after spending so many summers in the highest and finest part of the Sierra Nevada.

But now I saw that Olancha Peak was over 12,000 feet, with a granite summit well above timberline, and there were smaller peaks as far as I could see to the south. My obsession with the southern Sierra had prevented me from seeing how this range of mountains formed by the Pacific Plate slamming into the North American Plate actually continued more or less unbroken from Alaska to the tip of Baja California, and the names we give various sections of it—Cascades, Sierra Nevada, San Gabriel, San Pedro Mártir—are arbitrary remnants of a time when distance meant something different than it does now. In the golden light of fall, I was able to see the wilderness as a whole, without governmental distinctions or my own prejudice.

By early afternoon, with the sun beating down on us from the west, the day was getting warm, and Norm and I had to stop to peel off layers of our cold-weather gear. I was happy just to be there with my friend, climbing into that perfect fall sky, but Norm was in another state of mind, one much more intent. I'd hunted a lot growing up and thought I knew something about it. But after I hunted with Norm, I realized I didn't know half of what he knew. While Norm enjoyed hunting, he didn't consider it sport. Taking an animal's life was a serious matter to him, and talking with me only distracted him from doing what he needed to do. So I tried my best to keep quiet.

The higher we climbed, the more focused Norm became. As the route became steeper, and the granite rocks became monolithic blocks, I knew we wouldn't be able to go much farther leading a horse. I was about to say something to Norm about turning back, when a big buck leaped out ahead of us about a hundred feet away, moving in long, bounding strides. I would have waited until it paused, hoping for a still shot where my chances of hitting it were better. But Norm fired at that buck on the run, and he dropped it. I'd never seen a shot like that in my life, and I don't expect to ever see one like it again.

That night hunters from other camps came and went, and we all celebrated by stuffing ourselves with liver, heart, and freshly baked biscuits. One old cook insisted we eat the deer testicles, too, saying, "You young fellas are still growing. You know, you gotta eat a part to build a part!" Norm laughed so hard, tears came to his eyes.

Later, after everybody had gone, Norm asked me, "So what happens next year? You still have more work to do at Rock Creek?"

I hadn't told anybody what I'd been thinking all that summer, but I knew Norm would understand. "I don't think I'm going back," I said. "I still love the park, but I'm getting to where I can't stand the park service. I think it's time for me to move on."

Norm didn't hesitate. "I don't blame you. One of these years—maybe next year—I'll quit too."

Next morning Norm told me he wasn't ready to leave Summit Creek yet, that he wanted to hang around with the other hunters for a few more days, enjoying his favorite time of year. We'd planned for that likelihood by leaving my truck at the parking lot at Sage Flat, just over Olancha Pass, so I stuffed my ice-glazed deer quarters into my rucksack, swung that hundred-pound load onto my back, and said goodbye. Norm, who was always embarrassed by goodbyes, gave me his standard western farewell, "See you in the fall if I see you at all."

〰〰

That was October of 1983, and I never worked for the park service again. I moved to Encinitas and began writing full time for the *San Diego Reader*. But I sorely missed being in the backcountry every summer. I tried to compensate by focusing on stories that got me out into the desert wilderness of southern California, the Mojave, the Anza-Borrego, the Chocolate Mountains. I climbed El Picacho del Diablo, the highest and most remote peak in Baja, by myself. I became a scuba diver, a kayak fisherman, and an avid surfer. I learned that the ocean is the wildest place left on Earth, and that you can find the process of wilderness at work in any backyard. I took time off every fall to go on long backpacking trips alone, focusing on places I hadn't seen enough of, like the Ansel Adams Wilderness, and southern Yosemite. I made a tour through Alaska, hiking the Chilkoot trail with park service friends who'd gone there to work. I took two months off to wander through Chile, Bolivia, and Peru. I made manic loops through Utah, Colorado, Montana—the entire American West—as if I were afraid I might not see it all before I died. I stayed in touch with my winter snow survey buddies, too, so I could always spend a week or two in the Sierra backcountry every winter. But the truth was, I still longed to be up high in those beautiful meadows, in the summer, surrounded by white granite.

One Saturday evening in December 1984, as I was getting ready to go out on the town, I got a phone call from my old friend Tim Stubbs, who was still working at Sequoia. "I'm afraid I've got some really bad news for you," he said.

"All right," I replied. "Go ahead."

"A couple days ago, Norm Jefferson and Bruce Flom were killed in an auto accident near Mulegé, in Baja."

I sat down before that crushing news could knock me down. "How did it happen?" I asked.

"We don't know much about it. Apparently, they were four-wheeling in the mountains and their truck went off the road and rolled over. If we can find out more, I'll let you know."

But we never did really find out more. Another park employee who knew Norm and Bruce made a special trip down to Baja to learn what he could, but he came back saying it was pretty much a mystery. Later, I made a formal request, in Spanish, to the government of Baja California Sur, asking for more information about the accident, but no one replied.

In a few more years I found a beautiful and intelligent woman who thought maybe she could live with me. She'd heard my stories about living out of a backpack, or sometimes out of the back of a truck, and about the women who came and went as easily as moving camp. She took note of all the bad habits I'd acquired regarding laundry management, kitchen cleanliness, and a cowboy diet. She'd met some of my friends from the old days and saw that they drank too much, shaved rarely, and almost always lived alone. It was a big gamble she took, one I wouldn't have advised any woman to take. But Claudia and I have been together now for more than thirty years. She has indulged my wanderlust, tolerated my irresponsibility, corrected my selfishness, and reminded me almost every day that I'm no longer the foreman of a twenty-person crew eager to obey my every wish. When I told her I wanted to move back to Three Rivers, she said, "I think that's a great idea." But then she added, "You want me to go, too, right?"

We bought eight acres of oak woodland on the South Fork

of the Kaweah River, where I built a comfortable two-story house. We drilled a well 400 feet deep into Sierra granite and drank the purest water on Earth. We planted a small orchard and a large garden, bought an Australian Shepherd who loved to run wild, harvested our own bay leaves and pennyroyal, and put in enough firewood every summer to heat the house all winter long. All I lacked was a way to make a living.

In those days, Sequoia and Kings Canyon National Parks existed in the shadow of Yosemite National Park, which, though smaller, received nearly three times as many visitors. To casual tourists who might have only a day or two to see the parks from their automobile, Sequoia and Kings Canyon doesn't appear to be as photogenic as its more glamorous sister. Yosemite's waterfalls and lush meadows can be captured in a snapshot with no more effort than rolling down the car window, and because Highway 41 slices through the heart of Yosemite's backcountry, even the laziest tourist can witness something like the beauty of the wilderness without taking a single step. Those who know both parks well understand that Sequoia and Kings Canyon has a larger and more rugged backcountry, far more sequoia groves, and a more interesting and diverse foothill belt than Yosemite. But it's hard to appreciate such a large and varied park like Sequoia and Kings Canyon without getting out of your car and taking the time to walk around. No photographs come close to doing the wilderness justice, and even the famous sequoia groves, which aren't hard to get to, are notorious for being almost impossible to photograph. Their awe-inspiring presence has to be witnessed in person and at close range.

The problem was that so many visitors didn't even know where to start. In those days, Sequoia and Kings Canyon didn't have a guidebook describing day hikes suitable for people who knew nothing about the parks. My work throughout the parks had provided me with intimate knowledge of every corner of them, my experience as a journalist had given me the ability to write about them, and now that I had a young family of my own, I found it interesting and rewarding to try to see the parks from the point of view of first-time visitors with children.

So I set out to write a guidebook that described fifty day hikes in Sequoia. Though I'd already traveled those trails many times in a park uniform, to write about them I had to hike each of them again. In addition, I had to draw a simple but accurate map for each trail. It was a big task, taking most of year, but one I enjoyed very much. I spent almost an entire autumn hiking every trail out of Mineral King Valley, which at that time of year is heartbreakingly beautiful, with its aspens turning yellow and red in the golden light. The fall is a uniquely nostalgic time, and sometimes it felt odd, or even lonely, to be hiking those trails without my old cohorts. But I had a job to do, even if I had to do it on my own.

After I'd finished writing *Day Hiking Sequoia*, my old friend Jerry Schad, a UC Berkeley graduate who taught physics at Grossmont College, wrote for the *San Diego Reader*, and had published hiking guidebooks himself, convinced me that the desktop computer had made it possible for anybody to publish a book on their own. Furthermore, after Jerry explained the economics and price structure of book publishing to me, I realized that by publishing the book myself, I could easily earn six or seven times more than I would if I handed it over to an established publisher. So, with help from Claudia, who was a computer programmer and understood the new technology far better than I did, I published the book myself.

At first I was afraid my guidebook would meet resistance by the park management, which, after all, had its own staff of interpreters whose job it was to explain the park to visitors. But the opposite turned out to be true. John Palmer, the retired chief naturalist at Sequoia who'd become head of the non-profit Sequoia Natural History Association, welcomed my book into the park's visitor centers, where it sold very well.

I immediately went to work writing a companion guidebook, *Day Hiking Kings Canyon*, and it also sold well.

I was surprised, and gratified, by how many people who read my guidebooks took the time to write me a letter thanking me or asking for more information about their favorite areas. A family with three young children sent me a letter with crayon drawings they'd made while in Giant Forest. I received several letters in garbled English written by European visitors thanking me for introducing them to the parks. And an older woman told me she hadn't known what she was going to do in her retirement until she read my guidebooks; now her goal was to hike every one of the trails I described. Even local people who were fairly familiar with the parks told me they'd had no idea some of the trails were there until I wrote about them.

Now every summer, rather than backpacking with my old buddies, I took my two young boys on fifty-mile loops through the backcountry, traveling just short distances each day, and stopping to fish along the way. I became the mule on those trips, carrying almost all our gear to remind myself not to move too fast for my young companions. At the end of each day, when we arrived in camp, I'd collapse in exhaustion, while my boys would toss off their light daypacks and wrestle in the dirt until dark. Those were the most enjoyable backcountry trips I ever made in my life. But as often as I could, mostly in the fall when my boys were back in school, I still slipped away to get lost in the wilderness by myself.

Three or four times every winter, I'd ski alone into Mineral King Valley. The road was closed to vehicle traffic after the snow fell, but anybody could ski in from the campground at Atwell Mill. I liked to camp on the valley floor, beside the creek, then climb the peaks and ridges early the next morning before the snow became too soft. Unlike most of the southern Sierra, which consists of hard granite, Mineral King is made of metamorphic rock, which fractures and erodes much more easily. Rather than presenting steep rock faces, the bowls above Mineral King Valley lie at the angle of repose, which for fractured rock is about forty degrees. That makes for challenging but not dangerous backcountry skiing. What the Disney Corporation had tried to turn into the largest ski resort in California, I had entirely to myself on a sunny winter day.

※

In the fall of 1989, while hiking near the Sherman Tree in Sequoia, I happened to run into Truman James, the Native American tree climber I'd always admired so much for his work ethic on our hazardous tree crew. He was still working on the crew, and I caught him at the end of the day coiling his climbing rope and storing it in the crew's boom truck. Truman had done hard physical labor all his life, and though he never complained about it, I could see the effect on his body. His shoulders were stooped like those of a man much older, and he constantly twisted his back and neck as if trying to work out a painful kink. But seeing Truman standing there in that golden fall light brought back a flood of memories about the times we'd spent working together. I told him how much I missed seeing him, and Truman suggested we meet after work at the Gateway Inn, just below the park entrance, to have a drink.

We sat at the bar and recalled with fondness that wonderful day at Cedar Grove when we finished our work in the first snowfall of the year, went back to the fire dorm wet and exhausted, and ate the biggest breakfast of our lives. In those days Truman had been trapped in an unhappy marriage, but he finally divorced, then remarried, and was now living with his new wife in a mobile home down in the foothills town of Lemon Cove. He seemed happy—maybe as happy as I'd ever seen him. Before we went our separate ways, I asked Truman how much longer he had to work before retirement. "Ten years," he said, "but I don't know if my body will last that long. I can't hold on to a climbing rope the way I used to."

As we parted, I shook Truman's hand and couldn't help but notice how gnarled and bony his grip had become.

In April of 1990, when Truman was fifty, he was working with the forestry crew at Sentinel Campground in Cedar Grove, where the park had a bad problem with dwarf mistletoe in pine trees. If the trees were left untreated, they would weaken, become deformed, and eventually die. The best treatment, crude as it might seem, was to climb each infested tree to the top, set a climbing rope, and descend to the bottom, cutting out damaged or infested limbs as you went.

Near the end of the day, just before quitting time, Truman fell at least 150 feet from a pine tree he'd been working in. Amazingly, the fall didn't kill him instantly, but it did burst his aorta. Truman tried to stand, but his fellow workers held him down. His face turned bright red, and he coughed up blood. A helicopter was summoned to fly him to the hospital in Fresno, about seventy miles away, but it was already too late.

According to the park service, an accident like that should never have happened because a climber is supposed to be tied in at all times, either by his climbing rope or by his flipline. But anyone who's ever climbed trees knows that's impractical. Tree workers free-climb through branches all the time simply because to do otherwise would require far too much time and energy. Why Truman fell that day, I don't know, and I doubt anybody else knows, either, regardless of what the official investigation says. It might have been due to some equipment malfunction, but more likely it was due to the fatigue a fifty-year-old man with arthritic hands felt at the end of a very difficult day. In the park service, law enforcement and firefighting personnel are granted early retirement because their jobs are considered dangerous. But are their jobs really more dangerous than climbing and topping 150-foot trees with a chainsaw? Although I don't hold any single person responsible for Truman's death, I do blame the government for the insensitivity with which it treats its blue-collar workers, and I despise the maddening ease with which it can absolve itself of responsibility.

One July morning in 1996, I read in the news that backcountry ranger Randy Morgenson, who'd so resented my crew's presence at McClure Meadow nearly twenty-five years earlier, had disappeared from his backcountry station at Bench Lake. It wasn't unusual for backcountry personnel to fail to make radio check with headquarters at Ash Mountain when their radio batteries went dead, but after a few days without hearing from Morgenson, the park organized a search that included more than sixty people, five helicopters, dog teams, and even a psychic. Because Morgenson was having marital problems, had recently broken off a relationship with a female backcountry ranger, and was known by his closest friends to be depressed, there was speculation that Morgenson might have taken his own life, or perhaps had left the backcountry in secret to begin a new life elsewhere. After two weeks of searching, not a trace of him was found.

A few weeks after the search had been called off, I was sitting on my front porch in Three Rivers one morning when a green park service pickup truck pulled into my driveway. Two rangers in uniform got out, said they knew I'd worked with Randy Morgenson in the backcountry, and wondered if I'd spend a few minutes telling them what I knew about him. I explained that he and I had never been close friends, and I didn't really know him well. "That's okay," one of the rangers said. "We've already talked to his friends. We'd appreciate anything you could tell us about him."

It was an uncomfortable situation for me. Although I still spent a lot of time hiking in the park with my family, I avoided most park rangers, who I thought had become too rigid and authoritarian. Because of the way park rangers hopped from one park to another, I thought their knowledge of Sequoia was superficial, or worse. On one hand I didn't really trust these guys, but on the other hand I wanted to do anything I could to help. "Randy Morgenson was a complicated guy," I said. "He loved the backcountry of Sequoia and Kings Canyon and had probably seen more of it than anybody ever has. But he disliked dealing with the public, and I think he was frustrated and unhappy with his job."

One of the rangers asked me if I'd ever had problems with the park's backcountry radio system during the years I'd worked there. Another backcountry ranger, they said, had expressed frustration with the radio system, implying that if it had worked better, Morgenson would have been found.

"In the fourteen years I worked in the backcountry, I never had a radio fail me," I said. "There were certainly dead spots, where the repeaters couldn't reach, but that would be true in any mountainous region. I could always make radio contact when I wanted to. Sometimes I *didn't* want to, and I assume Morgenson was the same."

And finally one of the rangers asked me if I thought it was possible that Morgenson had faked his disappearance.

"I suppose it's possible," I said, "but I really have no idea."

〰️〰️

In September 1997, I'd just completed a solo backpacking

trip to Little Five Lakes. As I was driving away from the parking lot at Mineral King, I noticed a park employee tossing fifty-pound trash bags into the back of his service vehicle like they were lunch sacks. The guy had shoulders like a bear, legs like oak stumps, and a familiar sweat line running down his spine. I had the feeling I knew this person, but I had to watch him for a few moments more before I could place him. When he finally turned around, I called out to him, "Frank Walter, you crazy sonofabitch!"

Frank ducked like a criminal on the run. If he'd had a gun, I think he might have shot me. He gasped for air, clutched his chest, and said, "Sorensen, don't ever do that again!"

I teased Frank about being a trash collector, until I saw that he didn't think it was funny. No tree faller with his experience should ever have to bag trash. "They wouldn't give me my old job back," he shrugged. "But I guess it don't really matter. I just needed to get back in the mountains again."

Frank had lost fifty pounds, which put him at about 250. He looked like he could have been a linebacker on any football team. But there was something that wasn't right about him. His eyes lacked their old devilish sparkle. He wasn't the carefree young man who'd sat at the bar of the Whitehorse Inn sipping Skip-and-Go-Nakeds all night long. I knew he'd been badly hurt when his wife Karen left him, but that had been years ago. He should have gotten over it by now.

I took a scrap of paper from my truck and drew Frank a map to my house on the South Fork. "Stop by," I said. "Come meet my wife and kids. We'll have a beer and talk about climbing trees, just like the old days."

Over the next couple of years, Frank would stop by my place at all times of the day or night, but mostly late at night, always drunk, highly emotional, sometimes crying. But my wife and kids loved him. They thought Frank was like a grizzly bear with a growl two octaves higher than it should have been.

He'd stay for dinner, or breakfast, or whatever, but what he really wanted was to reminisce with me about those days when we'd worked together on the hazardous tree crew, before Karen, before he had screwed things up. He would lie on my couch where he had a view out the window of snow-capped Case Mountain. I'd put an oak log in the wood stove, and we'd talk as long as he wanted to talk, until he would surrender to sorrow and fatigue. But I never figured out what I might say that would ease his pain.

Late one afternoon in December, Frank stopped by my house on the South Fork. There had been heavy snowfall in the mountains, followed by a warm rain, and all the rivers were flooded. Just before dark, Frank and I walked over to the bridge near my house to watch the mad torrent of silty water pass below. We could hear granite boulders colliding against each other, and in the fading light we could sometimes see sparks under water. Walking back to the house, through the full-length windows, we could see Claudia cooking dinner, and see our boys on the floor in front of the wood stove doing their homework.

"Sorensen," Frank said sadly, "You've always been a lucky guy."

For some people, even common failures like divorce can become life-crushing experiences. And for some like Frank, the fear of failure can become its greatest cause.

Frank quit the park service again, and I didn't hear from him for a while. I called Jimmy Castro, who was still living in Visalia and had been sober for several years by then, to ask if he knew anything about Frank.

"Oh, yeah, I get calls from Frank in the middle of the

night," Jimmy said. "He's living with his grandma up in Springville, and besides the drinking, he's into cocaine and amphetamines now. Frank's in a really bad way. I've gone up there a couple of times to talk to him, but until he decides to quit using drugs and alcohol, I don't think there's much we can do for him."

Not long after that, I heard the terribly sad news that Frank had died. I never saw an obituary, but friends told me he'd been found lying on the steps of a storefront in a Seattle suburb. The cause of death was a drug overdose.

≈≈≈

In March of 1998, I was finishing a weeklong backcountry snow survey in the southern Sierra Nevada with my friend Nick Hartzell. We'd started at Cottonwood Meadow, skied to Tunnel Meadow, Big Whitney Meadow, Rock Creek, Crabtree Meadow, and Tyndall Creek. That was considered the greatest prize in California snow surveying because it followed the route of the Kern Plateau, just below the great 14,000 foot peaks of the southern Sierra. Each night we stayed at one of the small but cozy cabins built and stocked by the California Department of Water and Power.

Nick had grown up in Three Rivers, where his father had been the assistant chief ranger at Sequoia and Kings Canyon National Parks. After high school Nick went to work at Kirkwood ski resort, where his job was to ski across the ridges in the early morning to trigger avalanches before the paying customers arrived. Sometimes his crew could start an avalanche with nothing but their skis and poles, but sometimes they were given sticks of dynamite to make the job easier. What could possibly be more fun for a young man than setting off on skis in the morning with a few of your buddies and a pack full of dynamite? Later, Nick went to the University of California,

Berkeley, where he took a degree in history. He became an excellent climber, and for several years he worked on Denali (the highest peak in North America) as a rescue ranger. Together with his old buddy Dave Beck, Nick pioneered the now famous Sierra High Route, a weeklong trans-Sierra ski route from Symmes Creek on the east side of the Sierra to Wolverton Corrals on the west side. A few years earlier, I'd had the pleasure of following that route with Nick.

On the final day of our snow survey, we planned on crossing the crest by way of Shepherd Pass and continuing down to the trailhead at Symmes Creek, where a forest service truck was waiting for us. By that route, we knew we had to down climb Shepherd Pass, which is no problem in the summer but in winter is steep and icy. And we'd have to do it carrying our packs and skis—an awkward load—wearing clumsy ski boots. We figured we could manage it, but we weren't looking forward to it.

Then Nick said, "I have a better idea."

Nick had flawless judgment in the mountains, and I was willing to try whatever he had in mind. Rather than continue on to Shepherd Pass, Nick suggested we climb an unnamed 13,100-foot peak just south of the pass, which we did. Below us, to the east, was an avalanche chute about 300 yards wide that funneled with almost perfect symmetry to 30 feet wide at the bottom. "I tried this a few years ago," Nick said, "but it was all frozen crud, like skiing over rocks. What do you think?"

The chute looked steep, but the avalanche danger at that time was minimal, and it was still early enough in the day that the surface of the snow was firm but not icy. Still, I preferred to defer to Nick. "I dunno, what do you think?"

"Well, the worst thing that could happen is one of us would break a leg and we'd be stranded on the side of a thirteen thousand foot peak in winter," Nick said. "I guess I'm ready if you are."

The technology of backcountry skiing had changed dramatically in the previous few years. In the seventies, we'd used narrow Nordic skis that were almost straight, with wooden edges; they were equipped with lightweight but rather flimsy three-pin bindings. Instead of real ski boots, we had thin shoes that were cold and offered almost no ankle support. That kind of setup was the sort of thing Norwegian hunters might have used a thousand years ago. We couldn't really carve a fluid turn on those skis, relying instead on crude step turns, or at best a jerky stem christie. Back in those days, on steep terrain we were forced to make long traverses, come to a complete stop, lift one ski out of the track, twist it around 180 degrees, then begin another long traverse—a so-called kick turn. It had been safe and effective, but dull. Now, though, all that had changed. We had lightweight composite skis with wooden cores, plastic bottoms, and metal edges; the skis had deep side cuts that allowed us to carve smooth, precise turns; we had stiff but lightweight boots that gave us the support we needed to drive those skis; and we had strong cable bindings with a free heel that gave us the flexibility to move in unpacked conditions. The new setups weighed a bit more, but they were worth it. With practice we had become good Telemark skiers, which gave us complete control in even the most challenging terrain. Backcountry skiing had become like surfing now, an exercise in artistry and freedom, and it was so much fun.

Nick and I bailed off that peak in long traverses, but rather than pause at the end, we planted our downhill poles, bent our knees just a bit, then came up and around in one smooth motion. We were airborne for eight or ten feet, but when we made contact again, we were immediately in control. It felt like flying, and in just a few thrilling minutes we had descended more than 4,000 vertical feet. When we kicked off our skis at the bottom of the avalanche chute, near Mahogany Flat, we were already in the arid zone, surrounded by cacti and mountain mahogany.

The sad part was that now there was nothing left but to load our skis on our packs and trudge down the trail like mere backpackers.

When we got close enough to the trailhead to see the cars in the parking lot, we noticed a lone figure plodding slowly up the trail toward us. He was carrying skis on his pack, had his head down, and appeared to be limping. We got a little bit closer and saw that it was Scott Erickson, the fire guard I'd burned shake piles with at Redwood Mountain back in 1972. I hadn't seen Scott in twenty-five years, and Nick hadn't, either. We'd heard that Scott had gone to work at the new Boise Interagency Fire Center and had used his computer programming and organizational skills to revamp the way the government responded to wildfires. We knew Scott had become a superstar in the park service. But we had no idea what he'd been up to lately.

After a lot of back slapping and hearty handshakes, Nick asked, "What are you doing here?"

"Well," Scott replied, "I'm doing the High Route."

"But you're already limping," I pointed out. "And you have fifty miles ahead of you!"

"Yeah," Scott shrugged, apparently not concerned. "I blew out my Achilles tendon jogging a few months ago. It's getting better, or at least I think it is. I've been camped here a week now, and this is the farthest I've gotten so far. But at least I'm making progress. I guess I can go back to the trailhead now."

Scott's explanation of course made no sense at all. Though he was obviously happy to see us, he didn't look well and his thinking seemed muddled.

We all drove into the little town of Independence, bought a twelve-pack of beer, then went to the county park, sat on a picnic bench under the cottonwood trees, and talked.

Since we had seen him last, Scott explained, he'd gotten married, had a child, and gotten divorced. He'd quit the park service, then asked to be reinstated. His request had been granted, but as a form of penance, his new assignment was in Los Angeles, not exactly the land of dreams for park service employees. But at least his job there was an interesting one. The park had been expanding the Santa Monica National Recreation Area, a sprawling patchwork of land mostly in LA County, and the expansion required complex negotiations between the federal government, the State of California, and several private landowners who were interested in selling or donating their land to the park service. Scott's job, as assistant to the park superintendent, was to act as a liaison, or ambassador, a position for which he was highly qualified. The only problem was that he hated it.

"I spend all my time driving around on the freeways with a cell phone stuck in my ear, talking to rich assholes who want to know what kind of tax credits they can get for donating a parcel of land," he said. "Every day I miss my son so badly. Honestly, I don't know how much longer I can go on like this. I saved up all my vacation time for this ski trip, and now I can't even get four hundred yards out of the parking lot."

As Nick and I drove back to Lone Pine on Highway 395, the sun had already set below the Sierra crest, and gloomy shadows were creeping across the Owens Valley. Gazing up at the mountains, we could see the avalanche chute we'd skied down, more than 8,000 feet above us now. In the flat light, it looked impossibly steep, yet there were our tracks crisscrossing each other, carving our signatures down a route we wouldn't have considered skiing just a few years earlier. Nick and I talked about Scott, trying to understand what had happened to him.

Among my old park service friends, he'd been one of the smartest and hardest working, and his future seemed the brightest. Yet he was profoundly unhappy with his government career and frustrated to the point of madness by the circumstances in which he found himself. But that alone couldn't explain the person we met and talked with earlier that day. Scott seemed like somebody we didn't know.

It was only a few months later that I heard Scott was in a hospital in LA with terminal brain cancer. Of course he'd been suffering from his illness when we'd seen him at Symmes Creek—that explained his odd behavior. Just a few weeks later, I heard that Scott Erickson had died.

In July of 2001, five years after Randy Morgenson disappeared, his remains were found in a creek northeast of Window Peak by members of a CCC crew hiking on their day off. What they found were a boot with bones still inside, a pack, a backcountry radio, and a uniform shirt with Morgenson's name tag on it. It was an area that had been searched several times in 1996, but it was thought that perhaps the remains hadn't been seen at that time due to deep snow and high water levels in the creek. It was speculated that Morgenson had drowned while attempting to cross the creek, perhaps on a snow bridge.

For me (and others) the discovery of Morgenson's remains didn't explain anything—in fact, it just raised more questions. With his years of backcountry skiing experience, Morgenson knew that snow bridges are treacherous even in the middle of winter, when the snow is frozen solid. He wouldn't have dared cross a snow bridge in summer, when the snow is rotten, unless he was intentionally inviting disaster. If he'd been trying to wade across the creek, he certainly knew as well as anybody that it's almost impossible to stay upright in a fast-moving current. At the very least, he would have unfastened the waistband of his pack, which allows a hiker to free himself from the pack if he goes down in the current. But the park service said his waistband had been found fastened.

Part of the joy of traveling in the wilderness is coping with risk. So many times I've been on a climb, or a backcountry ski trip, when the success or failure of the entire trip came down to one dangerous move. To decline the risk meant failure, or at least disappointment and a frustrating retreat. But to accept the risk, and survive, could bring a kind of elation. And that's how risk taking becomes addicting.

I don't know what Morgenson's state of mind was the summer he disappeared, but by all accounts it wasn't good. I can't believe he was playing with danger in a joyful mood, and I can't believe a ranger with his experience made a mistake so foolish that it cost him his life. It's useless to speculate now, I suppose, but I suspect that Randy Morgenson went into the wilderness that July day not wanting to come back.

≈≈

For several years, my close friend Tim Stubbs and I had parallel paths in the park service. We both became tree fallers, learned to climb and top trees from Charlie Castro, fought wildfires, worked in the backcountry, and drank and caroused in the bars of Three Rivers.

Tim Stubbs had grown up in Los Angeles, where his father had been a child actor. At a young age, Stubbs developed a love of plants, and a marvelous green thumb, from his mother. Stubbs was introduced to Sequoia when he attended Boy Scout camp at Wolverton. After high school, he began working toward a degree in botany at San Diego State and moved to the little beach town of Encinitas, where he became a good surfer. During the summer months, to help pay for college, Stubbs began working seasonally for Sequoia and Kings Canyon National Parks, which is where I met him. Later, when I moved to Encinitas to begin working for the *San Diego Reader*, Tim let me crash on his sofa until I found a place of my own, and he introduced me to the woman who would later become my wife. When I began experimenting with meadow restoration projects in the backcountry, Stubbs helped me identify each of the plants I was working with and understand the role they played in meadow ecology, and he loyally defended my projects in park service meetings when I was in the backcountry and couldn't defend myself.

Our paths diverged when I chose to leave the park service and begin working full time as a writer. Almost simultaneously, Tim took a full-time job in the resource management division at Sequoia. At first I thought it was a good move for Tim to take a permanent position with the park service. He had job security, health and retirement benefits, a small house with cheap rent at Ash Mountain, plus, with his permanent status, he had hold of the bottom rung of a career ladder he could climb as high as he wanted. I was happy for Tim, he seemed happy too, and I sometimes wondered if maybe I was making a mistake by not following his example and taking a permanent job with the parks. Our diverging paths set up a comparative experiment in career choices that took nearly thirty years to play out.

Before long, Stubbs's park service career veered toward firefighting, and he became a fire behavior specialist. His most common task on wildfires was aerial reconnaissance—he was the eye in the sky on large wildfires, the person who sees the big picture from a plane or helicopter in a way those working on the ground can't. His radio handle became AirBear, and he was known to firefighters all over the West as someone whose primary concern was the safety of those working on the ground, an approach that sometimes got him into trouble with his supervisors. He took several jobs at various parks, but it didn't really matter much where his home base was because during fire season he traveled almost constantly. Whenever his travels led him back to Three Rivers, which was often, he'd stop by my house, lie on the couch looking out the window at Case Mountain, like so many of my old park friends, and unload his burden of woe. I tried not to offer advice, since I had none, but I always tried to listen.

Over the years, Stubbs married, started a family, divorced, moved and moved again, began drinking too much, put on weight, and lost the remarkable fitness and strength he'd had in his youth. The biggest change I noticed, however, was that he was becoming increasingly bitter, and for that he always blamed the park service.

"One of my supervisors, who's thirty years older than me, insists on calling me sport," he'd fume. "Now, how in the *hell* am I supposed to have a professional relationship with somebody who thinks he can call me sport?"

On one wildfire, Stubbs got into a huge argument with the fire boss when a crew of hotshots was sent to the top of a ridge to try to cut off a fire that was out of control and running rapidly uphill. "That's not what we were taught in fire school!" he told the fire boss. "You never put workers in front of a heading fire! That's how firefighters get killed!" Stubbs lost that argument and was forced to leave the fire in shame.

Another time Stubbs told me he got into a shouting match with a fire boss in Texas who'd called in heavy equipment from a private contractor when the equipment wasn't really needed.

"That guy had a sweetheart deal with the contractors and got a kickback every time he used their equipment," he said. "It was totally corrupt, and everybody knew it, but nobody had the guts to stop it!"

As the years passed, I didn't see Stubbs quite as often, but he emailed me from time to time, mostly wanting to reminisce about the old days, trying to reconnect emotionally, like many others, with a time when we still had our youth to squander. He became fire management officer at Guadalupe Mountains National Park in Texas, a nice promotion and a job I figured he could ride for another ten years or so to retirement. Then one day Stubbs sent me an email saying he'd accepted early retirement from the park service and moved to Carlsbad, New Mexico. He didn't sound well, said he urgently needed to talk to me, and I decided I'd better drive out to New Mexico to see what was going on with my old friend.

I found Stubbs living alone in a semi-rural neighborhood of Carlsbad, in a run-down house on a large lot. Besides a dog and several cats, he had a pig, a few goats, a flock of geese, chickens, and ducks, all running free in the backyard. Stubbs had let his hair and beard grow long and scraggly, like a backwoods hillbilly, and he smelled like he hadn't bathed in days. He spent nearly all his time sitting in an easy chair in the living room, with the curtains drawn, watching CNBC on the television with the volume turned up loud. Like many other workers who ran chainsaws when they were young, he was more than half deaf.

"I lost a bunch of my retirement money in the stock market," he said. "That's why I watch these guys on CNBC all day, hoping they'll tell me how to get it back. Problem is, they're the same assholes who stole it from me."

Even though it was midmorning when I arrived, Stubbs offered me a can of beer, tossed his empty in a plastic garbage can in the corner, and popped a fresh one himself. He drank all day long, somehow managing, like a lot of alcoholics, to never get sloppy drunk.

"What I really need to tell you," he said, bellowing over the TV, "is that I didn't leave the park service willingly. Those knuckleheads convinced me I couldn't afford *not* to take early retirement, that I'd lose money if I didn't, and I believed them. But I realize now they forced me out. So what the hell am I supposed to do now with the rest of my life?"

"Maybe go fishing?" I suggested. "You always liked growing stuff. Maybe you could start a pot farm."

Stubbs ignored my advice and launched into a long tirade about everybody and everything he hated in the world, but mostly about the park service, beginning in 1969 and continuing through the present. His face turned red, his eyes bulged out, and the veins in his neck throbbed. When he finished his tirade, he started over again, as if I hadn't heard it the first time. I knew Stubbs didn't expect me to provide him with answers—he shouted over anything I tried to add to the conversation—but he desperately needed me to listen. I was the only person left who had seen the entire arc of his park career and understood the risks and advantages he'd assumed from the start. So I sat there for something like eight hours, sharing his anger and frustration.

That evening we drove into town to have dinner at Stubbs's favorite bar, a sad little joint on the main drag, next to a 99 Cent store. Dinner turned out to be a bowl of mixed nuts and a microwaved hot dog, a routine Stubbs said he followed almost every night.

Early the next morning, I told Stubbs I had to be moving on. Claudia and I had two sons heading off to college, and I wanted to be home when they left. The sun hadn't come up yet, but Stubbs had already put away a couple of beers. "Let's go backpacking like the old days," he said. "We'll get Mike Palmer and Jimmy Castro together. Maybe make a big loop through Rattlesnake Creek and the Kern."

"I'm all for that," I said. I left him a card with my cell phone number and said, "If you want, come to Three Rivers and stay with us awhile." Stubbs always loved Three Rivers and still had friends there, and I thought it would be good for him to get in touch with them again.

"I'd like that," he said.

In December I got a call from Tim ex-wife, Barbara. Tim had died of a heart attack, and she was calling his old friends and coworkers to let them know. She'd found my card sitting on the lamp stand next to his easy chair.

♒

After the summer of 1968, when Doug Tompkins had given me my first rock-climbing lessons in Yosemite Valley, he took the money he'd made selling The North Face and funded a legendary road trip to South America with three of his climbing and skiing buddies: Yosemite climber Yvon Chouinard, who would go on to found the outdoor clothing company Patagonia; renowned British climber Chris Jones; and former Olympic skier Dick Dorworth, who held the world record for speed skiing. Filmmaker Lito Tejada-Flores also went along to document the trip. Tompkins had told me that summer of 1968 that he was planning a trip to South America, but he seemed reluctant to talk about it, perhaps because he was worried that people might consider it a foolish and irresponsible adventure. I recall him explaining the trip to me as if it were something he had to do, even though it made no sense. It was the feeling of trepidation anybody has before setting out on a risky adventure. But Tompkins saw that most people avoided risk so effectively that their lives became dull and almost meaningless. For him and others like him, adventure was an essential, though sometimes illogical, part of mental health.

What Tompkins and his young band of misfits did was drive a battered Ford Econoline van 8,000 miles from California to southern Chile, where they climbed Mount Fitz Roy, considered one of the most dangerous mountains in the world because of its atrociously bad weather and remote location. (The peak had been climbed first by the great French alpinist Lionel Terray, who had been on the French expedition to Annapurna in 1950.) Tompkins and his party put in a new route on Mount Fitz Roy, which they called the California Route, and they made a film of their entire adventure, *Mountain of Storms*, which has become a classic in the genre of low-budget, slightly goofy adventure films. For Tompkins the experience began a lifelong love affair with southern Chile and the Patagonia region. For Yvon Chouinard, the image of Mount Fitz Roy became Patagonia's corporate logo.

After returning to California, Tompkins's more practical nature prevailed, at least for a while. He and his wife, Susie, started a clothing and manufacturing company, Esprit, that catered to the fashion-minded consumer. When I first read about that, I had a hard time imagining Tompkins working in the fashion industry. In 1968 he'd already been an ardent and well-informed environmentalist, the first I had ever known, and I couldn't see him fussing over a new line of summer dresses or making trips to Paris to select fabric for next year's fall season. Yet I knew Tompkins saw things from a different perspective than most of us; he'd succeeded at everything he'd ever tried (except high school) and he needed an outlet for all that talent and energy. I suspected he had a plan—probably a good one—I just couldn't see what it might be.

Esprit soon became highly successful, thanks to Susie's fashion sense and Tompkins's gift for business. In a few years, Esprit was doing sales of $100 million per year and would eventually go on to do even more. But in spite of that phenomenal success, which might have jaded anybody else, Tompkins was still the idealistic person I'd known back in Yosemite. I laughed out loud when I read in the newspaper one day that he'd advised the customers of Esprit to "buy only what you need," and I figured it was only a matter of time before he left the fashion world behind. For all his social skills and business savvy, Tompkins belonged outdoors. He hated the corporate world, his dissatisfaction put a strain on his marriage, and eventually something had to give. Tompkins sold his shares of Esprit for many millions of dollars, he and Susie divorced, and once again he had to figure out what to do with himself. Later he said, almost guiltily, "I was selling useless stuff to people who didn't need it."

Tompkins went back to southern Chile, where he used his money to begin buying large parcels of land in Patagonia, a wild and fantastically beautiful region that had been under intense pressure from logging companies and hydroelectric developers. Over time, working with local environmentalists and wealthy donors, he established Conservación Patagónica, which eventually put into protection more than two million acres— an area larger than Yosemite, Sequoia, Kings Canyon, and Lassen National Parks combined. And he had plans to acquire up to eight million acres more. Although the purchased land was being held in trust, his ultimate goal was to turn the protected land over to the Chilean government. The man I'd known as the manager of the hot-dog stand at Camp Curry created one of the greatest national parks in the world.

Although Tompkins and I never crossed paths again, we had several friends in common, and I always thought we might run into each other and have a chance to reminisce about those few weeks we spent climbing together in Yosemite. I would have loved to hear about his adventures in Chile, and I believe he would have been interested in hearing about my efforts to

## Ghost Sickness

restore meadows in the Sierra Nevada backcountry. I had been thinking about volunteering to work on wilderness restoration projects, and with my experience living and traveling in Latin America, Conservación Patagónica would have been a good choice. But it didn't turn out that way.

In December of 2015, I read in the *New York Times* that Doug Tompkins, then seventy-two, had died while kayaking on Lago General Carrera in Chile. Powerful winds had created six-foot waves on the lake, and his kayak had capsized. After surviving two hours in water below forty degrees, he was flown to the nearest hospital, where he died of hypothermia.

〰️〰️

I was called a liar once for telling this final story. Even when people are too polite to say it to my face, I can see the discomfort in their eyes when they hear me tell it. That's why I saved it for last. I don't want to damage my credibility too much until the very end. I should add that I don't believe storytellers should always be held to a strict definition of the truth. Otherwise, how would we have fiction? Norm Jefferson, who was a good storyteller, once said, after hearing a preposterous story told around the campfire, "I can listen to a lie . . . if it's told right." Still, I insist that every word of this story is true. It might seem improbable, but that would be a poor reason for not telling it. Besides, the number of people left on this earth who could hurt my feelings by calling me a liar has grown so small that I'll accept the risk.

Deadman and Cloud canyons are twin canyons running parallel to each other in southern Kings Canyon National Park. If you've never been there, you might want to put them on your list of places to see before you die. If they were better known, they might be considered two of the most beautiful places on Earth. But for a lot of folks, a place doesn't exist if you can't drive to it, so I suspect both canyons will remain relatively unknown, which is a good thing. Part of what makes wilderness so beautiful is that it can't be consumed effortlessly like fast food, pop music, or a movie. The time and effort required to get there is part of the experience, and part of the reward.

Deadman and Cloud were both heavily grazed by sheep in the late 1800s, which we know now was a terrible mistake. But looking at it from the sheepherders' point of view, it's easy to see why they favored those places. Although the canyons are nearly surrounded by high peaks, the elevations along the canyon bottoms aren't extreme, making the summers there mild and pleasant. Water and firewood are plentiful. The long, fairly narrow canyon bottoms are plush with meadows but have steep passes at their heads, making it difficult for sheep to escape. A sheepherder with a good border collie could block the trail below his camp with a crude fence and not do much for the rest of the summer except eat sourdough biscuits and nap in the shade of a Jeffrey pine. That's probably what Alfred Moniere, a Basque sheepherder, was doing when he died in Deadman Canyon in 1887, giving the canyon its name.

My old packer Slim Knutsen thought so highly of Deadman Canyon that when he got married during the Great Depression and didn't have so much as a dollar to spend on his honeymoon, he took his bride to Deadman Canyon by horse and mule, riding all the way from Badger, practically the San Joaquin Valley floor, up through Redwood Canyon, Big Meadow, Sugarloaf, and Roaring River. Of course he had to buy food, but people have to eat no matter where they're at.

Once, back in the seventies when I was rebuilding drift fences in Deadman Canyon with my backcountry crew, we marveled at a place we'd found along Deadman Creek where the glaciers had molded a long stretch of granite with twists, rolls, and banked curves, all of it perfectly sculpted, with scarcely a sharp angle anywhere. "It looks like a skate park,"

Mike Palmer said. So when Slim Knutsen rode out for our next resupply, I asked him to stop by my truck parked at Ash Mountain and pick up my skateboard lying in back. (As a landlocked surfer, I got my speed thrills skateboarding the paved roads around Three Rivers.) For three weeks my crew and I spent every evening after work riding that Deadman skate park, and somewhere somebody might have the photos to prove it.

There used to be a backcountry ranger at Roaring River, just below where Deadman and Cloud canyons meet, by the name of Gustafson. He was from Arizona, into transcendental meditation, and had spent some time in India at the ashram of the Maharishi Mahesh Yogi when the Beatles were there. He swore that the Beatles wrote a line in their song "Get Back" about him:

> *Jojo was a man who thought he was a loner*
>
> *But he knew it wouldn't last,*
>
> *Jojo left his home in Tucson, Arizona*
>
> *For some California grass.*
>
> *Get back, get back,*
>
> *Get back to where you once belonged.*

I don't know if the song was really about Gustafson or not. It seems improbable, but who am I to call him a liar? I know for certain we loved to hear Gustafson *say* the song was about him, and we liked to think we were friends with a friend of the Beatles. Gustafson also played the guitar and could sing a version of "Ghost Riders in the Sky" that could make a grown man afraid of the dark.

When I decided it was time for me to return Deadman Canyon in the 1990s, I chose a route so ridiculous that it seems like madness to me now. Rather than follow the maintained trail through Rowell Meadow, Sugarloaf, and Roaring River, I decided to take an almost entirely cross-country route, beginning at Lodgepole Campground, climbing Silliman Pass and heading almost due east, crossing Crowley Canyon, the East Fork of Sugarloaf Creek, the West Work of Ferguson Creek, and Ferguson Creek, which meant I was descending about a thousand feet to the creek bottoms each time, then immediately climbing up the other side. That amounts to a total ascent and descent of several thousand feet, through rattlesnake-infested brushlands and treacherously steep terrain, by myself, all in one day, while carrying a fifty-pound pack. It's impossible to explain why I would do something that foolish, except to say that I figured it had probably never been done before.

Shorty Lovelace, the legendary fur trapper who operated in Kings Canyon before it became a park in 1940, built several cabins throughout the Roaring River drainages, the largest being at Crowley Canyon, near Comanche Meadow. Shorty, who'd been born and raised in Three Rivers, was an alcoholic half the year and a teetotaling hermit the other half. In the summer months, he'd squander his earnings from the previous year, carousing around the San Joaquin Valley, then, come fall, he'd settle down and begin stocking his chain of backcountry cabins for the coming winter, which he would spend trapping fishers, wolverines, and especially pine martens.

Pine martens, which are closely related to the Russian sable, are highly adapted to living in snow and have thick, soft, luxurious fur. But their populations are not dense. A trapper seeking them had to have a large network of traplines in order to be successful. And Shorty was definitely successful, earning $2,000 for a winter's work during a time when that was more than the annual income in the United States. I once asked an experienced wildlife biologist why we don't see more pine martens in Sequoia and Kings Canyon. His answer was, "I don't know. Maybe Shorty trapped them all."

Well, I know Shorty didn't quite trap them all because in 1980 I saw a pine marten at Scaffold Meadow (right in the heart of Shorty's territory). It was broad daylight, and the marten scampered out of the brush and up a lodgepole pine, where there was a bird's nest. The marten quickly ate the eggs in the nest, then scurried back down the tree and into the brush. The entire appearance didn't last thirty seconds. What surprised me most about the marten was not only how sleek and agile it was, or how small—only about sixteen inches long, including the tail—but how quickly it moved, as if its internal clock was running twice as fast as that of any other animal I'd ever seen. The next day, at exactly the same time and place, the marten appeared again. Of course there were no eggs in the nest this time, but the marten couldn't resist trying again. It's the same animal behavior that causes lonely cowboys to return to the same empty bar where they'd gotten lucky one Saturday night many years earlier.

Slim Knutsen told me that once, back in the forties, he'd been riding out of the mountains leading a string of mules and had passed Shorty Lovelace on the trail, hiking in. Shorty had a gallon of wine dangling from each index finger, a loaf of bread tucked under one arm, and was so drunk he never even looked up to acknowledge Slim or his string of mules. Outside the Crowley cabin today stands a mound of empty, one-gallon wine bottles, which demonstrates that while in the backcountry Shorty tried to stay as drunk as he could as long as he could, until the logistics of hauling that much wine into the mountains became impossible, and sobriety became his only choice. Sometimes it's difficult to reconcile Shorty the drunken fool with Shorty the resourceful mountain man who traveled hundreds of miles alone each winter through the backcountry on a pair of homemade skis. At other times, though, he reminds me very much of the backcountry skiers, climbers, trail runners, and other outdoor junkies I've known. Some people have said that Shorty used the mountains and trapping to overcome his alcohol addiction, but I don't think that's quite right. I think Shorty substituted one addiction for another. Alcohol was his summer preference, and endorphins were for the winter.

I once went to see an orthopedist about pain in my knee. He took my pulse, which was fifty-two, scowled, and said, "Well, I can see you're a runner. Do you do marathons?"

"Some," I admitted, not sure why I should feel guilty about it.

"You'll have to quit," the doctor sputtered.

"I can't quit," I said. "Running is the only healthy habit I have."

The orthopedist went into a rage, growling, "You do whatever you want, but I've seen a hundred guys like you come in here addicted to your endorphins! In five more years you'll need a knee replacement."

It's been twenty years since then, the two knees I was born with still work just fine, and that orthopedist is forty pounds overweight. But he was correct in pointing out that endorphins, our body's natural painkillers secreted by the central nervous system, are powerfully addictive drugs. I think Shorty understood that instinctively years before science explained how endorphins actually work.

Another thing that's so fascinating about Shorty is that he was traveling through the backcountry on skis at a time when Nordic skiing wasn't well known in the United States. Even alpine skiing wasn't common in the US until soldiers coming back from World War II began to popularize the sport they'd tried in France, Austria, and Italy. Snowshoes, which are native to North America, had long been considered the accepted means of travel through snow in this country. But snowshoes are awkward, heavy, and slow. Shorty had somehow learned that skis were much more efficient, especially downhill, where an accomplished skier can travel in minutes what a plodding snowshoer might take all day to cover. Even traveling uphill, skis require much less effort than snowshoes. Without the benefit of modern ski waxes to aid a skier moving uphill, Shorty had to use climbing skins strapped to the bottoms of his skis, and there can be no better skin for that purpose than the hide of a marten; it's finely textured fur grows at a backward angle, allowing the skis to glide smoothly forward while sticking to the snow when slipping backward. How Shorty figured out the many complexities of Nordic skiing on his own, I don't know, but there can be no doubt that he was a clever and resourceful man.

The line cabins Shorty built throughout the backcountry were tiny—just five feet by ten—with dirt floors, a platform bed at one end, and a rock fireplace at the other—scarcely big enough for a hobbit. Over the years, I've visited many of Shorty's cabins, stooping under the low door headers, and curling up to try out his tiny beds. Some of the cabins are still in remarkably good shape, but others have been almost completely destroyed. Around 1978, while working in Granite Basin, I hiked to Granite Pass to see Shorty's most famous cabin. Like so many others, it was hidden in plain sight. You could walk within a few yards of the cabin and not see it unless you were paying close attention. Fifty years had only disguised it more, weathering the lodgepole logs almost to the color of gray rock. And like so many of his cabins, it was built in a beautiful spot.

That cabin at Granite Pass figures large in Shorty's history because he came very close to dying there. In the late 1930s, a powerful winter storm blew a tree across the cabin while Shorty was inside. He was struck either by the tree or the collapsed roof, and even though he didn't suffer any broken bones, he had internal injuries of some kind that left him in a great deal of pain. Even worse, the falling tree had smashed his rock fireplace, which in turn started a fire in the cabin. Shorty was trapped there, in a howling winter storm, severely injured, without adequate shelter, at least fifty miles from another human being, and more than a hundred miles from a hospital. Those weren't flatland miles either, but some of the most rugged terrain in North America. Yet somehow Shorty made that 6,000-foot descent, through heavy snow, to Cedar Grove, where he had yet another cabin. We don't know how long Shorty stayed there, but sometime that winter he climbed out of Cedar Grove, probably by way of Sphinx Creek, and eventually returned to his main cabin at Crowley Canyon. The entire journey from Granite Pass would have been at least forty miles, and he was still another forty miles from a place where somebody might help him—perhaps at Hartland or Badger. In March a snow survey crew found Shorty at his Crowley cabin and they offered to help him out, but Shorty declined their offer and made his own way out after the snow melted.

It has been estimated that Shorty built as many as thirty-six cabins throughout the southern Sierra, though nowhere near that many have ever been found. But how, I wondered, could they be found if somebody didn't go looking for them? What a joy it would be to come across one of Shorty's cabins exactly the way he'd left it more than fifty years ago! And what might one find? A rumpled letter from a sweetheart? A recipe for elderberry wine? An AA membership card with his name on it? I knew the odds were slim that I'd ever find a previously unknown cabin of Shorty's, but I wanted to look, and I figured the most likely place to find one was on those seldom visited forks of Ferguson and Ellis creeks.

I won't describe the tedium of that day's journey across all those drainages to Deadman Canyon, except to say that the canyons were narrow, with just trickles of water in their V-shaped bottoms. After seventy years of fire suppression in the parks, the drainages were a snarl of manzanita, ceanothus, and chamise, making travel up and down them nearly impossible. I saw no sign of Shorty having ever been there, or anybody else for that matter. Maybe he ran traplines up those creeks—I believe he might have—but the canyons felt cramped and spooky to me, and the winter days there would have been dark and gloomy. Shorty had an eye for beauty and preferred to spend his days in more open country. Beauty, after all, can be addictive, too.

When I finally reached the top of that last ridge above Deadman Canyon, the day was nearly spent. I was thirsty and exhausted, and all I wanted to do was point my weary bones downhill for a final thousand-foot descent. Already I could hear the delightful sound of Deadman Creek flowing below. As near as I could tell, I'd be arriving at the canyon floor near a place called the Grave, where the old sheepherder, Alfred Moniere, was said to have been buried more than a hundred years earlier. I had worked near that area before, but I'd never gone looking for the grave or even knew if a marker still existed.

At Deadman Creek, I stopped to drink my fill. I was too tired and weary to eat, and I could think of nothing but finding a place to spend the night. In the dim light I could see a gravel flat just ahead, and beyond that a large tree with long, low-slung branches. I hadn't brought a tent, and I figured those branches would offer protection if it happened to rain during the night. I unrolled my foam mattress, pulled off my boots, lay down, drew my sleeping bag over me, and in a few seconds I fell asleep.

Normally I sleep fitfully my first night at elevation, but that night I scarcely moved. When I finally opened my eyes, I saw the ridge top to the west beginning to glow pink. I rolled over once, remembered where I was, and sat up to take in my surroundings. Directly at the head of my bed was what appeared to be some sort of manmade object, perhaps a crude marker of some kind. Scooting closer I saw that it was an old, badly weathered sign, and in the dim morning light I could barely make out these words:

Here Reposes Alfred Moniere, Sheepherder, Mountain Man, 18— to 1887

Call me a liar if you will, but I swear I had unwittingly spent the night sleeping exactly on top of the Grave.

♒

Around the new millennium, those of us who loved the southern Sierra had to take notice of the problems brought about by climate change: reduced winter snowpack, fewer conifers at middle elevations and more chaparral, drier meadows, increased stress on endangered animals like the bighorn sheep, the California condor, and the yellow-legged frog. A lifetime might be too short for a person living in the Sierra Nevada to notice some of those symptoms, but the record of climate change could be read clearly in other ways. Ice cores taken in Greenland and Antarctica clearly showed that carbon dioxide in the ice began increasing dramatically after the beginning of the industrial age, around 1760, when humans began burning fossil fuels in great quantity. It made me sick to see the massive die-offs of ponderosa and sugar pines at lower elevations due to bark beetles, a sign that the trees had been weakened by drought and thus less able to fight off the beetle attacks. But there was evidence that those die-offs had happened before, and perhaps what we were seeing was a cyclical pattern, not a new catastrophe. Wildfires all over the West were increasing in both frequency and intensity, and that in itself was an indicator of higher temperatures and reduced precipitation. But after forty years of prescribed burning,

Sequoia and Kings Canyon had greatly reduced the threat of devastating wildfires. I participated in many of those burns, was given responsibility to conduct some on my own, and that knowledge gave me confidence that the parks could cope with a future that included higher temperatures.

Another thing that gave me hope for the future of the southern Sierra Nevada was visiting the nearby White Mountains, a starkly beautiful range that lies just east of the Owens Valley. White Mountain itself, at 14,225 feet, is taller than any mountain in the Sierra except for Mount Whitney and Mount Williamson. But because the Whites are in the rain shadow of the Sierra Nevada, they are very dry. Trees are small and scraggly there, and meadow vegetation is scarce, yet a bristlecone pine in that range is the oldest living tree in the world, at 5063 years. The bristlecone pine, which is closely related to the foxtail pine that grows at high elevation in the Sierra, is clearly a tree that has evolved to survive in dry conditions. Maybe the White Mountains are an indication of what the Sierra Nevada might look like in a drier future. Many species might not survive, but others will adapt.

I was never as pessimistic about climate change as most of my wilderness friends. The Earth has gone through five massive extinctions in which more than half the species were lost, and it's likely we're seeing a sixth extinction now, this one brought about by man. But the Earth recovered after each of those mass extinctions. Maybe our anxieties about the future of the planet are mostly about our limited time reference and our own fear of mortality. Change isn't just a part of nature, it's the very essence of it. And it isn't Earth that's dying—it's us, the human race. While that thought might have terrified me long ago, more and more I have found it oddly reassuring.

After I turned fifty, my backcountry trips became mostly solo adventures. My sons, who had shared my trips for twenty years, now had lives and interests of their own. Jimmy Castro and I made a few loops together out of Mineral King, but most of my wilderness-loving friends were either more bunged up than I was, or dead. Wandering through the backcountry was still my favorite way to spend four or five days, though, and I was going to keep on doing that, even if I had to do it alone. The combination of solitude and beauty still calmed my nerves and renewed my appreciation for life. For people like me who were raised on religion but can't swallow the old biblical mythologies anymore, pure nature is the greatest spiritual experience we can know. Wilderness is like a chapel, offering shelter for the soul, and providing a sense that all is well with the world, in spite of the damage we've done to it.

Wandering the wilderness alone, though, can leave an older person vulnerable to ghosts. The noise and clutter of civilization, all our electronic distractions, our sense of urgency and self-importance—all that is gone in the wilderness, and what is left is nothing at all like the reality we've grown comfortable with. Call me fanciful or superstitious if you like, but only after you've spent four nights in the wilderness alone.

I once told Norm Jefferson that, while exploring a remote canyon in Baja, I'd spent the night alone in a cave that had been used as a human shelter perhaps hundreds of years earlier. A rubble wall had been built to partly close off the opening, and the floor was littered with pottery shards. That night I was visited by the ghost of a young man who'd once lived there. He refused to enter the cave but peered in at me from the entrance, and his image was frighteningly real. The ghost told me he didn't object to my use of the shelter, he just wanted to make sure his woman wasn't lying with me. I gathered up my sleeping bag and spent the rest of the night outside the cave.

I asked Norm if he thought maybe I'd experienced some kind of hallucination, maybe caused by spending too many days alone. But Norm just laughed, shook his head, and said, "Ghosts aren't hallucinations, and you don't have to go to the wilderness to find them. You just have to shut up long enough to notice them."

My list of dead friends was growing every year: Craig Thorn, the fifteen-year-old packer who'd tricked me into riding a mule, died after rolling his truck on Highway 198. Steve DeBenedetti, who'd convinced me to begin our meadow restoration projects, died of cancer. My neighbor of twenty years, Gary Kenwood, who had warned me about the dangers of lightning, also died of cancer. Pete Lewis, who'd dared to wear his African dashiki at Wolverton Corrals, had passed away, too. Norm Jefferson, Bruce Flom, Frank Walter—I was beginning to see that if you live long enough, everybody you know will die, a thought that had never even occurred to me forty years earlier. I might have been able to accept death as natural in a biological sense, but I missed those old friends dearly, and I couldn't see how the world I knew could ever be the same without them. My friends and I had been reckless and foolish when we were young. We had worked and played as if our bodies would last forever and we could never be hurt. I had barely avoided death many times, but they hadn't, and I could see that the difference between life and death is so often just a chance occurrence, an accident, a thing of no substance or meaning at all.

I began having conversations with my dead friends, sometimes explaining why I'd done something to disappoint or anger them, but other times just telling in story form the adventures we'd lived together. The dead are better listeners than the living, they aren't as critical, they laugh easier, and are much more patient. If speaking with the dead was a form of madness, I didn't care. I enjoyed it. But I did worry that by encouraging my dead friends to come around, I was slipping into their world little by little and leaving this world behind.

The Paiutes describe the symptoms of ghost sickness as nightmares, insomnia, hallucinations, visitations, and sometimes a sense of impending danger. Except for the sense of danger, I had all those symptoms, and I thought I'd better do something about it before it was too late.

In 2007 my wife and I decided to leave Three Rivers, where we'd raised our sons and had lived almost all our married life. I was approaching sixty, though I didn't feel so old, and I certainly wasn't ready to become an arthritic graybeard sitting by my wood stove, waiting for hapless visitors to turn up my driveway so I could unload my memories on them. But I had developed a strong intolerance for the cold. Forty years earlier, I'd gone on weeklong ski trips through the backcountry wearing a light sweater and a thin windbreaker, and I'd surfed in forty-five-degree water without even a wetsuit. Now I cringed at the sight of frost in the fall and wore woolen socks late into June. Most people would consider the Mediterranean climate of the southern Sierra Nevada foothills almost ideal, and for eight months out of the year I might agree with them. But more and more, I found myself longing for a place where I could feel the heat in my bones year round.

To show my appreciation to the Sequoia Natural History Association for buying so many of my guidebooks over the years, I donated the publishing rights for those books to the association with the agreement that they'd remove my name from them. Novice hikers are injured or killed in the parks every year—walking off cliffs, being swept over waterfalls, or simply getting lost—and I was always worried that my guidebook might be found in one of their packs, and their family might try to sue me. Also, several imitations of my guidebooks had appeared on the market, sometimes copying almost the exact language I'd used. While it's possible to copyright a text, it isn't possible to copyright a trail, and as long as my imitators changed their words just a bit, there wasn't much I could do about it without taking them to court. But, honestly, I no longer cared. I'd moved on to other writing projects, and I knew that if I donated my publishing rights to the Sequoia Natural History Association, my books would always find a favored spot on their shelves, even if my name wasn't on the cover.

In 2008, after our two youngest sons went off to college, Claudia and I sold our place in Three Rivers and moved to Mexico, on the eastern tip of the Baja peninsula, sometimes called the east cape. It wasn't that I'd grown tired of the Sierra, rather that my concept of wilderness had been expanding for years into deserts and oceans, and I figured if I ever wanted to know those places as well as I knew the mountains, I'd better do it soon.

My plan was to give up climbing, backpacking, and backcountry skiing—those sports were just an excuse to be outdoors anyway—and spend a few years surfing and kayak fishing before I got too arthritic to do that, too. For older extreme-sports junkies, landing on water is a lot easier than landing on rock or ice.

In Baja I began spending almost every morning on the ocean, usually surfing with a band of new friends who reminded me very much of those I'd left behind: reckless, impulsive, often funny, and tenaciously devoted to using their bodies while they still had them. But other times, just after daylight, I would paddle my kayak straight into the Sea of Cortez, three or four miles, and sit there by myself without another human being in sight. I wasn't standing on top of a 14,000 foot peak, I was sitting exactly at sea level. But the benefit was the same, and the risks similar. The water was always alive with turtles, sea lions, and curious fish. Sometimes I could hear the call of humpback whales through the hull of the kayak, and I marveled at their size and grace as they appeared just a hundred feet away. If the wind came up quickly, as it often does on the east cape, it took every bit of strength I had to beat my way back to shore.

After witnessing a few tropical storms in Baja, with absurd amounts of wind and rain, I began to appreciate where those summer rain squalls in the Sierra Nevada really came from. *Chubascos* are just the remnants of a tired, blown-out hurricane. The Pacific Ocean south of Baja is the birthplace of *chubascos*, and the American Southwest, including the southern Sierra Nevada, is where they go to die.

As much as I loved having new deserts and ocean to explore, after just one year in Baja, I told my wife I couldn't bear being away from the high mountains every summer. I never wanted to be cold again if I could avoid it, but I needed to hear the sound of a creek flowing, see the tops of ponderosa pines swaying in the wind, and breathe mountain air—at least during those magical days of late summer. So we bought a small motorhome just big enough for two people who like each other, and we began spending every August and September exploring mountainous regions all over the western United States. For years I'd ridiculed park visitors who traveled by motorhome, and for that I sincerely apologize. It took me fifty years, but I'm beginning to understand the wisdom of toilet seats, warm showers, and soft beds with clean sheets. A motorhome might be a violation of my old wilderness ethic of traveling light, but it's a compromise imposed by age, and one I'm willing to make, even though I can hear my ghostly friends laughing at me. They might not have lived long enough to feel their gnarled joints crack and their frayed tendons knot with pain, but I have.

After seeing a lot of the western states, my wife and I decided there was no summer place we liked better than the eastern Sierra, between Lone Pine and Bridgeport. For all the beauty and variety of the American West, there's nothing more spectacular than those white peaks and those blue, blue skies. Every few miles along Highway 395, there's another rugged canyon with trails leading toward the high passes: Lone Pine Creek, Independence Creek, Glass Creek, Walker Creek, and so many more. Those passes are where the Paiutes met their Miwok and Monache neighbors long ago to trade obsidian for seashells, pine nuts for acorns, and wives or husbands just for the night. Instead of carrying a heavy pack and staying out for days at a time, like we did in the old days, my wife and I carry light daypacks now and explore as much new country as we can manage. On our best days, we might reach the rocky summits, trying like Coyote to grab hold of a branch of the sky so we can peek over the Sierra crest and spy on our old friends to the west.

Holding on to a branch of the sky might sound illogical. But back in the old days, Miwok and Paiute children entertained themselves by bending a pine sapling, grabbing hold of the highest branch, and rocking back and forth from the tip like a metronome. Young men scrambled up pinyon pines and edged out on their long limbs so they could knock down the cones and recover the pine nuts before the squirrels got them. A branch of the sky is really no more illogical than our concept of heaven. And as somebody who has climbed to the top of a dead sugar pine while lightning crashed all around, I can tell you I would gladly grab a branch of the sky if nothing else were available.

≈≈

In January 2016, I read in the *Visalia Times-Delta* that Osmund "Slim" Knutsen, the skinny cowboy who had taught me how to identify a mule's sex using Morse code, had passed away at the age of ninety-six. At the time of his death, Slim had four children, nine grandchildren, twenty great-grandchildren, and seven great-great-grandchildren. I read that one of his grandsons, Nick Knutsen, had been crowned world champion mule packer at the annual Bishop Mule Days competition, something I'm sure made Slim very proud. But what really moved me about Slim's obituary was the final paragraph, which read, "A note from Slim was found that pretty much summed up what kind of man he was; it stated, 'Besides God, family, and friends, I loved the backcountry and the high mountains.'"

Though I usually do my best to avoid funerals, which can only aggravate ghost sickness, I would have liked to have gone to Slim's funeral because I knew it wouldn't be a sad event. When someone as unique as Slim Knutsen lives to be ninety-six, that's cause for rejoicing, not grief. But it was already too late. That's all right, though, because I know it won't be long before I see Slim's ghost slipping through my bedroom window at two in the morning. And I already know what I'll say to him: "Hey, Slim, remember when we listened to Hank Williams Junior on the radio back in Rattlesnake Creek in 1971, and you said he couldn't hold a candle to his daddy? Well, I just heard Hank Three on the radio the other day—that's Hank Junior's son, Hank's grandson. And guess what? He can't hold a candle to *his* daddy!"

After we've had a laugh about that, I'll say, "And tell me, Slim. What's the use of hiding the fact that your real name is Osmund all your life, only to have it announced to the whole world in your obituary?"

〰︎
〰︎

Although I had moved to Baja to get away from my ghosts, I soon learned, that Mexico is one of the most ghost-infested places on Earth, with a long tradition of *fantasmas*, or ghostly apparitions. Mexicans are less willing than gringos to accept the boundary between life and death as anything but a temporary border, and unlike us, they refuse to forget their dead. While *norteamericanos* might acknowledge their ghosts one night a year, mostly by handing out candy to children, in Mexico *el Día de los Muertos* lasts at least three days, with festivals, parades, and family gatherings at the cemetery to visit dead relatives. In Mexico the dead aren't buried and forgotten, they're encouraged to hang around as long as they like, to eat, drink, and party with the living. I might have thought I was running away from my ghosts by moving to Mexico, but after living here awhile, I saw that time and distance mean nothing to ghosts, who are patient and persistent, and can easily find me no matter where I go.

The ghostly visitations come almost every night now. Because of the way I chose to live my life, and the people I chose to live it with, my cast of ghosts is larger than it should be. So many of my old friends were carefree types, full of mischief, and overly fond of drinking and carousing. I suspect the only reason some of them come around now is to find a good-time buddy to share a laugh and a drink with, like the old days. They can still be pleasant company at two in the morning, as they were in life, but they fail to understand that it was mostly the drinking that killed them, and sometimes it saddens me to know that even in death they can't satisfy that need.

As a person who believes in science, I can't explain my apparitions in any logical way, and that embarrasses me. But as a writer, I take satisfaction in knowing that ghosts appear in the greatest literature, especially the works of Shakespeare, who came along too early to be embarrassed by science. I also find some comfort in knowing I'm not the only person visited by ghosts. As a boy, I once heard a man in our church say he'd fallen asleep while driving and woke to find two arms not his own handling the wheel. And a fellow I worked with in the backcountry at Sequoia saw the same ghostly figure so many times that he finally gave him a name, George Peripheral.

An old friend who'd committed suicide visited me perhaps a hundred times in my sleep, taking perverse pleasure in shocking me with the graphic violence of his death. I was never sympathetic, and in fact I told him several times how angry I was with him for using such a selfish act as suicide to punish his family and friends. Eventually, his ghost lost interest, and I haven't seen him now in years.

During a very difficult time in my life, after a loved one had suffered a serious injury, I was visited in a vivid dream by an ancestor who came to offer his solace. I call it a dream, even though I was fully awake at the time. The vision was in my mind, and not physical in any regular sense, but it was still shockingly real. My ancestor, whom I recognized from an old photo in a family scrapbook, spoke to me without saying a word, saying he couldn't change what had happened, that all he could offer was his love and concern. To my surprise, though, that helped a great deal.

It puzzles me that the ghosts of my ex-girlfriends never come around to see me during those restless hours before dawn. A few of them have died now, and if any ghosts ever wanted to cause me grief, they would surely be the ones. Women, though, have a greater ability than men to be done with their romantic past. They may struggle with rejection at first, but once they decide to move on, it's like you never existed for them—which is okay with me. Their wrath was frightening enough in life, and I'd be horrified to meet them as ghosts. Still, I must admit it hurts my feelings that they have no interest in reliving the intimacies we once shared. Maybe I'm wrong, though. Maybe some of those female ghosts *have* lingered outside my window on a moonless night. And once they glimpsed the lovely woman lying next to me, they lost heart and fled shrieking into the dark.

My ghosts appear most often in my sleep, with a vividness and authenticity that jars me awake. It's a clever, almost infallible strategy to steal my attention. Sometimes I explain to them that I don't believe in a soul that survives in an afterlife, and therefore they don't exist. But they don't mind. Their existence belongs outside logic or anybody's religious preferences, and they know it. My ghosts differ from other ghosts I've heard or read about in that they aren't strangers to me. They're almost always the spirits of people I knew and loved when they were alive. Many of them died too soon, and I often feel they need me to help them understand a life left unfinished. They aren't malevolent. They almost never come to threaten, warn, or frighten me. I only find their presence troubling because my ghosts bring with them deep, heartfelt memories, and a profound sense of regret that the joy and wonder we shared in life can never be again. Their regrets are the same as mine.

Younger people shouldn't have to think too much about death. For them, ghostly visitations might be a warning of danger to come, perhaps even an early end. For somebody my age, though, conversations with the dead are a graceful way to begin making peace with the inevitable. If I truly wanted to rid myself of ghostly visitations, I'd do exactly what the Paiutes advised a long time ago: leave the dead alone, stop thinking about them, stop speaking with them, and stop dreaming of them if you can. Like so many ancient customs that don't conform to our scientific models of the world, the Paiute cure for ghost sickness contains a lot of wisdom. But because I live in Mexico now and have seen how Mexicans deal with their ghosts, I've come to think that the Mexican way is a healthier one.

I still need my old friends, whether they're dead or not, and I welcome their visits: Frank Walter standing in the morning sunlight with a cigarette tucked behind one ear; Truman James sitting in a smoky bar gleefully telling an off-color joke; Bruce Flom in a white apron cooking dinner over a wood stove; or Norm Jefferson shouting victory after he's come from behind to beat me at horseshoes, his laughter echoing off granite walls.

# A Branch of the Sky

# Photos

Doug Wiens, a shy Mennonite who learned rock climbing while working as a busboy in Yosemite, became one of the greatest adventurers of his generation.

*Photo: Wiens family collection*

Doug Tompkins was a rock climber, hot-dog stand manager in Yosemite, founder of The North Face and Esprit, and later became the mastermind behind the creation of Conservación Patagónica.

Mike Palmer, Larry Cook, Steve Sorensen, and Norm Jefferson, members of the Soil and Moisture Crew, pose after finishing a check dam at Sugarloaf Meadow, 1974.

*Photo: Curtis Cohoe*

Mineral King Valley, once targeted by the Disney Corporation as a potential ski resort, is now part of Sequoia National Park. The valley is a major trailhead, with routes leading in all directions.

*Photo: NPS Archive*

Master tree faller and climber Charlie Castro receives an award for working twelve treacherous hours to extinguish a fire in the California Tree in Grant Grove, 1967.

*Photo: NPS Archive*

Cedar Grove was like Yosemite but without the crowds.

*Photo: NPS Archive*

The Soil and Moisture Crew built hundreds of checkdams, like this one at Sugarloaf Meadow, throughout the backcountry to help restore damaged meadows.

*Photo: NPS Archive*

Jimmy Castro was the cook on the Soil and Moisture Crew. He beat alcoholism and spent years helping other people recover from drug and alcohol addiction.

*Photo: Mike Palmer, 1979*

Williams Meadow is covered with hummocks, some of them three feet high—no place to land an airplane. The Silliman Crest can be seen in the background.

*Photo: NPS Archive*

Navajo crewmembers: Ernie Cohoe, David Beaver, Jerry Martine, Amos Pino, and Leonard Jose pose after finishing a checkdam at Williams Meadow, 1974. Jerry prescribed corn pollen to prevent accidents but later died in an automobile accident himself.

*Photo: Mike Palmer*

The Pear Lake Cabin serves as a winter shelter to backcountry skiers and marmots, and features the luxury of an indoor toilet.

*Photo: NPS Archive*

Giant sequoia loggers pose at Converse Basin, about 1900. The largest trees in the world were cut down to make fence posts and roof shingles.

*Photo: NPS Archive*

Steve Sorensen sizes up a trail erosion control project at Big Arroyo, 1980. The multiple ruts channel water away from the meadows, eventually damaging or destroying them.

*Photo: NPS Archive*

This is a meadow erosion scar, about ten feet deep, at Sugarloaf Meadow caused by livestock grazing before Kings Canyon became a national park. The Soil and Moisture Crew built check dams here to try to heal the scar.

*Photo: NPS Archive*

Norm Jefferson on a hunting trip in the Inyo Mountains. Norm didn't like to speak of the dead and wouldn't have approved of this photo.

*Photo: Steve Sorensen, 1979*

Members of a California Conservation Corps crew are working on a trail scar at Rock Creek. . The impacted soil had to be loosened by hand before fresh soil could be added. Mount Langley, 14,032 feet, can be seen in the background.

*Photo: Steve Sorensen, 1982*

Black Kaweah, 13, 675 feet, is the most beautiful and rugged peak in the Kaweah Range.

*Photo: NPS Archive*

Siberian Outpost looks austere but it is also very fragile. A California Conservation Corps crew worked here two summers restoring damaged meadows.

*Photo: NPS Archive*

Steve Sorensen at Woods Lake, 1979. The straw hat signifies the lowest possible level of proficiency at mule packing.

*Photo: Norm Jefferson*

Norm Jefferson leads a string of mules across the Kern Plateau, 1979.

*Photo: Steve Sorensen*

Deadman Canyon was named after the body of Alfred Moniere, a Basque sheepherder, was found there in 1887. Packer Slim Knutsen took his bride there on their honeymoon during the Great Depression.

*Photo: NPS Archive*

Legendary fur trapper Shorty Lovelace relaxes in front of his Cedar Grove cabin, about 1940, not long before the government banned him from trapping in Kings Canyon. Besides being an alcoholic, Shorty was a skilled mechanic and a master backcountry skier.

*Photo: NPS Archive*

Kern Ranger Station

*Photo: NPS Archive*

Norm Jefferson on the crest of the Inyo Mountains

*Photo: Steve Sorensen*

# Author Profile

Steve Sorensen was born in San Francisco, grew up in the San Joaquin Valley, and graduated with a degree in English from California State University at Fresno. He spent fifteen years supervising a backcountry crew in Sequoia-Kings Canyon National Park and conducting winter snow surveys. After being warned by his college professors that it would be impossible for him to earn a living as a writer, he sold the first feature story he ever wrote to the *San Diego Reader* and spent the next twenty years writing for that same paper. He's an avid surfer, climber, and kayak fishermen. He and his wife Claudia, who have three grown sons, now live on the east cape of Baja California Sur. His other books include: **Morning Glass:** *The Adventures of Legendary Waterman Mike Doyle*, and **Heap of Bones:** *A Baja Surfer's Chronicle.*

www.ingramcontent.com/pod-product-compliance
Lightning Source LLC
Chambersburg PA
CBHW020923090426
42736CB00010B/1013